Withdrawn from
Davidson College Library

Library of
Davidson College

POLITICAL THEORY AND POLITICAL PHILOSOPHY

Seventeen Volumes of Previously Unavailable British Theses

Edited by
MAURICE CRANSTON
London School of Economics and Political Science

A Garland Series

PROGRESS AND DEMOCRACY
William Godwin's Contribution
to Political Philosophy

Frederick Rosen

Garland Publishing, Inc., New York & London
1987

Copyright © 1987 by Frederick Rosen
All rights reserved

Library of Congress Cataloging-in-Publication Data

Rosen, Frederick
Progress and democracy.

(Political theory and political philosophy)
Revision of the author's doctoral thesis.
Bibliography: p.
1. Godwin, William, 1756–1836—Contributions in
political science. I. Title. II. Series.
JC176.G85R67 1987   320.5′092′4   86-26979
ISBN 0-8240-0829-4

All volumes in this series are printed
on acid-free, 250-year-life paper.

Printed in the United States of America

PROGRESS AND DEMOCRACY:

WILLIAM GODWIN'S CONTRIBUTION TO

POLITICAL PHILOSOPHY

by

Frederick Rosen

For my Mother and in memory of my Father,
David Rosen, who died in 1965, the year
the thesis was completed.

PREFACE

The publication of one's doctoral thesis more than twenty years after it was written requires some explanation, if not justification, especially since Godwin studies have blossomed since the early 1960s. At that time I felt that exploring the ideas and life of William Godwin was a relatively novel enterprise for the aspiring Ph.D. student, even though good work had recently been done by Priestley, Monro, Marken and Pollin. But there were then relatively few attempts to explore Godwin's political ideas by carefully examining his philosophic and practical writings (both published and unpublished), and the thesis still seems sufficiently novel and interesting to appear as a publication two decades later. Were I to write a study of Godwin now, it would differ in many respects from that which I have written. Many years of research on the life and times of Jeremy Bentham have given me a more confident grasp of the historical period and in the theoretical material I should also develop and emphasise more strongly both Godwin's utilitarianism and his development from within the Dissenting tradition.

In some respects, the thesis was a child of its time. Its very subject reflects the libertarian aspirations of the 1960s, but the approach of the author reveals a certain disenchantment with those aspirations. My preoccupation with the status of the intellectual in politics and the paradoxes surrounding the establishment of a science of politics also reflect this period. I could not approach these subjects today in the same manner, although I should note that the interest in Greek political thought which emerges in these pages, with important references and allusions to Plato and Aristotle (and their interpreters), has been an abiding one ever since.

For this revised version of the thesis, I have omitted numerous appendices and other historical material which filled out the thesis but now seem superflous to the main account of Godwin's political ideas. I have also omitted the lengthy bibliography of Godwin's writings which has been superseded by the work of Pollin and others. In addition, the opportunity has been taken to correct numerous minor errors of typing and transcription which crept into the thesis. But I have not attempted to rewrite the text, and in spite of some defects in argument and conception, the final form more or less follows the original thesis. In allowing Godwin to speak for himself in much of the thesis, I acknowledge the extent to which I remain impressed with the originality of his thought and the liveliness of his prose. I can only mention here the contributions made by Pollin, Clark, Locke, Marshall, Kramnick, and Philp to Godwin studies. To incorporate and deal critically with their contributions I would have had to rewrite the thesis.

Since completion in 1965, I returned briefly to Godwin in two articles:

> 'Godwin and Holcroft', English Language Notes, Vol.5 (1968).
>
> 'The Principle of Population as Political Theory: Godwin's Of Population and the Malthusian Controversy', Journal of the History of Ideas, Vol.31 (1970).

More recently, the relationship between Godwin and Bentham was explored in: 'Utilitarianism and Justice: A Note on Bentham and Godwin', <u>Enlightenment and Dissent</u>, No.4 (1985). For the most part, I have put the thesis to one side, though I have thought that I might eventually use the material in another context to explore the connection between English radicalism and early socialism during this period. Godwin's thought and influence would play no small role in such a study.

In both the writing and the revision of the thesis there are numerous debts to acknowledge. I am most indebted to Professor Maurice Cranston, my thesis supervisor, whose encouragement and editorial skills were invaluable to me, and to the late Professor H.B. Acton who was a most sympathetic and helpful External Examiner. To Edward Andrew, Henry Drucker, Robert Lamb and the late John Parsons, who, as fellow-students at LSE during this period, I remain grateful for advice, criticism and patience at my efforts to interpret and expound Godwin's ideas. For the revised version, I thank the members of the staff of the Bentham Project for tolerating my sudden preoccupation with Godwin which required more trips to the British Library than I had originally planned, and my family for allowing me the extra time to complete the work in the evenings and during weekends. Mrs. Paula Da Gama Pinto has enabled me to approach the revised version with confidence that it would be completed. I am most grateful to her for producing the final typescript.

Thanks are due to the librarians and staff of the British Library, Bodleian Library, Dr. William's Library, Senate House Library, British Library of Political and Economic Science, and the University College London Library for assistance in finding various books and articles which enabled me to check the references of the original thesis. I am also grateful to the following for permission to quote from unpublished sources: Lord Abinger for permission to use and quote from the Abinger Manuscripts; the Librarian of Dr. William's Library for permission to quote from Henry Crabb Robinson's *Letters* and *Diary*; the Keeper of Manuscripts, The British Library, for permission to quote from the Place and Mackintosh papers. I am also grateful to the Keeper of Western Manuscripts, Bodleian Library, for access to the microfilm of the Abinger Manuscripts which was used in the original thesis, and, more recently, to the Abinger Manuscripts on deposit in the Bodleian. Dr. B.C. Barker-Benfield was especially helpful in assisting me to relate the microfilm references to the original manuscripts.

Fred Rosen
The London School of Economics
University of London
March 1986

TABLE OF CONTENTS

I.	AN INTRODUCTION TO WILLIAM GODWIN	1
II.	NATURE, PROGRESS, UTILITY	10
III.	POLITICAL PRINCIPLES	38
IV.	DEMOCRACY	61
V.	LIBERTY	77
VI.	ECONOMICS	100
VII.	POPULATION	120
VIII.	THE EARLY WRITINGS	144
IX.	THE FRENCH REVOLUTION	154
X.	THE LATER WRITINGS	181
XI.	PROGRESS AND DEMOCRACY: THE MEANS	209
XII.	PROGRESS AND DEMOCRACY: THE ENDS	233
XIII.	GODWIN'S CONTRIBUTION TO POLITICAL PHILOSOPHY	242
NOTES		258

CHAPTER I

AN INTRODUCTION TO WILLIAM GODWIN

'My creed is a short one. I am in principle a Republican, but in practice a Whig', wrote William Godwin to Lady Caroline Lamb. 'But I am a philosopher: that is, a person desirous to become wise, and I aim at that object by reading, by writing, and a little by conversation.'[1] This casual remark reveals an important characteristic of Godwin's thought which has hitherto been largely ignored. Godwin was able at the same time to be a Whig, Republican, and Philosopher. The distinction is reflected in his writings by a division between what might be called his theoretical and his practical works. Godwin's own words may again be quoted: 'My political creed may be stated with great brevity and clearness. It consists of two parts, speculation and practical.'[2] This is a distinction which was appreciated by some of Godwin's contemporaries. In a letter written in 1829, Francis Place, the Charing Cross tailor and reformer, wrote:

> The 'Enquiry concerning Political Justice' should be read by **every body**. Some of its speculations are pushed nearly to absurdities, but as the reader is informed that they are to be considered only as speculations, advised to examine them for himself, and recommended to take nothing for granted, even these speculations deserve more indulgence than it has been the fashion to bestow on them.[3]

Godwin wrote a number of pamphlets and articles (most of these published in the <u>Morning Chronicle</u>) which dealt with specific questions and events of public importance. His earliest pamphlet, published in 1783, was entitled <u>A Defence of the Rockingham Party, in their late Coalition with the Right Honourable Frederic Lord North</u>. Among his manuscripts is a draft of a petition to King William IV concerning the Reform Bill of 1832. Godwin's practical writings thus span a period of fifty years. These pamphlets and articles were concerned with particular issues, and Godwin would seldom argue in terms of the abstract principles which abound in his more speculative books. His practical writings were designed to complement, rather than merely to translate his speculations into more workable principles. Thus, a principle emerging from one of his pamphlets may appear to be contradicted by a principle stated in his speculations, although, ultimately, the two might be seen to complement each other. For example, in <u>Political Justice</u>, Godwin conceived the role of the state solely as a coercive instrument which should be increasingly limited until it 'withered away'. However, in his pamphlets, Godwin was intensely concerned with government in its numerous aspects revealing what might be considered a very 'political' disposition in contrast to the 'anti-political' character of <u>Political Justice</u>. Nevertheless, the apparent contradiction is resolved when we appreciate the place Godwin believed his speculations should have in the whole of human activity.

> It has been said of Political Justice that its
> views and aspirations are too high to accommodate
> themselves to human frailty and 'man as he is',
> and therefore it has been condemned.
> But this is unjust. Supposing, but not granting,
> that the period of the improved state of society
> delineated in that book will never arrive. Yet I
> should think the writer is a public benefactor,
> and worthy of honour, who sets before our minds the
> finest standard, who assists us in our contemplations,
> if not in the scenes of real life, to rise above the
> grossness, the sordidness, the empty delusions, the
> wandering, fleshly lights of our nature and enable
> us, in our early youth and in our generous moods
> and in our solitary contemplations, to fix our
> thoughts on shining and spotless excellence. The
> true path of a noble ambition is to aspire to the
> highest model: it is likely that we shall never
> entirely reach to be what we contemplate but yet
> we shall be the better for the contemplation.[4]

Godwin's speculative principles may be found in six productions: The *Enquiry concerning Political Justice* (1793, 1795, 1797); *The Enquirer* (1797); *Thoughts Occasioned by ... Dr. Parr's Spital Sermon, etc.*, (1801); *Of Population* (1820); *Thoughts on Man* (1831); and his *Essays* (published posthumously in 1873). He intended *Political Justice* to be a contribution to the new science of politics. He described his two-fold task: to compile the new discoveries in political science which had recently superseded old ones, and to add some reflections of his own to those he had accumulated.[5] His treatise, he said, was one of the 'disquisitions of science'.[6] There has been some discussion of the modifications made in the three editions of Political Justice, and some writers have suggested that Godwin changed some of his doctrines in this period, partly in response to the French Revolution.[7] Godwin, himself, was quite explicit on the subject. In 1824, he wrote:

> The book was first published in 1793. It was afterwards twice revised by me in the editions of 1795 and of 1797. But the alterations and additions were made in the same spirit in which the work was written. They were the fruits of careful and severe meditation upon these momentous topics: but they flowed from the same erect and unbending mind. They were improvements in the detail of my system and principles; but they had no regard to the predilections and good will of any man or body of men on earth. My object had a higher scope.[8]

Godwin's second theoretical work was The Enquirer of which he occasionally spoke when he referred to Political Justice. The Enquirer contained his thoughts on education as well as several chapters on economic problems. In the preface to the volume, he explained that, unlike Political Justice, which was rigidly deductive in formulation, The Enquirer consisted of a series of essays, each complete in itself. Though he dealt with his themes in a more informal manner, he certainly regarded the essays as speculations, though of somewhat more modest stature than Political Justice.[9]

The full title of the third work was Thoughts Occasioned by the Perusal of Dr. Parr's Spital Sermon, Preached At Christ Church, April 15, 1800: Being a Reply to the Attacks of Dr. Parr, Mr. Mackintosh, the Author of an Essay on Population and Others. The pamphlet was intended to answer the mounting criticisms of his philosophy. His estimation of it may be found in this note in his manuscripts dated June 8, 1801, ten days before the pamphlet was published.

> It is my will that, in any future editions of the Enquiry concerning Political Justice, my pamphlet in answer to Dr. Parr & c., be annexed to the work, in place immediately following the prefaces to the different editions; not so much to perpetuate the fugitive and obscure controversies which have been excited on the subject, as because it contains certain essential explanations and elucidations with respect to the work itself. Let the title then stand, Defence of the Enquiry concerning Political Justice.[10]

Godwin never published another edition of Political Justice. He attempted to do so in 1832, and he even prepared a prospectus for possible publishers. It is not known whether at that time he would have inserted the Defence as earlier he had intended.

Godwin's next major book was his full reply to Malthus, Of Population, which was perhaps his most important writing after Political Justice. The dispute over the relationship between the increase of population and the increase in food production was more than a dispute over population and production statistics; it raised questions of crucial importance to politics and philosophy. This major reply to Malthus was first, a study of population, but, in addition, it provided further dimensions to the doctrines of Political Justice.

In a draft of a letter to a prospective publisher on June 1, 1830, Godwin stated his opinion of Thoughts on Man. 'It is the fruit of thirty years meditation, (it being so long since I published Political Justice and the Enquirer), and has been composed by me in the full maturity of my understanding.'[11] The book was a collection of essays dealing with many issues specifically raised in Political Justice, and may be regarded as Godwin's substitute for a new edition of that work.

Godwin's last theoretical work was his study of Christianity which was uncompleted at his death. Before he died he wrote to his daughter, Mary Shelley, urging her to ensure that it would be published and that it would be entitled The Genius of Christianity Unveiled: in a Series of Essays.

> I am most unwilling that this, the concluding work of a long life, and written, as I believe, in the full maturity of my understanding, should be consigned to oblivion. It has been the main object of my life, since I attained to years of discretion, to do my part to free the human mind from slavery. I adjure you, therefore, or whomsoever else into whose hands these papers may fall, not to allow them to be consigned to oblivion.[12]

Godwin's words were only partially heeded. Nearly forty years after his death, the essays were finally published under the modest title, Essays, Never Before Published, a far cry from The Genius of Christianity Unveiled.

In addition to the six theoretical works and the large number of practical political pamphlets and articles, Godwin wrote a number of histories, novels, and books for children. Although many of these are of interest because of their particular subjects, these productions are clearly subordinate to the six speculative works.

My interpretation of Godwin's political philosophy relies to an extent upon Godwin's papers, the Abinger Manuscripts. A selection from these papers was made by C. Kegan Paul and published in 1876 under the title: <u>William Godwin: His Friends and Contemporaries</u>. This edition, though useful, was neither complete nor wholly accurate. Microfilm copies of the papers were made in 1953 and these repose at the Bodleian Library, Oxford and at Duke University in the United States. This thesis was originally written using the microfilm on deposit at the Bodleian Library. Since that time, however, the manuscripts have been placed on deposit at the Bodleian Library by Lord Abinger.[13] With the exception of Kegan Paul's selection, Godwin's manuscripts have thus only recently become available for the general use of scholars. In addition, other manuscript collection at the British Museum, the Bodleian Library, and Dr. William's Library have been consulted.

Nearly half of the Abinger collections consists of Godwin's unusual journal which is a daily record kept from 1788 until several days before his death in 1836. The entries are terse summaries of the day's reading, the names of the people with whom he dined or took his tea, his writing, a note of an important political event, or the publication of a book or article. There is no commentary in the journal, and, indeed, there are few complete sentences. The whole is strictly a record, but nevertheless a useful one. With the journal, Godwin's friends, some of his activities, and most of his publications during that period may be identified. In spite of a number of enigmatic references to the political events of the day, the journal is also useful in estimating Godwin's role in English radical politics.

Besides the journal, the Abinger Manuscripts consists of drafts of various articles, a partial autobiography, and a considerable correspondence. Here may be found correspondence with Coleridge, Shelley, Lamb, Mackintosh, Place, Wedgwood, Holcroft, Wollstonecraft and many others. Some of the letters have already been published, but seldom have the various series of correspondence been considered (or even published) as a whole. Godwin's correspondence is particularly valuable, because he practiced 'sincerity' in all of his writing, and some of his letters are highly revealing of his life and activities.

The thesis is divided into three parts. The first presents Godwin's moral and political philosophy, which begins with his ideas of nature, progress and utility. These concepts lay the foundation for his political theory and are analysed insofar as they provide this foundation. In the next chapter I move to his political theory and examine the principles which surround his idea of justice. In the following two chapters I deal with the specific concepts of democracy and liberty which are central both to his philosophy and to the solution of several major problems in his thought. In the next chapter Godwin's economic doctrines are considered, and this leads to an examination of his dispute with Malthus over the relationship between the increase of population and the increase of food production. With the dispute with Malthus, I begin to consider Godwin's practical politics and some of his more polemical writings. This introduces the second part of the thesis, in which I examine Godwin's pamphlets and articles. The first of these chapters deals briefly with his early writings, where I show how Godwin became established as a political journalist. The second deals with his activities at the time of the French Revolution, when Godwin was put to a rigorous test as a pamphleteer. The third treats Godwin's later pamphlets and some of his personal relationships with various poets and reformers. In the final chapters I attempt to bring Godwin's political philosophy into focus by considering his works as a whole and attempting to discern his broader intentions in politics and philosophy. Here, the theoretical and practical are joined to provide first an overall view of Godwin's writings and then some assessment of his contribution to political philosophy.

CHAPTER II

NATURE, PROGRESS, UTILITY

Godwin never looked on 'nature' as a pivotal concept, but he was eventually forced to appreciate its importance and to give it a more central position in his theory. This change of emphasis or focus was stimulated by the dispute with Malthus over the principle of population, a dispute which ultimately turned on a disagreement about not only the effects of certain human propensities but also the intentions of all nature. It is not surprising that an enquiry concerning the capacity of man to eliminate poverty and create new societies should raise questions about nature as a whole as well as about human nature.

In Political Justice, Godwin abandoned the use of the word 'nature', because it was open to many conflicting interpretations.[1] If following nature consisted in accommodating oneself to appetites such as hunger and thirst, Godwin was ready to admit that 'follow nature' was probably a valid maxim, though it might lead to excess which would have to be corrected, not by consulting the appetites, but by the exercise of reason. Following nature could not mean that men should follow instinct, because the human species had no clear instincts to follow. Current human behaviour should not be considered permanent and, hence, natural.

Only man's bodily structure could properly be said to be natural to him, and even this was capable of modification. None of these ways of speaking of nature was satisfactory in Godwin's eyes. Another suggestion was that what was natural to man was what conduced to human happiness. Godwin found some merit in this idea, but felt that calling it 'natural' seemed to confuse an otherwise clear idea.

In his posthumously published Essays, Godwin again wrote that 'nature is a term that has been so licentiously used, and with such a perplexity of senses'.[2] Nevertheless, the question of the intentions of nature, he admitted, could not be avoided on these grounds. 'There is ... a principle in nature', he wrote, 'which in a vast sum of instances works for good and operates beneficially for us'.[3] Godwin defined nature very broadly:

> Having first observed this vast machine of the earth and its inhabitants as at a given moment they stand before us, we next come to behold the revolutions that occur in the machine, and the various changes that take place around us. That I should call nature. How the universe came to be as it is, it is vain for man to endeavour to discover; but we can follow its operations, and to a certain extent minute down its processes as we see them succeed to each other. It is in this way that we ascertain Laws of Nature, and perceive that regular succession of antecedents and consequents that enables us in

many cases to predict what is about to happen, and to model our judgments and our actions accordingly.[4]

Within this universe stands man:

> Lastly, we come to man, the masterpiece of the earth in which we dwell. His form is in many respects similar to that of the nobler animals, but with immense advantages over them all. His erect figure speaks him at once the lord of the earth. His hands are most admirably calculated as instruments to produce the stupendous effects which form the history of man. His very nakedness essentially contributes to the rendering him the being that we find him. He requires clothing and shelter; and these wants imperiously stimulate his ingenuity to supply them. The countenance of man is a magazine for the expression of thoughts; and through it we awaken in each other sympathy and deference. But more than all the other characteristics which distinguish him is the faculty of speech, by which we impart to each other the knowledge of a thousand phenomena, together with infinite shades of sentiment and observation, and all the various subtleties of thought. It is this which brings us into societies and communities, and gives occasion to the co-operation we exhibit, whether of body or mind. By this we build houses and cities. By this we are induced to cultivate the arts of design and painting, of sculpture and architecture. Lastly, by this we are prompted to engage ourselves in the pursuit of science and literature, enabling one man to improve on the advances of another, to erect libraries, and to arrive at the mighty refinements which human nature has exhibited in the various ages of the world.[5]

This argument suggests that Godwin regarded human society and civilisation as having a 'natural' character. Furthermore, the arrangements of society and civilisation were most directly dependent upon the faculty of speech, found only in man, though his vulnerability, erect stature, and the condition of his hands were also important for the stimulation of his social sentiments.[6]

This understanding of nature was somewhat different from the summary treatment of it in Political Justice. In his later work Godwin detected a generally benevolent principle in nature.[7] Nature's beneficent intention was observable by man in the provision of his subsistence and comfort. Although this fact of nature implied no moral imperative, it provided a standard for evaluating the achievements of various societies. Assuming a freedom in the realisation of human capacity, a given society represented one of several possible achievements. These achievements, or the societies which embodied them, could be subject to different evaluations depending upon one's conception of the natural provision for man. Mandeville, for example, conceiving a great natural scarcity, considered poverty a condition more endemic to human kind. 'There is nothing Good in all the Universe to the best designing Man', he wrote. 'On the contrary, every thing is Evil, which Art and Experience have not taught us to turn into a Blessing'.[8] The cultivation of the arts and sciences may alleviate a condition of poverty, but this development of 'civilisation' did not create it. If nature's provision for man was scanty, poverty could not be attributed to human misconduct. Thus, in Mandeville's view, poverty was a natural phenomena. But according to Godwin, who found nature's intentions more beneficent, poverty was created by human action and could be prevented or overcome.

At the head of the second chapter in Of Population, Godwin inserted a quotation from Aristotle's De Caelo.[9] It is translated 'But God and Nature create nothing that has not its use'. That is, if man was intended to be, his needs should be provided for.[10] Though Godwin used Aristotle to indicate that in nature there was abundance rather than scarcity, he nonetheless extended his doctrine beyond the Aristotelian one. Godwin conceived the natural abundance to be sufficient to free the mass of mankind from necessary labour and the need for war.[11] With this conception of the constraints of nature, it was possible to transform the conditions of existence for whole societies.

Godwin's view of the intentions of nature was obviously tied to his complementary idea of progress. If nature was generally beneficent, a condition such as poverty could not easily be considered a natural one. Nor could excessive moral evil easily be assumed to be the work of nature.[12] The condition of nature appeared to set dimensions -- both the limits and the extent -- of progress. Godwin's idea of progress was a curious blend of optimism and pessimism.[13] He regarded much of the history of man as a history of domestic strife and foreign wars.[14] Wars between states depended on the capriciousness of princes. Wars within states resulted from the enslavement of the poor by the rich. However, none of this evil was necessary; it was not prescribed by nature; and human arrangements might be changed. Changing, reforming, or improving societies required dispositions toward these ends, and, if changes were to affect the whole of societies, these dispositions should be found in most of mankind. But Godwin did not find this tendency revealed in the history of man.

Godwin argued that while opinion favourable to reform had not predominated in the past, the fault lay less with human nature itself than with certain opinions which controlled men's minds, especially those insinuated by the presence of government. He admitted that the state of present opinion was still not favourable for great reform, but he insisted that there was no original determination in the mind which precluded the establishment of such opinion. This argument provided the basis for the element of universality in his doctrine of progress. That is, all men were considered capable of being educated to favour reform and establish improved societies. But another argument was required to make the case for the certainty of progress. If there was no reason to believe that reform would necessarily follow dispositions towards reform, actual improvement might not be worth the effort. In <u>Political Justice</u>, Godwin set forth two propositions: first, 'the actions and dispositions of mankind are the offspring of circumstances and events, and not of any original determination that they bring into the world'; and, secondly, that 'the great stream of our voluntary actions essentially depends, not upon the direct and immediate impulses of sense, but upon the decisions of the understanding'.[15]

As for the first proposition, Godwin presented arguments designed to demonstrate that neither innate principles, instincts, nor original alterations in structure such as impressions received in the womb, had a significant impact on the development of the mind.[16] He attempted to establish that no original bias existed in the mind, and, in addition, that no bias was permanent. He also noted that although brutes might be improved by breeding, man was improved only by the training of the mind.

The idea of the mind as a <u>tabula rasa</u> was of great importance to the reformer. However, the sceptic might argue that human conduct was determined not by the understanding but by the immediate impressions of the senses, and that feeling fought with reflection for control of conduct.

Godwin reacted to this argument by first pointing out the nature of the problem and its implications.

> If man be ... the subject of opinion, and if truth and reason when properly displayed, give us a complete hold upon his choice, then the search of the political enquirer will be much simplified. Then we have only to discover what form of civil society is most comformable to reason, and we may rest assured that as soon as men shall be persuaded from conviction to adopt that form, they will have acquired to themselves an invaluable benefit. But if reason be frequently inadequate to its task, if there be an opposite principle in man resting upon its own ground and maintaining a separate jurisdiction, the most rational principles of society may be rendered abortive, it may be necessary to call in mere sensible **causes to encounter causes of the same nature, folly may be the fittest instrument to effect the purposes of wisdom, and vice to disseminate and establish the public benefit.**[17]

Given this view, it was necessary to examine the operation of the mind, and this brought Godwin to consider the nature of voluntary actions. An involuntary action was one 'which takes place in us, either without foresight on our part, or contrary to the full bent of our inclinations'.[18] An example would be breaking into tears when attempting to remain composed. A voluntary action occurred 'where the event is foreseen previous to its occurrence, and the hope or fear of that event forms the excitement, or, as it is most frequently termed, the motive, inducing us, if hope be the passion, to endeavour to forward, and, if fear, to endeavour to prevent it'.[19]

Voluntary actions, then, contained the two distinct elements of _motive_ and _foresight_. Motive, for Godwin, was an operation of the intelligence that induced one to act, and it was applicable to both voluntary and involuntary action. A direct motive (in voluntary action) was present to the mind of the agent when he determined a course of action, and an indirect motive (in involuntary action) 'operates without being adverted to by the mind, whether in the case of actions originally involuntary, or that have become so, in whole, or in part, by the force of habit'.[20]

Foresight was a concept which was inseparable from the idea of voluntary action. It meant less a prediction of the future as a basis for action than a perception of a situation which prompted one to respond. It appears that Godwin used the term in an almost literal sense meaning 'before the sight' as opposed to 'out of sight'. Foresight followed experience.

Although foresight and motive were distinct, they were for Godwin intimately connected. If one saw or foresaw an event, the image raised desires which in turn became motives for action. Foresight determined motive, which was always the correct motive, if the action was perfectly voluntary. Error entered Godwin's system in two ways. First, if foresight was deceived, if things were not seen as they were, the wrong motives might be raised which would lead to the wrong actions. It was easy to be blinded by prejudice and self-deception or rationalisation. Secondly, few actions were wholly voluntary. Some acts were, in infancy, involuntary and became partially voluntary through the years. In maturity, numerous voluntary acts became habitual and the reason for performing them passed out of consciousness. As these actions were not perfectly voluntary, they were liable to be in error.

> Hence it appears that the voluntary actions of men in all cases originate in their opinions. The actions of men, it will readily be admitted, originate in the state of their minds immediately previous to those actions. Actions therefore which are preceded by a judgment, 'this is good' or 'this is desirable', originate in the state of judgment or opinion upon that subject. It may happen that the opinion may be exceedingly fugitive; it may have been preceded by aversion and followed by remorse; but it was unquestionably the opinion of the mind at the instant in which the action commenced.[21]

Thus far, Godwin has argued that 'in all cases of volition we act, not from impulse, but opinion'.[22] However, it has been pointed out that immediate sensations are stronger than judgment, that sense is stronger than reason. Godwin must refute Hume's remark that 'the most lively thought is still inferior to the dullest sensation'.[23] Godwin flatly denied that the pleasures associated with the understanding were inferior to those associated with sensation.

> Where ... is the man, who would sit down with
> impatient eagerness to the most splendid feast ...
> if he must sit down alone, and it were not
> relieved and assisted by the more exalted charms
> of society, conversation and mutual benevolence?
> Strip the commerce of the sexes of all its
> attendant circumstances; and the effect would be
> similar. ... It is probable that he who should
> form himself with the greatest care upon a system
> of solitary sensualism, would come at last to a
> decision not very different from that which
> Epicurus is said to have adopted, in favour of
> fresh herbs and water from the spring.[24]

Although it might be conceded that the pleasures of sense were trivial when compared with intellectual pleasures, the question of which was more powerful and seductive may still be asked. Godwin gave the example of a man engaged in the enjoyment of a most sensual scene. Other considerations have been put aside by this man. But tell him, or state that his father had died or that he had lost all his money, and the impact of the sensual scene would immediately disappear. This would show that statements may have a stronger impact on the mind than direct sense impressions.

A final objection with which Godwin dealt arose from the priority of sense impressions. Man depended upon his senses, and this had led some theorists to argue that immediate impressions must be more significant than those which resulted from the intellectual refinement of the sensations. Godwin admitted the priority of sensation, but he did not believe that the pleasures of external sense organs were higher or more exquisite than other pleasures. The pleasures of a brute or savage could not be compared with those enjoyed by a cultivated and refined man. Furthermore, while abstract ideas might be, as Hume wrote, faint and obscure, there was no reason why they could not be made more definite and precise.

Therefore, by arguing that human actions were the product of circumstances or events rather than an original determination of the mind, and that voluntary actions depended essentially on the decisions of the understanding, Godwin hoped to ensure the possibility of progress. These ideas established the potential universality of a disposition towards reform and a fair certainty that reform in action would follow reform in disposition. This certainty was enhanced by Godwin's doctrine of necessity.

In re-examining the idea of progress, Morris Ginsberg has pointed out that modern psychological theories 'expose the naivité of the assumption which earlier theories had taken for granted that intellectual advance will be necessarily reflected in improved human relations'.[25] He is anxious to discard these pre-modern psychological arguments. 'The optimism of the early theories of progress which assumed that intellectual development was the chief or sole determinant of social progress is dead and beyond hope of resurrection.'[26] Ginsberg's criticism of these theories, of which Godwin's represents an important example, is common, but is it a just criticism? I suggest that Godwin's optimism stems less from a _naive_ assumption of the relationship between intellectual advance and moral improvement, than from a conviction of the universality of possible progress and from the certainty that such progress will take place. One **can** believe that there is an intimate connection between intellectual advance and improvement in moral relationships without admitting a doctrine of progress. Consider the laborious training required to produce that type of person whose knowledge or wisdom is sufficient to guide his moral actions. Few men in a generation apply themselves to attain such knowledge, and **as this training** affects so few members of a society, it cannot be relied upon to generate great reforms.

Godwin built his political or ethical science on a belief that all men could easily obtain the ethical knowledge requisite for progress. He joined the rational to the experiential, and thus united knowledge and experience.[27] Ethical knowledge was a consequence of 'seeing things as they are' and all were capable of making these observations. These observations, in turn, stimulated a moral sentiment in the human heart, a sentiment which was easily cultivated.

Some examples of seeing 'things as they are' may be useful here. Hume used the example of the feelings aroused by the sight of a ship sinking close to the bank on which the spectator was standing so that he could perceive 'the horror painted on the countenance of the seamen and passengers, hear their lamentable cries, see the dearest friends give their last adieu, or embrace with a resolution to perish in each others arms'.[28] No man would fail to be aroused with feelings of sympathy.

A second example may be found in Godwin's first major novel, <u>Caleb Williams</u>, published in 1794. This book was initially entitled <u>Things as They Are, or The Adventures of Caleb Williams</u>, and it served as a record of tyranny, domestic and public. In his preface (omitted from the first edition because the publishers feared repression), Godwin wrote:

> The following narrative is intended to answer a purpose more general and important than it immediately appears upon the face of it. The question now afloat in the world respecting THINGS AS THEY ARE, is the most interesting that can be presented to the human mind. ... Accordingly it was proposed in the invention of the following work, to comprehend, as far as the progressive nature of a single story would allow, a general review of the modes of domestic and unrecorded despotism, by which man becomes the destroyer of man.[29]

The images of this record of despotism should have **led** one to express feelings in the direction of reform, if the reader truly saw 'things as they are'. Of course, popular prejudices or various kinds prevented one from making accurate observations. To the extent that these were overcome, and sentiments were refined, there could be progress in civilisation.

Monro has written that 'it is usual to regard Godwin as the supreme apostle of reason. But actually he wavered between two schools of thought; and in the end he is closer to Hutcheson or Hume than to Clarke or Price'.[30] Indeed, Godwin's ideas were much closer to the moral sense doctrine of Hutcheson and Hume, and Godwin employed that doctrine in a very radical manner. 'The voluntary actions of men are under the direction of their feelings', he wrote at one point.[31] 'The human mind is so constituted, as to render our actions in almost every case much more the creatures of sentiment and affection, than of the understanding', he wrote at another.[32]

What gives Godwin's doctrines their high intellectualist tone is his elimination of what has traditionally been called the moral virtues. The moral virtues, according to Aristotle, were based upon habit; Godwin sought to eliminate habit by increasing the number of voluntary actions.[33] But Aristotle thought that the intellectual virtues could only be given to a few because of the great time and effort necessary to teach individuals ethical knowledge and reasoning, i.e. to produce a philosopher. To discard Godwin's doctrine because it is too optimistic in exalting the intellect in social progress, as Ginsberg has discarded such theories, is to misunderstand the manner in which the intellect becomes so important for Godwin. The establishment of a science of politics and ethics, based wholly on experience and which enables all men to see 'things as they are' renders the moral virtues, necessary habits for those who do not wish to dedicate their lives to study and contemplation, inapplicable to human activity and even barriers to progress. The intellect thus becomes more important as the moral virtues are eliminated. Godwin has lowered, so to speak, the position of the intellect rather than elevated it. If he had elevated it, if he had made ethical knowledge more difficult, he would have had to abandon the universality of his doctrine and possibly adopt a conception of moral virtue. With the elevation of the intellect, progress must be necessarily slowed.

Thus, Godwin's doctrine of progress was radical, not because it emphasised the intellect, but because it was universal and made general progress possible for mankind. Societies, not merely individuals, could now be transformed. Evil was wholly the product of prejudice and of the institutions that maintained this prejudice. Since men needed less in order to be just, more was possible.

Nevertheless, Godwin's science of politics was not as optimistic as were numerous other doctrines in the nineteenth century. Godwin's ideas required much more than the mere destruction of institutions or the re-arrangement of economic relationships to establish an improved society. Progress depended upon changes in human dispositions which were highly conditioned by habit and prejudice. His optimism, which was tempered even more after the experience of the French Revolution, extended at its height only to the immediate establishment of republican institutions, in place of hereditary monarchy and aristocracy -- by non-violent methods. His theory of perpetual improvement related chiefly to a disposition in man and did not indicate a particular rate of improvement. What alarmed and excited Godwin's contemporaries was not his optimism but the radical character of his ideas in terms of their universal application.

Godwin is frequently compared with Condorcet, but apart from superficial similarities, there are great and fundamental differences. Condorcet's idea of progress was expressed in historical terms, his evidence was the growth of the arts and sciences, and his method was based on an examination of history and a use of the past to predict the future. Godwin avoided any historical argument for progress; progress took place vertically within societies rather than horizontally through historical epochs. While he admitted that the invention of printing and the influence of commerce had established conditions favourable to moral progress, he held that such progress did not depend upon a general improvement of the arts and sciences. Referring to conditions in England at the time of Chaucer, Godwin said that writers at that time suffered from papal superstition, the discredited position of the English language, and the paucity of books which kept literature out of the hands of the many and so prevented the accurate and minute studies which were possible in Godwin's own period. He added that 'they were prevented from being so minute and accurate in quotation as scholars of our own times frequently are, but not from being learned'.[34] Furthermore, Godwin did not feel that modern scholars or political leaders had progressed so very far beyond the older luminaries:

> I pity the being of slender comprehension, who lives only with George the Third, and Alexander of Russia, and Wieland, and Schiller, and Kant, and Jeremy Bentham, and John Horne Tooke, when if the grosser film were removed from his eyes, he might live and sensibly mingle with Socrates, and Plato, and the Decii, and the Catos, with Chaucer, and Milton, and Thomas **Aquinas**, and Thomas à Becket, and all the stars that gild our mortal sphere.[35]

Furthermore, Godwin's idea of progress was not dependent upon the development of technology or a high development of the arts and sciences in general. This conclusion also followed from his idea of natural abundance. The development of the arts and sciences was conducive, but not necessary for the achievement of the good life.

'The abuse showered on Mr. Godwin's book', wrote Francis Place, 'was mainly caused by its propogating Utilitarian doctrines'.[36] Attacking Godwin's system, Thomas Green said:

> That it is not with Mr. Godwin's System merely, but with the Principle from which that System is deduced, and which may briefly be defined 'the resolving morality into expediency', that I am really at issue in the following pages. This principle did not originate with Mr. Godwin: he found it where we may all find it, in most of the leading authorities of the age: he **assumed** it as a point established, beyond all controversy, in the general opinion of mankind: and he pursued it to conclusions. ...[37]

Green's attack on Godwin was not directed solely against his theory itself, but against it as representative of a philosophy he found prevalent since the time of Locke. The offence, as Green saw it, was that of defining virtue as utility. 'It cannot, I am sure, escape you, that what gives force to this principle, and, through this principle ... to the whole body of the New System of Morals is the opinion ... that it is the beneficial or pernicious tendency of any action, which alone constitutes it virtuous or vicious.'[38]

It is important to realise, as Green suggested, that utilitarianism was generally accepted by Godwin on trust, as part of that new science of politics to which he was attempting to contribute. However, it must be added that Godwin was not merely accepting the doctrine; he was also attempting to introduce modifications for its improvement.

After the first edition of Political Justice, Godwin continually stressed the hedonistic basis of morality. 'Good is a general name, including pleasure, and the means by which pleasure is procured. Evil is a general name, including pain, and the means by which pain is produced'.[39] If he had initially implied that morality was based on anything but pleasure, he tried to clarify his intention. He considered one of the three blemishes in Political Justice to be 'an inattention to the principle, that pleasure and pain are the only bases upon which morality can rest'.[40] In the Enquirer he remarked that 'morality is nothing more than a calculation of pleasures. ...'[41]

There is no doubt that morals for Godwin were analysable in terms of pleasure and pain. However, he did not wish to conclude that all pleasures were of equal value. Like John Stuart Mill after him he thought it better to be a dissatisfied human being than a satisfied pig.[42] In *Political Justice* he went so far as to construct a 'scale of happiness'.[43] In the lowest rank were the peasant and artisan whose lives were spent in perpetual toil and who had no opportunities to cultivate themselves and to enjoy their pleasures. As such, pleasure was transient, though the peasant was in some degree happy. Godwin concluded: 'He is happier than a stone'.[44] In the second rank was the man of wealth, who enjoyed many pleasures.

> This man is happier than the peasant. He is happier, by all the gratifications of neatness, elegance and splendour, in himself, and the objects around him. Every day he is alive, inventing some new amusement, or enjoying it. He tastes the pleasures of liberty; he is familiar with the gratifications of pride: while the peasant slides through life, with something of the contemptible insensibility of an oyster.[45]

Of higher development was the man of taste. He enjoyed the pleasures of wealth, and, in addition, had acquired a new range of pleasures. This man enjoyed the beauties of nature, the pleasures of study, the charm and grandeur of poetry. 'In this person, compared with the two preceding classes, we acknowledge something of the features of man. They were only a better sort of brutes.'[46] But, there was a final rank of man whose representatives enjoyed even more exquisite pleasures: the man of benevolence, who enjoyed the pleasures of distinterested action for the greatest happiness of man. This person put his knowledge and sensibility to use for the benefit of mankind.

> He enjoys all the good that mankind possess, and all the good that he perceives to be in reserve for them. No man so truly promotes his own interest, as he that forgets it. No man reaps so copious a harvest of pleasure, as he who thinks only of the pleasures of other men'.[47]

In addition to his 'scale of happiness' Godwin was anxious to clarify the role of reason and feeling in moral action. In the Summary of Principles attached to the third edition of <u>Political Justice</u>, he said: 'The voluntary actions of men are under the direction of their feeling'.[48] Writing of <u>Political Justice</u> in 1800, he noted 'an inattention to the principle that feeling, and not judgment, is the source of human actions'. This revision followed a reading of Hume's <u>Treatise of Human Nature</u> in 1795.[49] Godwin succinctly explained the rôle of reason in his Summary of Principles: 'Reason is not an independent principle, and has no tendency to excite us to action; in a practical view, it is merely a comparison and balancing of different feelings'.[50] Both reason and feeling appeared to play an important role in determining volition itself and its direction. Man could not act without desire and neither could he act voluntarily without exercising his foresight. Unlike

Helvetius, Godwin did not reduce everything to feeling.[51] Like Hume, he recognised that reason was dependent upon feeling for its direction. However, unlike Hume, he did not think that reason was the slave of feeling.

The point of issue was not whether reason <u>or</u> feeling determined moral behaviour, but to what extent reason could determine what was desirable for human action. In <u>Political Justice</u> Godwin initially left the impression that volition originated solely in the mind. He corrected this error and said that voluntary action was initiated by feeling guided by reason. Reflecting on past experience, one could exercise foresight in moral matters. Monro has charged Godwin with confusing feeling an emotion and seeing that it is the right emotion.[52] However, Monro has failed to see the limited sense in which Godwin used reason. Godwin never tried to envisage the good or best society, because reason could not determine what is good for man. His scale of happiness did not rise above a class of men who actually existed. And the greatest happiness principle followed merely from a recognition of the common physical and mental frame of mankind. What is desirable is what is desired, not because the two are confused, but because reason cannot conceive anything desirable beyond that which men are capable of desiring. Thus, what is desirable and what men desire were, for Godwin, coterminate though not necessarily confused or combined.

Godwin's utilitarianism may be further clarified by considering his discussion of self-love and benevolence. His argument began with psychological hedonism.

> The things first desired by every thinking
> being, will be agreeable sensation, and
> the means of agreeable sensation. If he
> foresee any thing that is not apprehended to
> be pleasure or pain, or the means of pleasure
> or pain, this will excite no desire, and lead
> to no voluntary action.[53]

Therefore, the desire for agreeable sensation, self-satisfaction, is at the root of all action. If my neighbour cries, I wish initially to help him in order to relieve the distress which his cries arouse in me.

> But it is the nature of the passions, speedily to
> convert what at first were means, into ends.
> The avaricious man forgets the utility of money
> which first incited him to pursue it, fixes his
> passion on the money itself, and counts his gold,
> without having in his mind any idea but that of
> seeing and handling it. Something of this sort
> happens very early in the history of every passion.
> The moment we become attached to a particular
> source of pleasure, beyond any idea we have of the
> rank it holds in the catalogue of sources, it must
> be admitted that it is loved for its own sake.[54]

Benevolence arose in this manner. What was done for a neighbour to alleviate the distress his cries aroused, soon became a disposition to help him for its own sake. The motive thus became perfectly disinterested.

Godwin had by no means completely made his case for benevolence, for he admitted that at this point self-interest and benevolence developed side by side. Why should benevolence be preferred to other motives?

> When once we have entered into so auspicious
> a path as that of disinterestedness, reflection
> confirms our choice, in a sense in which it
> never can confirm any of the factitious passions
> we have named. We find by observation, that we
> are surrounded by beings of the same nature with
> ourselves. They have the same senses, are suscept-
> ible of the same pleasures and pains, capable of
> being raised to the same excellence, and employed
> in the same usefulness. We are able in imagination
> to go out of ourselves, and become impartial
> spectators of the system of which we are a part.
> We can then make an estimate of our intrinsic and
> absolute value. ...[55]

Exactly what Godwin meant in this statement is difficult to say. At least, he meant that the choice was confirmed when an habitual action is turned into a fully voluntary one. If I see five people drowning and am moved by the situation to assist them at the risk of my life, I might act unthinkingly, because the motive of benevolence had become habitual and divorced from any feeling of self-satisfaction. However, if I were placed in this position and were then forced to choose between the motive of benevolence and a motive of self-satisfaction, I would always choose the motive of benevolence.

After this statement of his case for benevolence, Godwin turned to the arguments concerning self-interest. While it was admitted that one man might sacrifice his life for the lives of twenty men, the advocate of self-interest would argue that the determining factor was a release from uneasiness created by the situation and a feeling of exhaltation from performing an act of virtue. Self-interest, therefore,

> ... affirms that we are wholly incapable of
> being influenced by motives which seem to
> have an absolute power; that the philanthropist
> has no love for mankind, nor the patriot for his
> country; that no child ever had an affection for
> his parent, or parent for his child; in a word,
> that, when we imagine we are most generously
> concerned for another, we have no concern for
> him, but are anxious only for ourselves.[56]

The idea that uneasiness impelled a person to action, Godwin attributed to Locke, who wrote: 'The motive we have for continuing in the same state, is only the present satisfaction we feel in it; the motive to change is always some uneasiness: nothing setting us upon the change of state, or upon any new action but some uneasiness'.[57] Godwin replied that impatience and uneasiness were created when desires met opposition. Uneasiness resulted from an unfilled desire and was not antecedent to it. 'It is because I wish my neighbour's advantage, that I am uneasy at his misfortune'.[58] One felt uneasy, rather because he loved his neighbour and his desire for his neighbour's well-being was unfulfilled.

At the root of the problem, Godwin claimed, lay a misconception. More philosophers would have abandoned the doctrine of self-love had they taken into account the complexity of human motives. In every action there was a mixture of the voluntary and involuntary, of direct and indirect motives. Godwin admitted that the first indirect and original motive in man was the love of agreeable sensation. He also admitted that 'there is probably something personal directly and perceptibly mixing itself with such of our beneficent actions as are of a sensible duration'.[59] There was usually some feeling of self-approbation over a neighbour's well-being.

> Yet, after every deduction that can be made,
> the disinterested and direct motive, the
> profit and advantage of our neighbour, seems
> to occupy the principal place. This is at
> least the first, often the only, thing in the
> view of the mind, at the time the action is
> chosen. It is this from which, by way of
> eminence, it derives the character of voluntary
> action.[60]

Godwin admitted in <u>Thoughts on Man</u> that there was something that distinguished feelings for oneself from those towards others. Certainly a man felt differently about himself than he did about other people, but this did not prove for Godwin that men were motivated by self-interest. Man was a creature of his senses. As such, 'we can fly from others, but cannot fly from ourselves'.[61] When I was with a sick friend, I felt sorry for him and wished him well. When I left him, I was relieved. My wishing him well was motivated by benevolence. That I was relieved when I left only indicated that my actions were dependent upon my senses, and other matters absorbed me when the sick friend was not present. But no man could run away from himself. That the desperate man attempted to do so was indicative of a basic sentiment that was different from self-love. 'What the desperate man hates in his own identity'.[62]

> He knows he must act his part to the end, and
> drink the bitter cup to the dregs.... It is
> the consciousness of the indubitable future,
> from which we can never be divorced that gives
> to our present calamity its most fearful empire.
> Were it not for this great line of distinction,

> there are many that would feel not less for
> their friend than for themselves. But they
> are aware that his ruin will not make them
> beggars, his mortal disease will not bring
> them to the tomb, and that, when he is dead,
> they may yet be reserved for many years of
> health, of consciousness and vigour.[63]

Godwin's insistence that utilitarian doctrines rested on benevolence as opposed to self-interest has distinguished his doctrine from what might be called 'Benthamite Utilitarianism'. Monro has suggested that Godwin's utilitarianism 'is free from the inconsistencies in which both Bentham and Mill entangled themsleves, inconsistencies which, it is often said, were not plainly seen by anyone before Sidgwick'.[64] Godwin, himself, regarded Shaftesbury, Butler, Hutcheson and Hume as among the modern philosophers who based their moral philosophy on disinterestedness.[65] The origin of his doctrine, notwithstanding, Godwin's employment of his principle of disinterested benevolence did not involve an elevation of the rational faculty to perform tasks hitherto denied to it.

The question why a utilitarian philosophy requires benevolent motives, remains unanswered. Is not the important thing the tendency of the act to produce the greatest happiness? Yet, Godwin wrote of just men, virtuous men and duty as well as of just acts, virtuous acts and the tendency to promote the greatest happiness. Monro has suggested that Godwin felt that virtuous intentions would result in actions more virtuous than those produced without these intentions.

'The real point is that Godwin has no faith in lucky accidents'.[66] However, Hume also wrote that 'no action can be virtuous ... unless there be in human nature some motive to produce it'.[67] It seems that since reason is too infirm to justify a moral standard such as the principle of the greatest happiness, the feelings which direct action become very important. So it was with Godwin. Reflection only confirmed a choice between self-love and benevolence as motives, and the impartial spectator could feel greater pleasure in working for the **happiness** of others than for himself.

That Godwin introduced the 'impartial spectator' points to a certain strain in his system. The principle of benevolence was founded on a passion. As a passion, benevolent feeling was superior to other passions, and took its highest form in a universal benevolence. However, the cultivation of universal benevolence required that limited or particular feelings of benevolence were to be avoided. Hence, Godwin's initial **disavowal** of the domestic affections followed from his cultivation of the feeling of universal benevolence. Godwin, himself, became dissatisfied with his argument, and he devoted part of his novel St. Leon to demonstrating the importance of the domestic affections.[68] There he ignored his reasons for excluding the domestic affections in the first place, and seemed to see no problem in combining universal and particular benevolence. Furthermore, he did not question whether universal benevolence itself could be wholly based on passion, or suggest that perhaps, it might be an affair of reason to control and balance a tendency towards particular benevolence. It was only by stretching his theory that Godwin arrived at this solution.

CHAPTER III

POLITICAL PRINCIPLES

The title of Godwin's major work on politics, <u>Political Justice</u>, may be somewhat misleading, as Godwin's justice was not a 'political' idea in the traditional meaning of the term. For Godwin, justice was a social standard, and a just society was conceived as something that would replace government. The idea that government might be superseded by a just society came from Godwin's conception of the origin and purpose of government. He distinguished between society and government and said that government was devised to maintain order in a society which had been already established.

> Men associated at first for the sake of mutual assistance. They did not foresee that any restraint would be necessary, to regulate the conduct of individual members of the society, towards each other, or towards the whole. The necessity of restraint grew out of the errors and perverseness of a few.[1]

Although government arose to perform a negative function in society, Godwin asked whether it might not also bring with it evils of its own. He based his argument on Rousseau's ideas in the <u>Discours sur l'origine de l'inégalité parmi les hommes</u> where Rousseau dwelled on the evil effects of government itself.[2] While government may have been necessary, its effects were to perpetuate the evils it was supposed to alleviate. Godwin praised the English writers on liberty, from Locke and Sidney to Paine, but he suggested that they failed to appreciate the impact of government itself on the society.

> Perhaps government is, not merely in some cases the defender, and in other the treacherous foe of the domestic virtues. Perhaps it insinuates itself into our personal dispositions, and insensibly communicates its own spirit to our private transactions. Were not the inhabitants of ancient Greece and Rome indebted in some degree to their political liberties for their excellence in art, and the illustrious theatre they occupy in the moral history of mankind?[3]

To the extent that society could solve its own problems, government was unnecessary. A society which could solve them would be a just one, and here Godwin affirmed the intimate connection between politics and ethics. In order that a society might exist without the coercive element of government, it would be necessary that rules of conduct serve as effective restraints, and that ethics facilitate the determination of proper conduct. As a more recent writer has said, 'It may even be true that a society can afford to limit the constraints of the state only to the extent that public opinion furnishes _alternative_ constraints.'[4]

Godwin defined justice as 'that impartial treatment of every man in matters that related to his happiness, which is measured solely by a consideration of the properties of the receiver and the capacity of him that bestows.'[5] In the Summary of Principles in the third edition of <u>Political Justice</u>, he was more specific:

> Justice is a principle which proposes to itself the production of the greatest sum of pleasure or happiness. Justice requires that I should put myself in the place of an impartial spectator of human concerns, and divest myself of retrospect to my own predilections. Justice is a rule of the utmost universality, and prescribes a specific mode of proceeding, in all affairs by which the happiness of a human being may be affected.[6]

Godwin began his discussion of justice with the individual rather than with the society as a whole. A just man was one whose acts were most conducive to the general happiness. This idea might best be expressed in the maxim of loving others as we love ourselves. However, Godwin found this maxim insufficient, because justice must also depend on the individual capacity of each man. That is, the man who was more capable of acting for the benefit of mankind might be more just than he who was less capable.

> A man is of more worth than a beast;
> because, being possessed of higher
> faculties, he is capable of a more
> refined and genuine happiness. In the
> same manner the illustrious archbishop
> of Cambray was of more worth than his
> valet, and there are few of us who would
> hesitate to pronounce, if his palace were
> in flames, and the life of only one of
> them could be preserved, which of the two
> ought to be preferred.[7]

Furthermore, the valet should be willing to give his life for that of the bishop. If not, the action would be a breach of justice. Therefore, justice was more than the sum of individual acts contributing either to the public good or to the preservation of the society. A just society would be composed of individuals who were disposed to act for the public good or greatest happiness, and who acted according to their capacity. Individuals ought not to be treated the same, because those who had a greater capacity to contribute to the public good **were** superior to those who had a lesser one.

Godwin then considered two objections to his doctrine. The first was that in order to judge a man's moral worth, a certain personal acquaintance must be established. Thus, there was a tendency to favour closest acquaintances, although others might be morally superior. Godwin said that while this argument might serve as an apology for error, it would not defeat his doctrine. No one was expected to make perfect judgments, but they ought to attempt to make such judgments.

The second objection was that it was sufficient to produce the public good by increasing the mass of benevolent actions. To this, Godwin replied:

> Is the general good promoted by falsehood, by treating a man of one degree of worth as if he had ten times that worth? or as if he were in any degree different from what he really is? Would not the most beneficial consequences result from a different plan; from my constantly and carefully enquiring into the deserts of all those with whom I am connected, and from their being sure, after a certain allowance for the fallibility of human judgment, of being treated by me exactly as they deserved?[8]

In arguing that justice depended upon the worth of man, Godwin departed from the tradition of English liberal thought. Hobbes believed the negative statement of the 'Golden Rule' to be a sufficient maxim for estimating justice. Hume's restatement of Mandeville's thesis eliminated individual worth as a standard of justice in society and government, that being just which served to contribute to the preservation of society.[9]

There is a difficulty in Godwin's argument which might explain why other philosophers in this tradition avoided his conclusion. His idea of justice based on capacity recalls a portion of Aristotle's idea of justice. But Aristotelian teleology makes it easier to conceive capacity and merit in the natural relationship between potentiality and actuality. In Godwin's system, the capacity of the archbishop of Cambray is known only by his actions, but to judge him by his actions would be to ignore his capacity unless they happened to coincide. One might compare and contrast his actions with those of past archbishops and other famous men and reach a decision in this manner, or even invoke the scale of happiness. However, the decision would not be based on capacity, but on the actions themselves. What is required is an invention of an examination similar to that used supposedly to test 'intelligence', which might be applicable to morals. Obviously, like all 'intelligence tests', it would not be very satisfactory.

Furthermore, the difficulty of assessing capacity is compounded, because the determination of a man's moral capacity must depend on the feelings this person arouses in others. Godwin tried to get over this difficulty with his doctrine of impartiality. However, it might be easier to vindicate the impartiality of moral judgments in terms of an objective order comprehended by the understanding than in terms of a man making his passions impartial by going outside himself to become an 'impartial spectator'. At the root of the problem is an identification of love and justice, which becomes necessary in moral doctrines based on feeling, if one wishes to avoid identifying justice with interest. The universal benevolence of which Godwin wrote was a form of love or sympathy elevated and thinned to accommodate all of humanity. Doubtless, a man might have a benevolent feeling towards all of humanity. He might even subordinate domestic affections or any intermediate affections to this more universal love. However, this would be difficult, and

Godwin himself eventually elevated the domestic affections, but then ignored the problem of choosing between the archbishop and one's father who was the archbishop's valet. Perhaps, he intended one to save both or leave both to perish in the flames.

Basing justice on universal benevolence may be a seductive idea but also a faulty one. It is a worthy trait and mark of liberality to incorporate within oneself a love which leaves no man untouched. Yet, as justice frequently demands a choice between different objects of affection, universal benevolence leads to the confounding of choices and duties. Furthermore, from those who are not disposed to universal benevolence, one might still expect a measure of just treatment.

Though a benevolent disposition might be achieved by all, since it involves no more than the substitution of one passion for another, the attainment of universal benevolence looks more difficult. We are attracted to those with whom we are most familiar. In many instances benevolence directed at one group requires hostility towards another.

These difficulties lead to the conclusion that, whatever might be attained by a few, the mass of mankind may not be ready to be governed by a maxim that enjoins universal benevolence. Patriotism and the multitude of subordinate loyalties in any society are examples of the generally limited benevolence among men. Since limited benevolence cannot lead to justice (as favouritism would preclude it) and universal benevolence appears out of reach of the many, Godwin's idea of justice is unable to perform the function he conceived for it.

Furthermore, his doctrine of justice has also to be reconciled with his conception of equality. If men are judged by their capacity, all men should not receive the same thing. Society apparently is not an aggregation of equal individuals. But Godwin was supposed to be one of the great proponents of equality, and, thus, he has to reconcile the apparent contradiction. He began with the assertion that 'the principles of justice... proceed on the assumption of the equality of mankind.'[10]

> We are partakers of a common nature, and the same causes that contribute to the benefit of one, will contribute to the benefit of another. Our senses and faculties are of the same denomination. Our pleasures and pains will therefore be alike. We are all of us endowed with reason, able to compare, to judge and infer. The improvement ... to be desired for one, is to be desired for another.[11]

In answer to those who opposed equality, Godwin said that although men might appear in advanced society to be unequal, they were less so in their uncultivated state. Furthermore, a considerable degree of equality remained. Moral equality, 'the propriety of applying one unalterable rule of justice to every case that may arise', was derived from the fact that men were percipient beings, desiring pleasure and the avoidance of pain.[12]

Godwin admitted one species of moral inequality. 'The treatment to which men are entitled is to be measured by their merits and their virtues.'[13] He argued that this principle did not defeat the doctrine of equality; rather, it favoured it in the sense that equity had the same root as equality. Godwin wrote:

> Though in some sense an exception, it tends to the same purpose to which the principle itself is indebted for its value. It is calculated to infuse into every bosom an emulation of excellence. The thing really to be desired, is the removing... arbitrary distinctions, and leaving to talents and virtue the field of exertion unimpaired.[14]

Godwin appears to have developed an idea of a natural aristocracy, although it was different from that of Burke's, which was manifestly incompatible with a doctrine of equality. An emphasis on equality, for Godwin, should not rule out a similar emphasis on improvement. Emphasis on excellence should be a stimulus to reformation rather than to the institution of inequality. A doctrine of equality need not lead to a principle of 'levelling'.

The relationship between a just man and a just society was defined by rights and duties. There were two major questions to be considered here. The first was the distinction between rights and duties in general, their connection, and the emphasis to be placed on either rights or duties. The second was more specific and dealt with the various kinds of rights and/or duties to be established in a just society.

Godwin wrote:

> Duty is that mode of action, which constitutes the best application of the capacity of the individual, to the general advantage. Right is the claim of the individual, to his share of the benefit arising from his neighbours' discharge of their several duties....[15]

This distinction might be contrasted with Paine's definition of the relationship between rights and duties.

> A Declaration of Rights is, by reciprocity, a Declaration of Duties also. Whatever is my right as a man is also the right of another; and it becomes my duty to guarantee as well as to possess.[16]

Although, on the surface, rights and duties appear to be reciprocal concepts, there can be great differences in the way each is presented. The main difference is the priority given to either rights or duties. Godwin placed his emphasis on duties; rights depended upon man's fulfillment of his duties. Paine emphasised rights, and man's duties depended on the prior existence of these rights.

Thus, it may be asked whether men have rights which exist apart from, or prior to, their duties. Godwin argued that they did not.

> There is no sphere in which a human being can be supposed to act, where one mode of proceeding will not, in every given instance, be more reasonable than any other mode. That mode the being is bound by every principle of justice to pursue ... If then every one of our actions fall within the province of morals, it follows that we have no rights in relation to the selecting them. No one will maintain, that we have a right to trespass upon the dictates of morality.[17]

If there was a universally applicable standard of justice, men had a duty to live by that standard, and they have no right to live as they please or in opposition to it. Godwin, therefore, as opposed to Paine, turned away from the doctrine of rights, emphasising duties over rights. His doctrine of duties depended upon a standard of justice which he found in utility. From this basic concept of justice, he derived his ideas of duty and virtue.

In the same manner as he defined justice, Godwin defined virtue. A virtuous action is any action of 'an intelligent being, proceeding from kind and benevolent intention, and having a tendency to contribute to greatest happiness.'[18] Defining a virtuous man, he included an additional factor, human capacity. Although a man's conduct might be characterised by a higher proportion of beneficent motives and actions than of vicious ones, he might be doing a small percentage of what he was capable. The problems inherent in Godwin's idea of capacity have been discussed above, when applied to the concept of justice, and the same problems apply here.

Godwin argued that each man had a duty to act virtuously, to make the best application of his capacity for the general benefit. However, men derived from this no 'active' rights. 'Few things', Godwin wrote, 'have contributed more to undermine the energy and virtue of the human species, than the supposition that we have a right, as it has been phrased, to do what we will with our own'.[19]

> We have in reality nothing that is strictly
> speaking our own. We have nothing that has
> not a destination prescribed to it by the
> immutable voice of reason and justice....[20]

The miser had no 'right' merely to accumulate wealth; the man who lived in luxury had no 'right' to do so, when his indulgence left many in poverty. All were subject to moral law.

> There cannot be a more absurd proposition, than that
> which affirms the right of doing wrong. A mistake
> of this sort, has been attended with the most
> pernicious consequences in public and political
> affairs. It cannot be too strongly inculcated,
> that societies and communities of men are in no
> case empowered to establish absurdity and injustice;
> the voice of the people is not, as has sometimes
> been ridiculously asserted 'the voice of truth
> and of God'; and that universal consent cannot
> convert wrong into right.[21]

The active rights of man were, therefore, rendered null and void by the claims of justice. Man had no right to life and liberty. He had no right to life if his duty required him to give it. And the community could deprive him of life and liberty, if it was necessary to prevent a greater evil.

Although he excluded 'active' rights, Godwin recognised that man had 'passive' rights. 'Every man has a certain sphere of discretion, which he has a right to expect will not be infringed by his neighbours.'[22] The reason for this sphere of discretion was found in the nature of man. Since man were fallible, and there was no infallible guide for the resolution of problems, each man must make his own decisions. Even if there were an authority, men must still learn to recognise it, which was an affair of the understanding and which required a sphere of discretion.

> ... [E]very man should stand by himself, and rest upon his own understanding. For that purpose each must have his sphere of discretion. No man must encroach upon my province, nor I upon his. He may advise me, moderately and without pertinaciousness, but he must not expect to dictate to me.... Force may never be resorted to, but in the most extraordinary and imperious emergency. I ought to exercise my talents for the benefit of others; but that exercise must be the fruit of my own conviction; no man must attempt to press me into service.[23]

Godwin extended his idea of passive rights to include certain rights of property, arguing that a man should give to others the fruits of the earth, which accidentally came into his possession and were of no benefit to him. However, others had no right to take these goods from him by violence. They could only obtain such goods by convincing him of their value to them.

> Whatever then comes into my possession, without violence to any other man, or to the institutions of society, is my property. This property... I have no right to dispose of at my caprice; every shilling of it is appropriated by the law of morality; but no man can be justified, in ordinary cases at least, in forcibly extorting it from me.[24]

Of all the passive rights, the most important was the right of private judgment. Government, with its laws of libel, misprison of felony, treason, etc., prevented men from exercising this right. Godwin objected to those who would exclude government from matters of conscience but, nevertheless, advocated government regulation of civil matters. 'What sort of moralist ... is silent as to what passes in his intercourse with other men?'[25]

Godwin intended to demonstrate that in a society of just men, government would no longer be necessary. However, his discussion of justice may well have led the student of Godwin to conclude that no just society can be founded on a moral framework, based on passion or feeling. While government would not be necessary in a society of just men, Godwin's doctrine of justice might not create the just society he intended.

In setting forth his principles of government, Godwin devoted considerable attention to the theory of the social contract. At first, his argument followed Hume's whom he cited with approval.[26] Superficially, their arguments were similar. Both, for example, attacked the idea of consent, but each accomplished it in a different manner. Hume admitted that at the beginning of civil society, there might have been some consent which brought men together to form the original government. This consent was, however, imperfect and conceived among savages. It provided no basis for subsequent allegiance or non-allegiance. Hume argued:

> My intention here is not to exclude the
> consent of the people from being one just
> foundation of government where it has place.
> It is surely the best and most sacred of any.
> I only contend that it has very seldom had
> place in any degree and never almost in its full
> extent; and that therefore some other foundation
> of government must be admitted.[27]

Therefore, society could not be said to originate by consent or contract. Civil society originated from the necessity to maintain order in society. 'If the reason be asked of that obedience, which we are bound to pay to government, I readily answer, <u>because society could not otherwise subsist</u>.'[28] The purpose of government was to preserve society.

Godwin, who rejected the idea of contract, could not accept Hume's doctrine, because Hume derived the purposes of government from its origins, rather than from the best way a community should be organised. Hume used the same kind of derivation which had been used by the contract theorists. Thus, Godwin opposed both Locke and Hume more than he opposed the idea of contract. He opposed the determination of the role of government in society by its origins rather than by its tendency to promote the greatest happiness. Although government may have arisen either by contract or by the necessity to preserve society, it was not limited to the promises made under the contract or to the mere preservation of society. The principle of utility should be the deciding factor. Godwin's attack on the social contract idea should thus be interpreted, not as an affirmation of Hume's doctrine, but as a rejection of Hume's as well as those which Hume rejected.

Godwin presented two arguments against the idea of contract. The first attacked the ambiguities surrounding the idea of consent and the second dealt with the moral limitations on promises. He approached the problem of consent by asking a number of questions. Who were the contracting parties? There would be little value to the contract if one's ancestors formed it, and it was to bind everyone forever. If not, how long was it binding? When did one consent? Was one bound before he consented?

He asked: What was the form of the engagement? Many argued that acquiescence was sufficient, but if this was so, nearly all governments would be legitimate, however tyrannical. Like Hume, Godwin argued that acquiescence could not be construed to mean consent, and he attacked Locke's distinction between tacit and express consent.

> A singular distinction! implying upon the face of it, that an acquiescence, such as has just been described, is sufficient to render a man amenable to the penal regulations of society; but that his own consent is necessary to entitle him to the privileges of a citizen.[29]

Godwin then asked about the length of the contract. Assuming express consent, for how long a period was one bound?

Was it for one's entire life or only for an hour? To how many different things was consent given? It seemed ridiculous to expect anyone to be familiar with the volumes of laws of England to which one was supposed to consent.

Did the original consent extend to laws subsequently passed? Was one expected to consent to the laws after consenting to the contract? Godwin considered Rousseau's attempt to avoid this problem by making the people sovereign an impossible and superficial remedy.[30] At best, the people, gathered together, could only accept or reject; they could not deliberate under these conditions, as the people, collectively gathered, would be too tumultuous.

Finally, he turned Rousseau's own argument against him.

> ...[I]f government be founded in the consent of the people, it can have no power over any individual by whom that consent is refused. If a tacit consent be not sufficient, still less can I be deemed to have consented to a measure upon which I put an express negative. This immediately follows from the observations of Rousseau. If the people, or the individuals of whom the people is constituted, cannot delegate their authority to a representative, neither can any individual delegate his authority to a majority, in an assembly of which he is himself a member. That must surely be a singular species of consent, the external indications of which are often to be found, in an unremitting opposition in the first instance, and compulsory subjection in the second.[31]

The principle of the original contract rested upon the assumption that men were obliged to keep their promises. No doctrine of contract could exist without this assumption. Godwin argued that promises and compacts were not the foundation of morality. Justice was the foundation of morality, and justice for Godwin was unrelated to promises, being solely concerned with 'the wants of one man, and the abilities of another to relieve them'.[32]

> Why should we observe our promises? The only rational answer that can be made is, because it tends to the welfare of intelligent beings. But this answer is equally cogent, if applied to any other branch of morality. It is therefore absurd to rest the foundation of morality thus circuitously upon promises, when it may with equal propriety be rested upon that form which promises themselves derive their obligation.[33]

Godwin took his argument a second step by saying that promises were absolutely evil. They resulted in persons performing acts, not for their intrinsic recommendations, but because of the promises. They also limited what one could do for others. Promises did not take into account that men were always acquiring new knowledge and perspectives, and thus limited the use of this new knowledge.

He distinguished two reasons for breaking promises. The first involved a promise made without an intention to perform it. Breaking this kind of promise would indicate that one was 'deficient in delicacy of moral discrimination'.[34] The second resulted from additional information persuading one of the utility of breaking the promise. This might be justified.

With the attack on consent and promises, Godwin dismissed the idea of the social contract as the basis of government. He then proceeded to outline what he considered to be the rational basis of political authority.

> Government then being first supposed necessary for the welfare of mankind, the most important principle that can be imagined relative to its structure, seems to be this; that as government is a transaction in the name and for the benefit of the whole, every member of the community ought to have some share in the selection of its measures.[35]

Godwin argued that there was no satisfactory criterion for deciding which group of men should be placed over the rest. Since all men used reason and had access to truth, no potential wisdom should be excluded from such momentous affairs. Only after an event had passed, could we know which men were wise in guiding their fellows. Since government was instituted for the security of the individual, it was reasonable that each should have a share in providing for this security. Finally, a good effect of this participation was the opportunity it afforded for the exercise of private judgment. 'Each man will thus be inspired with a consciousness of his own importance, and the slavish feelings that shrink up the soul in the presence of an imagined superior will be unknown.'[36]

In place of the idea of the social contract, he introduced the concept of 'common deliberation'. Men discussed and agreed on matters; and a contract was irrelevant. According to this doctrine, there was no obligation, and no man was bound by a formal agreement in any manner. A person might participate because it was the best way to persuade the whole to accept his views. He might obey the decision, either because he approved, or because he feared that disobedience would create worse evils. He might also choose not to participate and not to obey.

What Godwin considered 'common deliberation' was not similar to Rousseau's conception of the operation of the General Will in Du Contrat Social. Where government was necessary, representation must be used. In small states, this would amount to the appointment of officers and administrators, and in large states, a house of representatives. There was a difference, he said, between the personal exercise of authority and its exercise when government was once admitted to be necessary. If it was an evil, it was a necessary one. 'The true and only adequate apology of government is necessity; the office of common deliberation is solely, to supply the most eligible means of meeting that necessity.'[37]

Assuming the necessity of government, for the present, Godwin raised the problem of obedience and authority. Rational obedience was not based on contract, and his arguments here were similar to those used for contracts and promises. He also wrote that there were three kinds of obedience. The first was purely voluntary, depending upon the value of the action to be performed, and not on the interference of another. The second kind occurred in a situation where 'confidence' was placed in someone to do something. 'To justify, in a moral view, the reposing of confidence, the only thing necessary is, that it should be fitter and more beneficial, all things considered, that the function to be performed should be performed by another person, than that it should be performed by me.'[38] The third kind of obedience was not prescribed by private judgment. I should obey 'merely on account of the mischievous consequences that I foresee will be annexed to my omission, by the arbitrary interference of some voluntary being'.[39] Compulsory obedience was often less injurious than forming a habit of the second kind. To repose excessive confidence was to give up one's independence and critical powers.

> Obey the unjust manadates of your governors; for this prudence and a consideration of the common safety may require; but treat them with no false lenity, regard them with no indulgence. Obey; this may be right; but beware of reverence. Reverence nothing but wisdom and skill; government may be vested in the fittest persons; then they are entitled to reverence, because they are wise, and not because they are governors....[40]

Authority, wrote Godwin, was the correlative of obedience. There were three kinds of authority, corresponding to the three kinds of obedience. The first was the authority of reason; the second depended upon confidence in another; the third arose with the conjunction of power and sanctions. Godwin worried most about the second type, about the loss of man's critical powers under government of any external authority. Freedom, for Godwin, ultimately depended upon the ability to remain critical about institutions and ideas. This is a disturbing conclusion to Godwin's principles of government. Since government is a necessary evil, it is, perhaps, better to have it consciously evil than unconsciously less than evil. The latter, though not as difficult to endure, may be more difficult to remove.

The importance of his conclusion is that it demonstrates how an emphasis on 'consciousness' rather than 'rightness' may lead to a condition where they conflict. In order to do what is good, men must 'see things as they are', and to 'see things as they are', they must be conscious of them. Godwin's science of politics cannot be cluttered with the dust of authority. To improve intellectually we must eliminate the acceptance of knowledge on authority, indeed, the acknowledgment of authority at all (unless absolutely necessary or in the sense of the authority of reason). In this process lies the hope of all moral improvement.

A moral doctrine based upon feeling and a political doctrine expressly excluding a reliance on what is traditionally referred to as moral authority, leads in two directions, however rapidly or slowly. It leads either towards a benevolent despotism or in the direction of a democracy of temperate men conducting their affairs in a manner conducive to the general happiness.

Godwin's notions of the right of private judgment and common deliberation tended to insure a movement in the latter direction. However, it is important to realise that the seeds for both types of regimes were being planted.

This difficulty, though endemic to his science of politics, might have been alleviated if government had not been regarded as wholly a necessary evil. There is a great distance between the English Constitution and 'common deliberation'. Conceiving most government as solely a coercive instrument prevents one from emphasising that it makes a difference whether it is more or less coercive. Although government is a necessary evil, Godwin might have devoted greater attention to making it less evil than less necessary. The juxtaposition of a more desirable 'common deliberation' to an undesirable state coercion does not resolve the interim difficulties.

CHAPTER IV

DEMOCRACY

Godwin claimed that all normal men had within their power the ability to comprehend and solve moral and political problems. A condition of society in which this activity took place, he called a democracy. As between monarchy, aristocracy and democracy, he favoured democracy, because it best met his criterion of the good society, that it least impeded the growth of knowledge.

Of monarchy, in general, he wrote:

> If we contemplate the human powers, whether body or mind, we shall find them much better suited, to the superintendence of our private concerns, and to the administering occasional assistance to others, than to the accepting the formal trust of superintending the affairs, and watching for the happiness of millions. If we recollect the physical and moral equality of mankind, it will appear a very violent usurpation upon this principle, to place one individual at so vast an interval from the rest of his species.[1]

Anyone seeking to contribute to the welfare of others must be adequately informed of their circumstances. He must also have the capacity to solve their problems.

> But for one man to undertake to administer the affairs of millions, to supply, not general principles and perspicuous reasoning, but particular application, and measures adapted to the necessities of the moment, is of all undertakings the most extravagant and absurd.[2]

Monarchy thus placed the ruler farthest from the ruled, although he should be close to the situation. It was absurd to think that one man could change the circumstances of so many. Godwin then argued that the idea that monarchy was more suitable to large states and republican governments to small ones was fallacious. The same criticism applied to the advocates of the virtuous despot. 'A despot, however virtuously disposed, is obliged to act in the dark, to derive his knowledge from other men's information, and to execute his decisions by other men's instrumentality.'[3] It was doubtful that his ministers and servants would be as virtuous as he.

Of crucial importance to Godwin was the influence of monarchy on its subjects. Monarchy was supported by an imposture maintained by regal splendour and the exaggeration of titles, duties and honours. This imposture generated an indifference to both real merit and truth, because distinctions were not based upon these qualities. Furthermore, the necessity to maintain imposture (or 'salutary prejudice', as Burke called it) stimulated artificial desires by the necessity of splendid and luxurious displays. Public spirit and personal integrity tended to be sacrificed in these practices.

Monarchy was not improved for Godwin by such variations as elected monarchy, limited monarchy, or the presidential system as it was organised in the United States. The purpose of an elected monarchy was to enable extraordinary men to be chosen for office or to prevent inferior men from succeeding to it. It was unlikely, however, that a man could be found sufficiently virtuous and wise to be a king. It was also unlikely that such a man would be selected. Godwin added that the defects of monarchy could not be avoided merely by electing the monarch. Limited monarchy added even more difficulties to the monarchical system. 'In a limited monarchy, there are checks, one branch of the government counteracting the excesses of another, and a check without responsibility, is the most flagrant contradiction.'[4]

In presenting the case against aristocracy, Godwin first considered the idea of hereditary distinction. Although children, in some ways, resembled their parents, this provided no basis for distinction based upon inheritance. 'The son of a poet is not a poet, the son of an orator an orator, nor the son of a good man a saint.'[5]

He acknowledged that the case for hereditary aristocracy had also been stated on moral grounds. It was important to sustain a class of men of superior education and moral qualities to oppose the 'unruly mob'. Although these qualities may not have been hereditary, they could be developed through education. A person raised in poverty and corrupted by a myriad of influences was not able to attain this refinement for which great leisure and uncorrupting surroundings were necessary. Therefore, an aristocracy might as well be based on hereditary distinction.

Godwin admitted that, in part, this argument was correct, but it was only partially correct.

> The sound moralist, will be the last man to deny the power and importance of education. It is therefore necessary, either that a system should be discovered for securing leisure and prosperity to every member of the community; or that a certain influence and authority should be given to the liberal and wise, over the illiterate and ignorant. Now, supposing, for the present, that the former of these measures is impossible, it may be reasonable to enquire whether aristocracy be the most judicious scheme for obtaining the latter.[6]

He argued that aristocracy was not the best way to obtain an ascendancy of the liberal and wise over the illiterate and ignorant.

> The plebian must expect to find himself neglected and despised, in proportion as he is remiss in cultivating the objects of esteem; the lord will always be surrounded by sycophants and slaves. The lord therefore has no motive to industry and exertion; no stimulus to rouse him from the lethargic, 'oblivious pool', out of which every human intellect originally rose.[7]

Furthermore, an aristocratic system could survive only on the basis of unearned privilege and a monopoly of wealth in the hands of the aristocracy. It could sustain itself only as long as it maintained a condition of ignorance elsewhere in society.

> Should the lower ranks of society once come to be generally able to read and write, its powers would be at an end. To make men serfs and villains, it is indispensibly necessary to make them brutes..., The resolute advocates of the old system have, with no contemptible foresight, opposed the communication of knowledge, as a most alarming innovation.[8]

It was thus doubtful that aristocracy produced conditions which led to the ascendancy of the liberal and wise. Burke's idea of a 'natural aristocracy' which combined an hereditary elite with an aristocracy of merit would be an impossible ideal for Godwin.[9]

Godwin insisted that democracy was the superior regime.

> Democracy is a system of government, according to which every member of society is considered as a man, and nothing more. So far as positive regulation is concerned, if indeed that can, with any propriety, be termed regulation, which is the mere recognition of the simplest of all moral principles, every man is regarded as an equal. Talents and wealth, wherever they exist, will not fail to obtain a certain degree of influence, without requiring positive institution to second their operation.[10]

He listed the evils alleged to accompany democracy. The unwise outnumbered the wise, and the latter were at the mercy of the former. The crafty demagogue obtained power by deceiving the multitude. A democracy continually wavered; 'the mass of mankind, as they have never arranged their reflections into system, are at the mercy of every momentary impulse, and liable to change with every wind.'[11] A democracy was liable to act with rash confidence at the prompting of passion. Finally, the people suspected the uncommon and virtuous man. Godwin replied that if these statements were true, not even monarchy and aristocracy could survive. But, he argued, the contemporary notion of man was of that type of man who had lived under monarchy and aristocracy; these regimes had undermined and destroyed his virtue.

> Democracy restores to man a consciousness of his value, teaches him, by the removal of authority and oppression, to listen only to the suggestions of reason, gives him confidence to treat all other men with frankness and simplicity, and induces him to regard them no longer, as enemies against whom to be upon his guard, but as brethren whom it becomes him to assist.[12]

Godwin pointed to ancient Athens, with all of its faults and imperfections, as an example of the democratic system.

> Shall we compare a people of such incredible achievements, such exquisite refinement, gay without insensibility, and splendid without intemperance, in the midst of whom grew up the greatest poets, the noblest artists, the most finished orators, and the most disinterested philosophers, the world ever saw, -- shall we compare this chosen seat of patriotism, independence and generous virtue, with the torpid and selfish realms of monarchy and aristocracy? All is not happiness that looks tranquillity. Better were a portion of turbulence

> and fluctuation, than that unwholesome calm
> in which all the best faculties of the human
> mind are turned to putrescence and poison.[13]

As an improvement on the institutions of the ancients, Godwin advocated the use of representative assemblies which would avoid the tumult associated with democracies. Representative bodies secured the 'pretended benefits of aristocracy, as well as the real benefits of democracy.'[14] In such councils public affairs were brought before men of superior education who generally followed the directions of their constituents; yet, the constituents at times act 'in the same manner as an unlearned parent delegates his authority over his child to a preceptor of greater accomplishments than himself.'[15] However, these assemblies created problems of their own. They compounded the problem of the tyranny of the majority by removing power and responsibility one step further from the people. 'Representation, therefore, though a remedy, or rather a palliative, for certain evils, is not a remedy so excellent or complete, as should authorise us to rest in it, as the highest improvement of which the social order is capable.'[16] With qualifications, Godwin thus approved the idea of representation. However, he did not extend that approval to the **institutions** of national assemblies. These, he felt, produced a fictitious and unnatural unanimity of opinion, and were especially degrading to the outvoted minority which must assist in carrying out decisions. Connection with sects and parties, fear of being disclaimed by associates, and the hope of success created uniformity. Furthermore, debates ended with a vote, distorting their reasonable tenor; it was perverse to believe that truth could be discovered by counting heads.

Like the use of Roman dictators, national assemblies should be convened for emergency situations or should meet for very limited periods each year. At first, these assemblies would exercise a sovereignty over subordinate units. Eventually, they might 'invite them to co-operate for the common advantage, and, by arguments and addresses, convince them of the reasonableness of the measures they propose.'[17] At the local level, Godwin envisaged the use of jury systems to perform most governmental functions.

Godwin's defence of democracy depended upon his refutation of a particular argument: 'the supposed necessity of deception and prejudice for restraining the turbulence of human passions.'[18] In examining the problem, he selected three cases where political imposture had been deemed necessary.

The first was the establishment of a doctrine of eternal punishments for evil acts committed on earth, allegedly necessary to restrain the passions and maintain order. Godwin pointed out that numerous civilisations had been able to survive without 'this dreadful apparatus of fire and brimstone, and a torment "the smoke of which ascends for ever and ever".'[19] A doctrine of a day of judgment was not essential to the religion of the Greeks and Romans. Furthermore, such doctrines were so foreign to experience that it was difficult either to accept or to understand them.

> If doctrines like these occupy the habitual reflections of any, it is not of the lawless, the violent and ungovernable, but of the sober and conscientious, overwhelming them with

> gratuitous anxiety, or persuading them
> passively to submit to despotism and
> injustice, that they may receive the
> recompense of their patience hereafter.[20]

The second example was taken from Rousseau's discussion of the 'Legislator' in Du Contrat Social, where he indicated the problems of instituting new laws by rational persuasion.

> There is this which has forced at all times
> the fathers of nations to resort to divine
> intervention and honour the gods with their
> own wisdom, in order that the peoples submit
> to the laws of the State as to those of
> nature, and recognising the same power in
> the formation of man and in the city, obey
> freely, and carry with docility, the yoke
> of public happiness.[21]

Rousseau was referring to the actions of Lycurgus at Sparta. In the account of the life of Lycurgus by Plutarch, Lycurgus went to Delphi _after_ the citizens had accepted the laws to obtain divine sanction for good measure. He also used this device only to ensure that the people would continue to obey his laws. Godwin would thus seem to be correct in asserting that Lycurgus appealed to the people's understandings through exhortation and persuasion.[22] Godwin argued that 'it is difficult to conceive a company of such miserable dupes, as to receive a code without any imagination that it is salutory or wise or just, but upon this single recommendation that it is delivered to them from the Gods'.[23] Furthermore, if it was desired to contribute to the welfare of the people, they should be taught to reason well rather than left to reason poorly. If prejudice was necessary to establish a regime, it was also necessary to maintain it.

Godwin's argument against Rousseau was that it was absurd to place power in the hands of the people without trusting their ability under a popular regime to exercise their reason. The use of prejudice prevented them from improving themselves to the point where a truly popular regime could be justified.

The third example, related to the second, was the belief, common to many political theories (and especially to be found in Burke) that obedience must be either courted or compelled. If imposture was not used to make citizens enthusiastically loyal, social order could be maintained only by the severity of punishment. Godwin replied:

> It [this argument for imposture] takes for granted, that a true observation of things, is inadequate to teach us our duty; and, of consequence, recommends an equivocal engine, which may with equal ease, be employed in the service of justice and injustice, but would surely appear somewhat more in its place in the service of the latter. It is injustice that stands most in need of superstition and mystery, and will most frequently be a gainer by the imposition.[24]

The use of imposture divided men into two classes, one to lead and the other to blindly obey. This, for Godwin, was an unwarranted distinction, considering man's basic equality. 'He that would reason with another, and honestly explain to him the motives of the action he recommends, descends to a footing of equality.'[25]

That Godwin directed much of his argument against Rousseau leads to the suspicion that his chapters on democracy were intended to refute Rousseau's doctrine, besides serving as a defence against such writers as Burke. Godwin's idea of democracy stood in sharp contrast to the Republican regime envisaged by Rousseau. The most critical difference was that Godwin's regime did not rest on juridicial foundations. Justice, but not law, was the foundation of society. When Rousseau wrote that 'democracy' was a government more suitable for gods than men, he was referring to democracy as a form of administration.[26] The laws had already been passed by the assembled citizens, and the question of forms of government was merely one of whether one, some, or all of the people should administer the laws. Rousseau rejected democracy because it was absurd for all men to administer their own laws. If they did, there was no need for laws or the social contract.

Godwin argued that if there were no laws, the people might be able to administer to their own needs. If there was a necessity for a system of administration, a legislative system was unnecessary. If men were moral, they did not need law, and in addition, law could only restrain but not reform them. Godwin saw in democracy the beginning of a society which could exist without government.

Both Rousseau's republic and Godwin's democracy must be considered popular regimes, as the people were ultimately responsible for their destiny. In this sense they agreed, although the two systems were very different. Godwin argued that each individual could know what actions contributed to the general welfare.

Rousseau said that the people were often mistaken about what was conducive to their own good. But he remedied what might be a deficiency in the individual by introducing an institution which was to correct this deficiency -- at least on a limited scale.

Godwin's solution again raises the question of the universality of his science of politics. Progress depended upon the minimization of imposture so that all men could obtain ethical or political knowledge. This could not be accomplished by institutions, as Rousseau would have it, because the institutions created and enforced imposture in society. However, if political knowledge could not be obtained by all men, because it required more than 'seeing things as they are', then the absence of institutions to impose moral authority on the people might lead to tumult and chaos.

Supposing that Godwin's idea of democracy was acceptable, the survival of such a regime in the midst of less virtuous neighbours posed a further problem. Godwin admitted that objections to democracy because of its alleged inability to conduct its foreign relations were as strong as those objections on the grounds of internal policy. In part, these objections were practical, founded on apprehensions of difficulties in reconciling the liberty of the regime with the discipline of an army. But Godwin felt he had avoided most of the practical problems by restricting the purposes of war to defence and advocating an army of citizen-guerrillas.

The major problem in foreign policy, as Godwin saw it, was defence in time of war. He believed that war was the product of a certain domestic order rather than a condition of international anarchy or hostility. Societies of just men would be little inclined to war. Although democracies were less adapted for offensive war than other regimes, the spirited pursuit of justice tended to equip them excellently for defence. Furthermore, as democracy was more just than monarchy and aristocracy, the tendency to war would decline with the establishment of the popular regimes.

Godwin was not a pacifist, though he believed that most reasons for war were untenable. Improving the character of the public, revenging private insults, anticipating hostilities of neighbours, drawing the line over small matters, or the vindication of national honour he regarded as illegitimate reasons for beginning a war. Only two legitimate reasons existed: the defence of one's own liberty and the liberty of others.

> This principle is capable of being abused by men of ambition and intrigue; but, accurately considered, the very same argument that should induce me to exert myself for the liberties of my own country, is equally cogent, so far as my opportunities and abilities extend, with respect to the liberties of any other country. But what is my duty in this case, is the duty of all; and the exertion must be collective, where collective exertion only can be effectual.[27]

Since defence was the only legitimate reason for going to war, the object of war should be limited to defence. War should not be used for purposes of reforming a society, restraining it from future acts, or indemnification.

> War... perhaps, never originates, on the offending side, in the sentiments of a nation, but of a comparatively small number of individuals: and, were it otherwise, there is something so monstrous, in the idea of changing the principles of a whole country by the mode of military execution, that every man not lost to sobriety and common sense, may be expected to shrink from it with horror.[28]

If war was the major concern of foreign relations, peace was the major object. There were two alternative viewpoints: peace was an arrangement between states, and peace was the result of arrangements within states. Adopting the second position, Godwin treated international relations in terms of the best regime, democracy.

Those who emphasised relations between states for the achievement and preservation of peace usually favoured commerce and republican institutions as means of maintaining some sort of international order. Commerce, wrote Paine, 'is a pacific system, operating to unite mankind, by rendering nations, as well as individuals, useful to each other.'[29] The extension of commerce would destroy the system of war. In the same vein, Montesquieu observed that peace was the natural result of trade.[30] Kant wrote that commerce would lead men to peace without establishing despotism.[31] The republican form of government was also believed to be conducive to peace. It was important to Kant, not because men would improve in knowledge and virtue, but because it, alone, was capable of ensuring the peace without resorting to Hobbesian despotism. Although Kant was obviously concerned with the goodness and badness of men, this question was unrelated to the one about the best form of regime. Republics were best suited to bring an end to war, because the subject as citizen would not approve measures which would result in so much misery and destruction for himself. A federation of republican states would ensure peace.[32] Montesquieu wrote that peace and moderation were the spirit of the republic, while war and expansion, the spirit of monarchy.[33] Since a republic need be small, it must federate to achieve peace.[34] He pointed out that the federation should consist wholly of republics, as a monarchy within a federation of republics would eventually destroy it, because of its spirit of war and expansion. Thus, Montesquieu also arrived at the same conclusion as Kant. In Paine, also, was the idea that republicanism was opposed to war.[35]

Godwin hardly used the term 'republic' in Political Justice. When writing of commercial societies he said that 'republicanism is not a remedy that strikes at the root of the evil. Injustice, oppression and misery, can find an abode in those seeming happy seats.'[36] At this point he was concerned with the distribution of property. The good and peaceful society depended as much upon this as it did on its republican institutions. Godwin argued in these terms because he did not believe that peace could be secured without the establishment of just societies, and societies were not just merely because they were republican. Since justice was a prerequisite for peace, neither republicanism nor commerce could alone or together establish a lasting peace.[37]

Godwin's defence of democracy was essentially negative. Of monarchy, aristocracy, and democracy, it was the best political regime; it was also capable of surviving in the midst of less virtuous neighbours. Although Godwin vigorously defended this form of regime, he considered it neither the ideal organisation of men nor an end in itself. Democracy was merely the best of all 'political' organisations, as it least impeded the growth of the intellect, but it suffered from the defects of all 'political' organisations.

Godwin's justification of democracy might not be adequate, however, if the universality of his science of politics is questioned. That is, if some men are found to be incapable of obtaining ethical and political knowledge, how can a regime based on the universality of this capability survive? What seems to be conclusive justification of a temporary regime, may require, in fact, a more problematic consideration of a more permanent establishment. If progress becomes problematical, so must the survival of the regime which is designed to ensure this progress.

CHAPTER V

LIBERTY

Liberty is an ambiguous term, capable of many definitions and applications, and Godwin's idea of liberty is not without its own ambiguity. It suffices to say that it includes, in Isaiah Berlin's terms, both 'negative' and 'positive' liberty.[1] And there is a sense in which it might be said that Godwin did not believe in liberty at all.

Godwin apparently was not disturbed by these difficulties (though he was vexed by the problem of the freedom of the will). Civil or political liberty does not seem to have been an end in itself for him. In *Political Justice*, he made one important statement about liberty:

> Superficial thinkers lay great stress upon the external situation of men, and little upon their internal sentiments. Persevering enquiry will probably lead to a mode of thinking the reverse of this. To be free is a circumstance of little value, if we could suppose men in a state of external freedom, without the magnanimity, energy and firmness, that constitute almost all that is valuable in a state of freedom. On the other hand, if a man have these qualities, there is little left for him to desire. He cannot be degraded; he cannot readily become useless or unhappy. He smiles at the impotence of despotism; he fills up his existence with serene enjoyment and industrious benevolence. Civil liberty is chiefly desirable,

> as a means to procure and perpetuate this
> temper of mind. They therefore begin at the
> wrong end, who make haste to overturn and
> confound the usurped powers of the world.
> Make men wise, and, by that very operation,
> you make them free. Civil liberty follows
> as a consequence of this; no usurped power
> can stand against the artillery of opinion.
> Every thing then is in order, and succeeds
> at its appointed time. How unfortunate is it,
> that men are so eager to strike, and have so
> little constancy to reason![2]

Although he did not hold political liberty in the highest esteem, he is consistently considered by modern writers as a 'liberal' or 'libertarian'.[3] He advocated limited government; he argued for the autonomy of the individual. In no sense can the man who said that 'excessive familiarity is the bane of social happiness' be considered a 'collectivist'.[4] Indeed, Godwin used many liberal ideas and arguments, though he was concerned with liberty (in its many variations) as a means to an end.

Many arguments which are connected with liberty are not arguments wholly about liberty. A liberal argument for limited government is as much an argument about the nature of government as it is one about liberty. An argument for individual rights may be as much an argument about human nature as it is about liberty. It may be rash to conclude that political philosophers are generally concerned with liberty as a means to an end, and thus, when they are affirming liberty, they are actually approving or condemning other values.

Nevertheless, it may be safely said that there are arguments which invoke the term 'liberty' which are not wholly about liberty. Godwin was fairly clear in his intentions: he was concerned with justice and happiness, and liberty was a means to another means (intellectual improvement) to these ends.

Of all of the problems which disturbed Godwin, one of the most important and unresolvable ones was the question of the freedom of the will. To suggest that he made a significant contribution to the technical solution of the debate between advocates of free will and necessity would be an overstatement. However, his dissatisfaction with the doctrine and the reasons for this dissatisfaction remain of interest in raising the question of whether there is a problem of the freedom of the will.[5] Godwin supported the doctrine of necessity. In Political Justice his arguments consisted primarily of a recognition of events in the universe, reducible to chains of cause and effect. His explanation of the doctrine added little that was new. However, from his idea of necessity, he devised his notions of duty, punishment, progress, etc. Indeed, the science of politics might lose its close relationship to human improvement if no necessary link existed between 'seeing things as they are' and acting to contribute to the general happiness. Godwin admitted that the terms used in explaining events according to necessity were somewhat at variance with common sense and discourse. He conceded that man's languages reflected the doctrine of free will. This, he maintained, needed to be changed, because 'accuracy of language is an indespensible prerequisite of sound knowledge'.[6]

By 1800, just three years after the third edition of
Political Justice, Godwin was no longer convinced of his own
argument.

> Too much stress is, I apprehend, laid in the
> *Enquiry concerning Political Justice*, on the
> inferences from the doctrine of necessity.
> That doctrine may perhaps be beneficially
> applied towards extirpating the odious sen-
> timents of revenge, and moderating the fury
> of political and private animosities. But we
> live in a world of delusion; we appreciate
> persons and things, not by an impartial
> standard, but from their nearness to our-
> selves; nor is this by any means without its
> use. We should lose the noblest emotions and
> sentiments of our nature by an indiscriminate
> application of the vulgar maxim, 'It will be
> the same thing an hundred years hence': and
> the moral feelings of approbation and dis-
> approbation, in their finest tones, would be
> extinguished within us, if we constantly viewed
> our fellow men in the light of machines.[7]

In *Thoughts of Man*, published thirty years later, Godwin
returned to the same problem. 'The question, which has been attended
with so long and obstinate debates, concerning the metaphysical
doctrines of liberty and necessity, and the freedom of human actions,
is not even yet finally and satisfactorily settled.'[8] He repeated his
case for the doctrine of necessity, and then questioned why it had not
been accepted. Godwin's own reply was that the human mind would reject
demonstrations and adhere to the senses. This had taken place with
respect to Berkeley's arguments for the non-existence of the external

world. People intuitively felt that they had a freedom of the will. Godwin called this the 'delusive sense of liberty'.[9]

> And, though the philosopher in his closet will for the most part fully assent to the doctrine of the necessity of human actions, yet this indestructible feeling of liberty, which accompanies us from the cradle to the grave is entitled to our serious consideration....[10]

He admitted that the language of civilisation, the language which illuminated the moral world, was dependent upon a doctrine of free will.

> It is to this we are indebted for all our refinement, and, in the noblest sense of the word, for all our humanity. Without it we should have had no sentiment ... and no poetry. -- Love and hatred, as we regard our fellow creatures, in contradistinction to the complacency, or the feeling of an opposite nature, which is excited in us toward inanimate objects, are entirely the offspring of the delusive sense of liberty.[11]

He also admitted the folly of attempting to change the language of common intercourse to incorporate the idea of necessity.

> The mode therefore in which the advocates of the doctrine of necessity have universally talked and written, is one of the most memorable examples of the hallucination of the human intellect. They have at all times recommended that we should translate the phrases in which we usually express ourselves on the hypothesis of liberty, into the phraseology of necessity, that we should talk no other language.... They did not perceive what a wide devastation and destruction they were proposing of all the terms and phrases that are in the communications between man and man in actual life.[12]

Godwin did not abandon his doctrine of necessity. In his closet, the philosopher could not but assent to the doctrine, and, as the number of educated persons increased, it would become more widely accepted. He counselled his readers to follow the axiom: 'think with the learned and talk with the vulgar'.[13]

The student of Godwin is left with no clear light to guide him on this problem. However, one point seems evident: the implications of the doctrine of necessity were for Godwin, as important as the doctrine itself. Without the idea of freedom of the will, duty, obligation and responsibility would become paradoxical. But with free will, punishment might be retributive. Godwin never challenged the analogy between the material universe and human psychology. He might have modified his whole notion of necessity to accommodate a measure of freedom. His omission provides a clue to his intention, that he was more concerned with the consequences of the respective doctrines for morals and politics. Without the doctrine of necessity, ethical education might not be possible in the sense that Godwin conceived it. This education was a precondition for the cultivation of justice. As more men adjusted their behaviour to the demands of justice, the tasks of government might be increasingly restricted. Thus, the acceptance of the doctrine of necessity was a prerequisite for the establishment of limited government. This argument should not be carried too far. One might think limited government was possible, without previously digesting an argument for philosophical necessity. Nevertheless, it is obvious that when mass education becomes easier, or when it may proceed with a greater certainty of success, the tasks of government, especially the coercive ones, might be more limited.

Necessity provided this element of certainty in Godwin's system and thus contributed to his doctrine of limited government. However, his argument for limited government required more than the doctrine of necessity. Limited government recalls the doctrine of Locke, which Godwin followed in conceiving the ends of government in a negative manner. Nevertheless, the two diverged significantly. For Locke, government should be limited so that men can 'order and dispose'. For Godwin, it should be limited because it was evil in the effects it created in society. For Locke, law should be consistent and government should not be arbitrary. For Godwin, all law and government were arbitrary. For Locke, law enlarged man's liberty, and protected man from man in society. For Godwin, men protected themselves from law in society. For Locke, individualism depended upon man being protected from his fellows. For Godwin, it depended upon man's social relations, individualism being necessary for improvement and progress.

These differences probably stem from Godwin's individualism which was closer to Rousseau than to Locke. Although Godwin resisted the idea that good laws made good men, his individualism was expressed in terms of an individual self-fulfilment. 'Man is a species of being, whose excellence depends upon his individuality; and who can be neither great nor wise, but in proportion as he is independent.'[14] However, man was not free to 'order and dispose'. He was free from government in order that he became virtuous. Furthermore his freedom from government depended on the ability of society to dispense justice; the constraints of government could be replaced only by a just society.[15]

Besides the themes of limited government and individualism, there are some additional ones to which a question of liberty is attached. The problem of rights and duties has already been discussed.[16] Another significant problem is that of resistance and revolution.

Godwin began his analysis of resistance by considering the right of resistance in 'the nation' as a whole. He said that a right of resistance to usurpation was usually taken for granted. However, if the problem was carefully examined, it would be found that this 'right' was attended with 'equivocal circumstances'.

> What do we mean by a nation? Is the whole people concerned in this resistance, or only a part? If the whole be prepared to resist, the whole is persuaded of the injustice of the usurpation. What sort of usurpation is that, which can be exercised by one or a few persons, over a whole nation, universally disapproving of it? Government is founded in opinion.[17]

Since government was supported by opinion, a government which had ruled for a time was presumed to be based on opinion. Otherwise, it would not have survived. It was absurd to urge resistance by violence, as no power could long rule without the favour of the people. Godwin qualified his words by saying that 'there can be little doubt of the justifiableness, of a whole nation having recourse to arms, if a case can be made out, in which it shall be impossible for them to prevent the introduction of slavery in any other way'.[18]

The reasoning applied to a whole nation might be also applied to instances where the rights of the majority were asserted. However, Godwin saw additional problems here. It was common to think one's own cause was supported by a majority when it was not, and a large number of that majority might be mere parrots who little understood the enterprise they advocated. Godwin's alternative to resistance by the majority was delay. In time, whether the people decisively desired to resist would become evident, and if the cause was just, men would eventually join it.

Godwin emphatically denied that a minority of a nation had a right of resistance. No small group had a right to use violence and disturb society, unless the group, as individuals, were acting in self-defence. Much of the difficulty in setting the limits and basis for resistance arose from the confusion of 'resistance' in a nation with 'self-defence' as it applied to an individual. An individual could be destroyed by one specific act, while a nation could not suffer in the same manner. Although men were bound to act in self-defence to avoid destruction, this did not extend to others in a political situation. At the least, resistance to government for the protection of others should follow from such considerations as whether this resistance would improve public institutions and whether the individuals involved deserved protection.

> The value of the individuals ought not to be
> forgotten; there are men whose safety should
> be cherished by us with anxious attention;
> but it is difficult to imagine a case, in which,
> for their sake, the lives of thousands, and the
> fate of millions, should be committed to risk.[19]

Resistance in the nation then should follow a careful assessment of the impact of the injury and its permanence. 'Resistance, by the very meaning of the term, as it is used in political enquiry, signifies a species of conduct that is to be adopted, in relation to an established authority: but an old grievance, seems obviously to lead, as its counterpart, to a gradual and temperate remedy.'[20]

The problem of resistance leads to the problem of revolution; and Godwin set forth several arguments against revolution. Revolution threatened and might destroy the freedom to speak and write opinions and to exercise individuality.

> Revolution is instigated by a horror against
> tyranny, yet its own tyranny is not without
> peculiar aggravations. There is no period
> more at war with the existence of liberty.
> The unrestrained communication of opinions has
> always been subjected to mischievous counter-
> action, but upon such occasions it is trebly
> fettered. At other times men are not so much
> alarmed for its effects. But in a moment of
> revolution, when every thing is in crisis, the
> influence even of a word is dreaded, and the
> consequent slavery is complete.[21]

Advocates of revolution usually replied that the oppressors could only be removed by silencing them with severe injury. Godwin answered, 'Is slavery the best project that can be devised, for making men free? Is a display of terror the readiest mode, for rendering them fearless, independent and enterprising?'[22] During revolutionary periods, enquiry and speculation were brought to a halt. The search for truth, on which human improvement depended, required calm and leisure, and in a disturbed period these were not available. Revolutions also produced bad moral effects on men and societies, not because men died, for death was not the greatest human evil, but because shedding blood brutalised people.

> The perpetrators, and the witnesses of murders, become obdurate, unrelenting and inhuman. Those who sustain the loss of relations and friends by a catastrophe of this sort, are filled with indignation and revenge. Distrust is propagated from man to man, and the dearest ties of human society are dissolved. It is impossible to devise a temper more inauspicious to the cultivation of justice, and the diffusion of benevolence.[23]

Finally, revolution was a crude method of change, and usually premature. Godwin preferred more gradual progress in its place.

> There is a condition of political activity best adapted to every different stage of individual improvement. The more nearly this condition is successively realised, the more advantageously will the general interest be consulted. There is a sort of provision in the nature of the human mind for this species of progress.[24]

Against those who were impatient of the long period necessary for truth to take effect in society, Godwin said that every attempt to move too rapidly was followed by calamity. Even the advocates of revolution admitted that 'a grand revolution includes in it the sacrifice of one generation'.[25] Furthermore, it was absurd to believe that violence and popular commotion were necessary for human improvement. Where political opinions changed, political institutions must relax their grip. Reform was not impossible; neither were its benefits as remote as some believed. Nevertheless, Godwin was aware that his words would not bring an end to revolution. 'The duty therefore of the true politician, is to postpone revolution, if he cannot entirely prevent it.'[26]

The right of resistance was usually defended by thinkers in the English liberal tradition; tyrannicide was generally condemned.[27] Godwin also opposed tyrannicide, but he did not oppose it with the strictness found, for example, in Hume.[28] His approach was more utilitarian. On balance, tyrannicide was not a good solution to the problem. Either a nation was ready for liberty or it was not; if it was, tyrannicide was only permissible if the tyrant was killed by someone whom he had attacked and if the killing occurred in self-defence. If the assassination failed, the tyrant was sure to become worse. Furthermore, assassination was accompanied by secret plots and intrigue; it was not frank and open, as political action ought to be.

Just as intrigue and assassination were inimical to the public good and understanding, so too were political factions which engendered tumult and restlessness. In the eighteenth century, many people favoured political associations as a means of spreading useful political information and influencing public opinion. Godwin's opposition to political associations rested on several grounds. Since all men could not participate in the affairs of an association, the views of a few stood for the whole. The formation of associations generated the formation of other associations to oppose them. 'Thus we should probably be involved in all the mischiefs of resistance, and all the uproar of revolution.'[29] Since political reform was based on an apprehension of truth, political associations were useless, because they succumbed to party spirit. Publications sponsored by such associations were seldom concerned with the truth or falsity of doctrines, but with arguing particular points of view. Political associations also tended to encourage conformity rather than individuality. To this attitude toward associations, Godwin made two exceptions. When a crisis occurred, associations might be necessary for safety, and *ad hoc* associations might be formed for some general reform or as a remedy for a pressing evil.

In delineating the role of government in society, Godwin set strict limits to the instances where the coercion of citizens was a legitimate function. As government arose to repair defects in society (and should be limited to that function), a major activity of government was the punishment of criminals. At the outset, Godwin dismissed the idea of retributive punishment. If all things were necessary, if 'the assassin cannot help the murder he commits, any more than the dagger', then suffering should not be inflicted on a vicious man.[30] The only legitimate reason for punishment was utility. The only purpose for which punishment might be inflicted on a person was to prevent future mischief.

Godwin wrote that punishment was supposed to serve either or all of these functions: restraint, reformation, and example. Of restraint, he asked how it was known that a man would commit another crime, merely because he had already committed one? If a person was known to be in financial difficulty and had other pressing problems, should he be locked up? Godwin also questioned the value of punishment for reformation. Coercion could never lead to a reform in character.

> Coercion cannot convince, cannot conciliate, but on the contrary alienates the mind of him against whom it is employed. Coercion has nothing in common with reason, and therefore can have no proper tendency to the cultivation of virtue.[31]

Punishment for purposes of example was the worst of the three. This system failed because example soon exhausted itself, and the effects were useful only as long as they were novel. The impression was easily lost, and it was unjust, because the victim was being punished for something he did not do.

With doubt cast on the supposed purposes of punishment, Godwin turned his attention to the problem of matching crimes and punishments. In his view there had never been two crimes exactly alike. Thus, it was impossible to reduce these acts to general classes. In considering a crime, should the criminal be punished for the act or the intention? Beccaria, wrote Godwin, considered only the action.[32] However, could all instances of a certain class be treated alike? Were all actions which resulted in death to be punished in the same manner? It was difficult to argue that a malicious murder deserves the same punishment as an accidental killing. Furthermore, crimes could not be classified solely by intention. For 'this attempt would lead, by a very obvious process, to the abolition of all punishment'.[33] It was impossible to determine the motives which led a man to perform a certain act. Usually, the person, himself, was not conscious of many of his own motives. How could the future motives of a person be predicted?

Godwin also opposed the view of punishment as a temporary expedient. 'Punishment has no proper tendency to prepare men for a state in which punishment shall cease.'[34] Societies might instead change their institutions which gave rise to these evils. While society in a corporate sense had no right to use coercion, individuals might use it as a temporary expedient. Godwin advocated private efforts at restraining wrong-doing, taking this function away from government.

> I ought to take up arms against the despot by
> whom my country is invaded, because my capacity
> does not enable me by arguments to prevail on
> him to desist, and because my countrymen will
> not preserve their intellectual independence in
> the midst of oppression. For the same reason I
> ought to take up arms against the domestic spoiler,
> because I am unable, either to persuade him to
> desist, or the community to adopt a just political
> institution, by means of which security might be
> maintained, consistently with the abolition of
> punishment.[35]

Godwin took great pains to distinguish this condition from anarchy. If it resulted in anarchy, it would be better to introduce some form of coercion. But, coercion for purposes of restraint could be legitimately introduced only as a temporary expedient. Neither corporal nor capital punishment had any justification.

Although Godwin attacked any privation of freedom, he admitted that it might be necessary. There were, however, different forms of restraint. 'Jails are, to a proverb, seminaries of vice; and he must be an uncommon proficient in the passion and the practice of injustice, or a man of sublime virtue, who does not come out of them a much worse man than he entered.'[36] Solitary confinement was a worse punishment. Its moral effects were disastrous, because man was a social animal who could not cultivate his sense of justice and benevolence alone. A method which appealed to Godwin was banishment and he favoured colonisation as the best form, although he recognised that there was no perfect solution. 'Men who are freed from the injurious institutions of European government, and obliged to begin the world for themselves, are in the direct road to be virtuous.'[37]

Godwin believed that even more important than restrictions on the coercive powers of government were restraints on government control of opinion.

> ...[I]f opinion be rendered a topic of political superintendence, we are immediately involved in a slavery, to which no imagination of man can set a termination. The hopes of our improvement are arrested; for government fixes the mercurialness of man to an assigned station. We can no longer enquire or think; for enquiry and thought are uncertain in their direction, and unshackled in their termination. We sink into motionless inactivity and the basest cowardice; for our thoughts and words are beset on every side with penalty and menace.[38]

Godwin opposed every possible kind of government control of opinion. As a result, he presented two arguments which run counter even to liberal thought. First, he opposed constitutions. Paine had written that 'government without a constitution, is power without a right'.[39] In opposition to Burke, Paine insisted that a real constitution was a written one as was the American constitution, and he challenged Burke to produce the English constitution.[40] But this dispute over the importance of constitutions did not seem to Godwin very important.

> If, by this objection, it be understood, that they have no written code bearing this appellation, and that their constitutions have been less an instantaneous, than a gradual production, the criticism seems to be rather verbal, than of essential moment.[41]

His concern with constitutions was more fundamental. He questioned the distinction which was generally made between fundamental (constituent) and temporary (legislative) laws. He said that if men had never known arbitrary and unjust rulers, they would never have thought it necessary to separate certain laws from the main body, and make the former more permanent than the latter. Men only began to ask questions about where power originated, when they were faced with the 'usurpations' of kings and nobles.

> But, if we saw no power existing in the state but that of the people, having a body of representatives, and a certain number of official secretaries and clerks acting in their behalf, subject to their revisal, and renewable at their pleasure, the question, how the people came by this authority, would never have suggested itself.[42]

Godwin then questioned the necessity of a constitution in a just society. Permanent laws were incompatible with the human capacity for improvement. Godwin did not mean that people had a right to govern themselves as they pleased. They ought, however, to be free from permanent laws to be able to determine what modes of conduct were just.

As an illustration, he examined the French constitution. In 1792 the convention assembled whose purpose was to draft a constitution which was to be submitted to the districts for their consent. Why were only the fundamental laws to be submitted to the districts?

asked Godwin. 'It is possible for the most odious injustice to be perpetrated, by the best constituted legislature that ever was framed.'[43] Godwin did not reject the idea of the consent of the districts to the laws. He wanted it extended to all laws, and he wanted the consent to be more than a simple affirmative or negative. It should be consent following the exercise of the understanding, and if men proceeded in this manner, they would never come to a conclusion.

> This principle of a consent of districts, has an immediate tendency to lead to the dissolution of all government. What then can be more absurd, than to see it embraced by those very men who are, at the same time, advocates for the complete legislative unity of a great empire? It is founded on the same basis as the principle of private judgment, which, in proportion as it impresses itself on the minds of men, may be expected perhaps to supersede the possibility of the action of society in a collective capacity.[44]

In Godwin's view, several consequences would follow a practice of the consent of the districts. The constitution would be reduced to a small number of articles, because few districts would agree. Soon, the districts would begin to legislate for themselves, and eventually, law would disappear.

> A large city, impelled by the principles of commercial jealousy, is not slow to digest the volume of its by-laws and exclusive privileges. But the inhabitants of a small parish, living with some degree of that simplicity which best corresponds to the real nature and wants of a human being, would soon be led to suspect that general laws were unnecessary....[45]

Godwin thus suggested how the strict application of a major principle of constitutionalism could lead to the eventual elimination of constitutions. At the end, he alluded to an alternative regime to the large commercial city, the small parish in which life was simple but cultivated. When government became unnecessary, Godwin could imagine a post-political way of life, built around small groups, as opposed to large commercial cities or nation-states.

Secondly, Godwin flatly opposed national education as a means of improving mankind.[46] National education produced permanent opinions on subjects. 'The moment any scheme of proceeding gains a permanent establishment, it becomes impressed, as one of its characteristic features, with an aversion to change.'[47] National education also required a unity of operation. Finally, it was in alliance with government.

> This is an alliance of a more formidable nature, than the old and much contested alliance of church and state. Before we put so powerful a machine under the direction of so ambiguous an agent, it behoves us to consider well what it is that we do. Government will not fail to employ it, to strengthen its hands, and perpetuate its institutions.[48]

J.S. Mill believed that the state ought to provide universal education, and enforce legislation requiring education.[49] However, Mill opposed the state direction of education. Godwin argued here, as he did earlier, that it could not be both ways: either the state was limited or it controlled the individual.

Despite Godwin's eloquent and often persuasive attack on government, we have still to ask whether he is to be considered a liberal (or libertarian). In the early novel <u>Caleb Williams</u>, he wrote:

'Curiosity, so long as it lasted, was a principle stronger in my breast than even the love of independence. To that I would have sacrificed my liberty or my life'.[50] Indeed, Godwin praised the love of learning more than he praised liberty, except as a means to that end. In his posthumously published *Essays*, he spoke of freedom in terms of those rhythms of solitude and conversation which permeated the lives of the scholar and poet. 'Man is especially characterised by two propensities', he wrote, 'the love of society, and the love of solitude'.[51] Of the latter, he said:

> Lord Shaftesbury has laid it down as a maxim, that soliloquey is a habit indispensable to an author. We love to be alone. ... And, when we are alone, how do we revel in the unbounded freedom of thought, conscious that we are under no restraint either of man or ... of God Himself; that, within the limits of honour and innocence, we shall be called to no account, neither by any human tribunal, nor by a tribunal, which many of us look for, beyond the grave.[52]

The man of thought required these conversations both with others and with himself. In order to engage in soliloquey, the mind must have an independence, an autonomy. For this reason, Godwin argued his case for liberty. However, Berlin's criticism of J.S.Mill may become relevant here: 'But the evidence of history tends to show ... that integrity, love of truth and fiery individualism grow at least as often in severely disciplined communities ... or under military discipline, as in more tolerant or indifferent societies; and if this is so accepted, Mill's argument for liberty as a necessary condition for the growth of genius falls to the ground'.[53] Even if Berlin is correct, it does not follow that Godwin's argument is damaged, because Godwin was concerned more with the emancipation of all men than with the cultivation of certain virtues. He pointed to the great philosophers of the middle ages who had developed their genius in the midst of barbarous feudal societies, but he did not find this to be surprising.[54] He did not deny that these virtues existed in societies which did not exalt liberty. Nonetheless, he believed that the progress of mankind, as a whole, depended on the value placed on liberty.[55] Furthermore, Godwin would be in partial agreement with Berlin in recognising that men, once conscious of their chains, could progress while they were in slavery.

Liberty was a means to an end for Godwin, although there is no doubt that it was an important means. What is at issue is whether the ends exclude the means, whether the kind of society Godwin hoped to see established would exclude liberty. Although he wrote little about it, Godwin envisaged a simple form of society which could exist without the institutions of government.

> If communities, instead of aspiring, as they
> have hitherto done, to embrace a vast territory,
> and glut their vanity with ideas of empire, were
> contented with a small district, with a proviso
> of confederation in cases of necessity, every
> individual would then live under the public eye;
> and the disapprobation of his neighbours, a
> species of coercion, not derived from the caprice
> of men, but from the system of the universe, would
> inevitably oblige him, either to reform, or to
> emigrate.[56]

Obviously, Godwin was interested in more than the fact of a society without government. Such a society presumed certain institutional arrangements within it. To be sure, it included an idea of liberty at its core. Nevertheless, it has been argued that 'utopian' speculations are often in conflict with traditional liberal thought.[57] It is not to be denied that some utopian doctrines do conflict with liberal ideas. But this is not a necessary consequence of what might be called utopianism, but rather the result of the nature of the utopia itself and the relationship between what is ultimately best and what presently exists. An ideal society which aimed to eliminate government and develop an autonomy for each individual must be considered to stress liberty.

But the means to achieve this ideal society might exclude liberty. If the relationship between means and ends excludes the possibility of liberty existing in the end society, Godwin might not be considered a libertarian. In a sense, this has been already noted. His concern with 'seeing things as they are' led to his acceptance of conditions of society which were antithetical to liberal sensibilities. However, this condition partly resulted from his refusing to accept a doctrine of moral authority, also antithetical to liberal sensibilities. And his willingness to accept a tyrant was only a temporary measure, and not one tied to his ideal society. The rate of progress from the real to the ideal did not seem to preclude a libertarian society in the end. Therefore, Godwin may be considered an advocate of liberty if it is understood that he placed liberty in a larger context by making it part of an ideal society. He showed that utopian and liberal thought need not be antithetical.

CHAPTER VI

ECONOMICS

Since the majority of a society have to labour, it is questionable whether they can also govern without the sacrifice of wisdom in deliberation or prosperity in the community. As Bentham put it:

> In the members of a Democracy in particular, there is likely to be a want of wisdom -- Why? The greater part being poor, are, when they begin to take upon them the management of affairs, uneducated.... Ignorant, therefore, and <u>unwise</u>, ... they <u>begin</u>. Depending for their daily bread on the profits of some petty traffic, or the labour of some manual occupation, they are nailed to the work-board or the counter. In the business of Government, it is only by fits and starts that they have leisure so much as to <u>act</u>: they have no leisure to <u>reflect</u>. Ignorant, therefore, they <u>continue</u>.[1]

This dilemma posed great problems for the advocate of the popular regime. There were those who argued that democracy and progress were incompatible.[2] However, Godwin's argument proceeded upon the assumption that nature was sufficiently beneficent to mankind, that men might satisfy their basic needs easily and efficiently. Unlike the popular regimes of the ancients, he believed that modern democracies did not require domestic slavery.[3]

Both the intention of nature and the organisation of political society were, for Godwin, keys to the problems of the economy. In turn, the economy was intimately connected to political society, and economic justice was a sine qua non of political justice. Godwin's arguments were pointed at the devotees of the new economic science which had its roots in such writers as Mandeville, Montesquieu, Hume, and Smith. He labelled them the 'commercial writers', as their political philosophy was directed toward the production of wealth and the expansion of trade.[4] Their arguments also offered a defence of 'luxury', a notion which was central to their economic science.[5]

Godwin was not the first to attack these writers. Kingsley Martin has claimed that 'the main stream of eighteenth-century socialism begins in 1755 with Rousseau's attack on private property in the essay on The Origin of Inequality'.[6] At any rate Rousseau began the attack on the commercial society, taken up in France by a number of writers, especially Mably and Morelly.[7] In England, Robert Wallace and William Ogilvie wrote in opposition to the supporters of the new economic science.[8] Furthermore, Paine and Joseph Priestley placed some reservations on the merits of society based upon these principles.[9]

Godwin's argument focused on a broadly defined conception of property.

> The subject to which the doctrine of property
> relates, is, all those things which conduce,
> or may be conceived to conduce, to the benefit
> or pleasure of man, and which can no otherwise
> be applied to the use of one or more persons,
> than by a permanent or temporary exclusion of
> the rest of the species. Such things in
> particular are food, clothing, habitation and
> furniture.[10]

His doctrine of property may, for purposes of this analysis, be divided into three parts: his critique of commercial society, his theory of property, and his defence of his theory. At one point in his argument, he advanced five major criticisms of the existing system of property.[11] First, the system of property created a sense of dependence of certain classes on others. He attacked the relationship established between pauper and benefactor, servant and master, and tradesman and customer. Through these and other relationships, nurtured by the organisation of property, the mass of men became wretched and servile. Instead of fostering independence and self-sufficiency, the system created a condition of dependency.

Secondly, the property system directed men's efforts, not towards distinction and excellence in general, but solely towards the acquisition of wealth.

> To acquire wealth and to display it, is therefore
> the universal passion. The whole structure of
> human society, is made a system of the narrowest
> selfishness. If the state of society were such,
> that self-love and benevolence were apparently
> reconciled as to their object, a man might then

> set out with the desire of eminence, and yet
> become every day more generous and philanthropical
> in his views. But the passion we are here
> describing, is accustomed to be gratified at every
> step, by inhumanly trampling upon the interest of
> others.[12]

Hence, although a child was educated to be a just person, as soon as he entered the world of affairs, he found that his ideas had to change.

Thirdly, the property system discouraged intellectual achievement.

> Accumulated property treads the powers of thought
> in the dust, extinguishes the sparks of genius,
> and reduces the great mass of mankind to be
> immersed in sordid cares; beside depriving the rich,
> as we have already said, of the most salubrious and
> effectual motives to activity.[13]

It was not equality, but the current system of property which was the great 'leveller' of man. Under it, Godwin felt the mass was reduced to a common wretchedness and the rich were robbed of incentive.

Fourthly, not only was intellectual improvement thwarted, but moral improvement was also prevented. With the abolition of property much crime and vice would disappear. The poor would not have to steal, as they would no longer be faced with a hopeless situation; the rich would have to temper their ambition and passion, as they would not be able to purchase other men's services. Furthermore, war might decline, because men must be promised something to be persuaded to fight a war. Without this material incentive, Godwin doubted that men could be led to kill other men. 'As long as this source of jealousy and corruption shall remain, it is visionary to talk of universal peace'.[14]

Finally, Godwin argued that the earth could support many more people than it did. Since population was related to subsistence and the amount of production was related to the organisation of production, the organisation of property might be blamed for not permitting more people to be born.

These criticisms did not complete his indictment of the property system, and in the *Enquirer*, he returned to the same theme. He did not agree with the Stoic maxim that riches were of no benefit and poverty, no evil. Poverty was an evil. 'He then that is born to poverty, may be said, under another name, to be born a slave.'[15] Poverty also shortened life, and deprived the poor of much enjoyment in life. There was no leisure for intellectual and moral improvement. Even those who had escaped total ignorance did not have sufficient leisure to develop themselves, and genius usually passed without notice among the poor.

It is important to appreciate the full scope of Godwin's indictment. Modern society did not merely fail to alleviate poverty or even only contribute to it; it actually created poverty.

> The earth is the sufficient means, either by the fruit it produces, or the animals it breeds, of the subsistence of man. A small quantity of human labour, when mixed and incorporated with the bounties of nature, is found perfectly adequate to the purposes of subsistence.[16]

The introduction of the division of labour, and subsequently, barter and sale, led to the conditions against which Godwin protested.

> The persons who first had recourse to these ideas, undoubtedly were not aware what a complication of vices and misery they were preparing for mankind. Barter and sale being once introduced, the invention of a circulating medium in the precious metals gave solidity to the evil, and afforded a field upon which for the rapacity and selfishness of man to develop all their refinements.
> It is from this point that the inequality of fortunes took their commencement. Here began to be exhibited the senseless profusion of some and the insatiable avarice of others.[17]

The division of labour and use of money thus stimulated the passions of avarice and greed. The dominance of these passions, which overwhelmed the simple virtues, led to a condition of society in which extremes of wealth predominated.

> The ideas of the division of labour, and even of barter and sale, first presented themselves, as conducive to mutual accommodation, not as the means of enabling one of the parties to impose an unequal share of labour or a disproportionate bargain on the other. But they did not long remain in this degree of purity. The sagacity of the human mind was soon whetted to employ these ideas as the instruments of fraud and injustice.[18]

Furthermore, since the division of labour and barter and sale were at the heart of commercial society, Godwin was attacking an entire social and political order, not merely or solely, rules of property.

It may seem strange that Godwin, who praised commerce at several points, should mount so fierce an attack on commercial society. He recognised that commerce freed men from traditional ties to church and state. But it also created conditions which were, in themselves, intolerable. Regarding the life and character of the tradesman in commercial society, he wrote:

> Yet this being, this supple, fawning, cringing creature, this systematic, cold-hearted liar, this being, every moment of whose existence is centered in the sordid consideration of petty gains, has the audacity to call himself a man. One half of all human beings we meet, belong, in a higher or lower degree, to the class here delineated. In how perverted a state of society have we been destined to exist.[19]

The 'perversion' here is commercial society, and Godwin proposed a solution to the problems it created. His theory might be called, as he and others referred to it, the system of equality.[20] For Godwin property was neither an extension of personality nor the way to protect human life and liberty. Neither was it a juridical concept. Its first basis was the recognition of an equality of claims for property and an equal right to subsistence. This might also appear to be the basis for chaos. Given equal rights, what happened when two people contended for the same goods? Would the old system of property have to be reintroduced? If not, might not a strong government be necessary to protect everyone's equality?

A second foundation for the system of property was thus necessary. This was the right of private judgment, the only 'active' right which Godwin admitted to be valid.[21] A person had the right to the forbearance of others, not because certain things were exclusively his, but because he must decide the best use of these goods in his possession. His decision should not be compelled; the clear exercise of judgment, accompanied by proper information was the road to moral improvement. Thus the right of property was founded in 'the sacred and indefeasible right of private judgment'.[22]

Godwin argued that property had to be considered on three levels. The first was the right to subsistence and basic happiness. How possession was taken of these goods was not an important factor, as long as the community generally acquiesced when the property was acquired. If the goods were of great importance to the person in possession of them, he had a right against any other person. Because of the right of private judgment, 'no man may, in ordinary cases, make use of my apartment, furniture or garments, or of my food, in the way of barter or loan, without having first obtained my consent'.[23]

The second level of property was the right to the fruits of labour regardless of whether they should be appropriated according to the rules of justice. Although a man must dispose of his property justly, as he was merely a steward, Godwin stated that he remained a steward in the sense that he retained full possession of the goods.

Since this degree of property went beyond subsistence and basic happiness, Godwin said that it was a form of usurpation. 'It vests in me the preservation and dispensing of that, which in point of complete and absolute right belongs to you.'[24] Nevertheless, the right remained with me to see that it was put to the best use.

The third level of property was in the labour of others, which was in opposition to the second. If men had the right to the produce of their own labour, it seems impossible for them to have a right in the labour of others; each having his own leaves none for another.

> Every man may calculate, in every glass of wine he drinks, and every ornament he annexes to his person, how many individuals have been condemned to slavery and sweat, incessant drudgery, unwholesome food, continual hardships, deplorable ignorance, and brutal insensibility, that he may be supplied with these luxuries.[25]

Godwin extended his critique of this form of property to include luxury which had been defended by Mandeville and Hume. He flatly stated that 'all refinements of luxury, all inventions that tend to give employment to a great number of labouring hands, are directly adverse to the propagation of happiness'.[26] The country gentleman, by spending on luxuries, might find employment for hundreds of workers, but he was not genuinely benefiting them in spite of his apparent generosity.

The essence of Godwin's argument was contained in this significant quotation:-

> Let us suppose that, in any country, there is now ten times as much industry and manual labour, as there was three centuries ago. Except so far as this is applied to maintain an increased population, it is expended in the more costly indulgence of the rich. Very little indeed is **employed** to increase the happiness or conveniences of the poor. They barely subsist at present, and they did as much at the remoter period of which we speak. Those who, by fraud or force, have usurped the power of buying and selling the labour of the great mass of the community, are sufficiently disposed to take care that they should never do more than subsist. An object of industry added to or taken from the general stock, produces a momentary difference, but things speedily fall back into their former state. If every labouring inhabitant of Great Britain were able and willing to-day to double the quantity of his industry, for a short time he would derive some advantage from the increased stock of commodities produced. But the rich would speedily discover the means of monopolising this produce, as they had done the former. A small part of it only, could consist in commodities essential to the subsistence of man, or be fairly distributed through the community. All that is luxury and superfluity, would increase the accommodations of the rich, and perhaps, by reducing the price of luxuries, augment the number of those to whom such accommodations were accessible.

> But it would afford no alleviation to the
> great mass of the community. Its more
> favoured members would give their inferiors
> no greater wages for twenty hours' labour,
> than they now do for ten.[27]

Thus, an increase in productivity would lead to an increase in poverty. The harder the poor laboured, the greater was the distance between the conditions of the rich and poor. It would seem to follow from this argument that luxury and the right of property in the labour of others should be abolished, but Godwin did not conclude that they should be immediately abolished.

> If, by positive institution, the property of
> every man were equalified to-day, without a
> contemporary change in men's dispositions and
> sentiments, it would become unequal tomorrow.
> The same evils would spring up with a rapid
> growth; and we should have gained nothing, by
> a project, which, while it violated everyman's
> habits, and many men's inclinations, would render
> thousands miserable.[28]

General security was necessary for the introduction of any major reform so that the people had the opportunity to determine what was best for themselves. Thus, the existing arrangements should be defended with coercion if necessary during that transition period. Property ought to be defended, but it was important to know why it was to be defended, i.e. to prevent a worse evil: chaos. We might well ask of what value is a theory which condemned and protected a system at the same time? Godwin's answer was his belief in gradual progress which followed change in general understanding. He believed that his doctrine might ultimately cause a revolution in the world, and such a revolution (as beneficial as this would be) could take place only gradually.

Godwin anticipated numerous objections to his radical arguments on the question of property. The first he considered was the common charge that it was too visionary.[29] Why should the rich give to the poor? Through a continual exposition of these truths, Godwin believed that they would eventually gain assent and that this would lead to changes in the organisation of society. If it were possible for the rich to know in a very direct and immediate manner, the consequences of their accumulation and expenditure in society, change would follow. What Godwin had in mind was a condition of society where everyone in the community utterly despised the rich and refused to serve or help them without obvious reluctance and even a measure of hatred. No man wished to be a social outcast, and he would soon see that his wealth was responsible for his condition. If his wealth made him more an object of antipathy than admiration, the system would soon change.

A second objection was that if the new system were introduced, it would soon disappear. In answer, Godwin said:

> Undoubtedly, this state of society is remote
> from the modes of thinking and acting which at
> present prevail. A long period of time must
> probably elapse, before it can be brought
> entirely into practice. All we have been

> attempting to establish is, that such a
> state of society, is agreeable to reason,
> and prescribed by justice; and that, of
> consequence, the progress of science and
> political truth among mankind, is closely
> connected with its introduction. The
> inherent tendency of intellect is to improvement. If therefore this inherent tendency
> be suffered to operate, and no concussion of
> nature or inundation of barbarism arrest its
> course, the state of society we have been
> describing, must, at some time, arrive.[30]

Godwin was concerned more with permanent than immediate changes. This was why he opposed revolutionary change, or the sudden introduction of great reforms by legislation.

A third objection was that if Godwin's doctrines were accepted, they would generate laziness and sloth. In commercial society there were incentives which led to increased activity and prosperity, and these incentives would disappear in Godwin's society. Godwin could see the danger, but he still held that sloth would not follow the introduction of equality. Since equality would be instituted only after great moral and intellectual improvement, there was no reason to think that a society of highly cultivated people would relapse into a state of barbarism as soon as a just system was introduced. Furthermore, nature was not as cruel to mankind as some of the commercial writers had supposed. Godwin estimated that the amount of labour required to supply the basic needs of men was one half hour per person per day.

Labour under these conditions would become merely good exercise.[31] People would be eager to do their small share and be done with it. Finally, he argued that the incentives to activity were not necessarily those incentives which were found in commercial society.

> We are deceived by the apparent mercenariness of mankind, and imagine that the accumulation of wealth is their great object. But it has sufficiently appeared, that the present ruling passion of man, is the love of distinction.[32]

Godwin placed great emphasis on this point, and it is a crucial one in his theory. In his ideal society, avarice would have been replaced by benevolence as the ruling passion. Mandeville had argued that without avarice the commercial society would disintegrate, leaving men without any of its benefits.[33] Godwin argued that men loved distinction. This pursuit of distinction took the form of avarice in the pursuit of wealth only in societies which honoured wealth. The basic passion could be channelled so as to produce the public good, if society was organised to reward properly those who served the public.

The final objection to his doctrine to be considered at this point was the objection from the benefits which luxury provided for mankind. Here, Godwin came directly against the doctrines of Mandeville and Hume. If it was assumed that refinement and cultivation were more desirable than ignorance and crudeness, then, according to Mandeville and Hume, luxury and inequality was necessary to society.[34] Great advances in the arts depended on great wealth and leisure in certain ranks of society. This argument was not without some force, though Godwin noted that 'it probably contributed to make Rousseau an advocate of the savage state'.[35] Godwin admitted that it might be necessary for mankind to pass through a period of inequality based on luxury as a necessary precondition for true civilisation, much as Marx believed that capitalism was a necessary stage in the journey to socialism. This stage, he said, might be necessary to distinguish his ideal state from the state of simple virtue which Rousseau preferred. Furthermore, Godwin did not consider all luxury to be evil.

> If we understand by a luxury, something which is to be enjoyed exclusively by some, at the expense of undue privations, and a partial burden upon others; to indulge ourselves in luxury is then a vice. But, if we understand by luxury, which is frequently the case, every accommodation which is not absolutely necessary to maintain us in sound and healthful existence, the procuring and communicating luxuries may then be virtuous. The end of virtue is to add to the sum of pleasurable sensation.[36]

Although the pursuit of luxury seemed to Godwin a waste of time, he did not exclude it as long as it did not harm anyone. The state of equality need not be one of stoical simplicity.

Thus far, Godwin cannot be said to have done much to refute the arguments of Mandeville. Although he argued that certain forms of luxury were not desirable, he was forced to admit that luxury might be necessary for the initial achievement of civilisation. He did, however, establish his point that the eventual achievement of a state of equality was not precluded, as Mandeville had argued, by the necessity of luxury and inequality.

Godwin returned to this theme in the Enquirer where he made a more direct assault on the theme of luxury.[37] Mandeville had argued that spending by the rich provided employment for the poor. Godwin replied by first pointing out that the employment of the poor in this manner degraded them, and robbed them of their individuality and integrity. Godwin's attack on luxury was soon expanded into an indictment of commercial society in general.

> Every man who invents a new luxury, adds so much to the quantity of labour entailed on the lower orders of society. The same may be affirmed of every man who adds a new dish to his table, or who imposes a new tax upon the inhabitants of his country. It is a gross and ridiculous error to suppose that the rich pay for any thing. There is no wealth in this world except this, the labour of man. What is misnamed wealth is merely a power vested in certain individuals by the institutions of society, to compel others to labour for their own benefit. So much labour is requisite to produce ... those superfluities which at present exist in any country. Every new luxury is a weight thrown into the scale. The poor are scarcely ever benefitted by this. It adds a certain portion to the mass of their labour; but it adds nothing to

> their conveniences. Their wages are not
> changed. They are paid no more now for
> the work of ten hours, than before for the
> work of eight. They support the burthen,
> but they come in for no share of the fruit.[38]

Beginning with the premise that all wealth was the result of labour, Godwin did not pass on to the usual Lockean conclusion, because he believed that happiness was basically unrelated either to labour or to the products of labour, whoever produced them. As Max Beer put it, for Godwin, 'real wealth was leisure'.[39] Though labour was the source of wealth, it was not to be praised or promoted. The achievement of the good life was possible only when man was free from necessary labour.[40] 'Mechanical and daily labour' wrote Godwin 'is the deadliest foe to all that is great and admirable in the human mind'.[41] Although profusion might lead to the employment of a million of the poor, they were not better off. They worked longer hours for the same amount of money. They did not produce the necessities which they themselves might need. Rather, they produced luxuries for the rich which did nothing to alleviate the condition of the poor. Godwin argued that if only necessities were produced, such necessities could be easily produced, if everyone laboured. Then all men could have leisure either to improve themselves or to produce luxuries.

> If the rich man would substantially relieve the
> burthens of the poor, exclusive of the improve-
> ments he may communicate to their understandings
> or their temper, it must be by taking upon himself
> a part of their labour, and not by setting them
> tasks. All other relief is partial and temporary.[42]

This discussion of the importance of labour led Godwin to an outline of the ideal society, though, like Marx, he never wrote directly in utopian terms. Godwin was anxious to avoid suggesting that he favoured any regimentation of life or diminishing of personal independence. He clearly recognised the tension which existed between the individual and society.

> On the one hand, it is to be observed that human beings are formed for society. Without society, we shall probably be deprived of the most eminent enjoyments of which our nature is susceptible....
> On the other hand, individuality is of the very essence of intellectual excellence. He that resigns himself wholly to sympathy and imitation, can possess little of mental strength or accuracy. The system of his life is a species of sensual dereliction.[43]

Godwin placed the greatest emphasis on individuality. At one point he wrote that 'every thing that is usually understood by the term cooperation, is, in some degree, an evil'.[44] He encouraged self-sufficiency, and opposed the division of labour which he believed led to cooperation. Although he granted that a certain division of labour was necessary, it should not be developed to the point where barter and sale was also necessary. Referring specifically to Adam Smith, he condemned the idea of the division of labour as it was presented in the Inquiry into the Nature and Causes of the Wealth of Nations.

> The division of labour, as it has been developed
> by commercial writers, is the offspring of avarice.
> It has been found that ten persons can make two
> hundred and forty times as many pins in a day as
> one person. This refinement is the growth of
> monopoly. The object is, to see into how vast a
> surface the industry of the lower classes may be
> beaten, the more completely to gild over the
> indolent and the proud. The ingenuity of the merchant is whetted, by new improvements of this sort,
> to transport more of the wealth of the powerful
> into his coffers.[45]

Marx also attacked the principle of the division of labour, linking it to human alienation. Like Godwin, he believed that commercial society, while increasing production was also increasing poverty and wretchedness. 'We shall begin from a <u>contemporary economic fact</u>', he wrote. 'The worker becomes poorer the more wealth he produces and the more his production increases in power and extent'.[46] In spite of the parallels between the two, a great difference remains because of their contrasting **attitudes towards** labour. Godwin never considered labour in any form to be desirable. His position led him to argue, as we have seen, that real wealth (in terms of the means of achieving human happiness) was to be found in leisure.

> The genuine wealth of man is leisure, when it meets
> with a disposition to improve it. All other riches
> are of petty and inconsiderable value.
> Is there not a state of society practicable in
> which leisure shall be made the inheritance of
> every one of its members?[47]

In the sense that Godwin considered the good life to exist wholly apart from that part of life which was devoted to the satisfaction of daily needs, he was closer to Aristotle than to nineteenth and twentieth century socialist thought.[48] According to Ernest Barker, 'Aristotle prefers to trust neither to a system of common ownership nor to a system of equal ownership... but to a system of moral training which affects the moral disposition and secures the right use of property'.[49] Excepting a stronger emphasis on equality, this summarises Godwin's position. Instead of making property collective, he seemed to do away with the very conception of it.[50]

CHAPTER VII

POPULATION

Neither Godwin nor Malthus initiated the population dispute. Godwin first considered it in a minor chapter in <u>Political Justice</u> in the last section on property. According to Robert Wallace (whom Godwin answered) increases in population relative to food supply would ultimately render an ideal world impossible.[1] Wallace was not pessimistic, as the earth was hardly cultivated, and many centuries would pass before population pressed on food supply. His doctrine merely set an ultimate limit to human aspirations, given the dimensions of the earth and the nature of human passions.[2] Godwin believed that Wallace's argument was neither accurate nor important.

> There is a principle in the nature of human society, by means of which every thing seems to tend to its level, and to proceed in the most auspicious way, when least interfered with by the mode of regulation. In a certain stage of the social progress, population seems rapidly to increase; this appears to be the case in the United States of America. In a subsequent stage, it undergoes little change, either in the way of increase or diminution; this is the case in the more civilised countries of Europe. The number of inhabitants in a country will perhaps never be found, in the ordinary course of affairs, to increase beyond the facility of subsistence.[3]

If there was a problem, Godwin suggested that there were numerous methods of solving it. The practices of exposing babies and procuring abortions, and the exercise of moral restraint had already been used in various countries, but even these, said Godwin, were generally unnecessary. 'But, without any express institution of this kind, the encouragement or discouragement that arises from the general state of a community will probably be found to be all-powerful in its operation.'[4] Besides, it would take a great period of time for mankind to overpopulate the planet, and by then, there would have been ample time to devise means to solve the problem.

While Godwin relegated the question of population to an obscure position in Political Justice, to be fairly summarily dismissed, Malthus was able to place it in the centre of political and economic controversy and to make all other arguments depend upon it. Malthus said that his doctrine was not new, but could be found in the writings of Hume and Adam Smith; what was new was the emphasis to be placed on it.[5] Both Hume and Smith assumed a condition of natural scarcity: failing to provide sufficiently for mankind, and working in part through the sexual urges, nature drove men to form societies which were in turn sustained by the necessity for the conquest and mastery of nature. Where Smith argued that this kind of society, organised by the division of labour to increase wealth, also led to an increase in human happiness, Malthus argued that the conditions of natural scarcity created a situation where there would always be pressure of population on food production.[6] Thus, an increase of wealth would not necessarily lead to an increase in happiness.

Malthus's argument that population constantly exerted pressure on subsistence, leaving a certain class in poverty and misery in spite of great wealth in the community, began with two 'laws': that food was necessary for human existence and that the passion between sexes was both necessary and constant.[7] Assuming these laws of nature, he wrote that 'the power of population is indefinitely greater than the power in the earth to produce subsistence for man. Population, when unchecked, increases in a geometrical ratio. Subsistence increases only in an arithmetical ratio.'[8]

Malthus intended not merely to force Godwin to modify his principles; he intended to destroy them. At stake was the idea of progress, itself. 'It has been said, that the great question is now at issue, whether man shall hence-forth start forwards with accelerated velocity towards illimitable, and hitherto unconceived improvement; or be condemned to a perpetual oscillation between happiness and misery, and after every effort remain still at an immeasurable distance from the wished-for goal.'[9] Malthus claimed that Godwin overemphasised the vices created by human institutions and political regulations.

> But the truth is, that though human institutions appear to be the obvious and obtrusive causes of much mischief to mankind; yet, in reality, they are light and superficial, they are mere feathers that float on the surface, in comparison with those deeper seated causes of impurity that corrupt the springs, and render turbid the whole stream of human life.[10]

Beneath all of the institutions to which Godwin alluded lay these laws of nature which Malthus claimed set limits and dictated action. If Godwin's ideal society were realised, the principle of population would lead to its destruction in thirty years.

In <u>Political Justice</u>, Godwin had appended some conjectures about the nature of the passions between the sexes, arguing that they might eventually be extinguished, or at least minimised. To this, Malthus took great exception, and stressed the constancy of the passions between the sexes. Godwin, according to Malthus, over-emphasised man's intellectual abilities and nearly dismissed his 'corporal propensities'.

> I am willing to allow that every voluntary act is
> preceded by a decision of the mind; but it is strangely
> opposite to what I should conceive to be the just theory
> upon the subject, and a palpable contradiction to all
> experience, to say, that the corporal propensities of
> man do not act very powerfully, as disturbing forces, in
> these decisions. The question, therefore, does not merely
> depend, upon whether a man may be made to understand a
> distinct proposition, or to be convinced by an unanswerable
> argument. A truth may be brought home to his conviction
> as a rational being, though he may determine to act contrary
> to it, as a compound being.[11]

Malthus admitted that pleasures of the intellect were superior to pleasures of sense. But, he asked, 'how am I to communicate this truth to a person who has scarcely ever felt intellectual pleasure. I may as well attempt to explain the nature and beauty of colours to a blind man'.[12] Malthus argued that this was impossible because unalterable laws of nature required a number of men to live in poverty and misery, and they were thus unable to experience intellectual pleasures.

On August 5, 1798, Godwin began to read the Essay on the Principle of Population. He wrote to the author, and ten days later, Malthus joined Godwin for breakfast. After their meeting, Godwin wrote again to Malthus, but the letter has unfortunately disappeared. The lengthy reply written by Malthus on August 20 remains: it is significant because the discussion centred around the introduction of prudence into Malthus's argument.

> The prudence which you speak of as a check to population
> implies a foresight of difficulties; and this foresight
> of difficulties almost necessarily implies a desire to
> remove them. Can you give me an adequate reason why the
> natural and general desire to remove these difficulties
> would not cause such a competition as would destroy all
> chance of an equal division of the necessary labour of
> society, and produce such a state of things as I have
> described?[13]

Even so, Malthus was willing to be convinced. 'If you can satisfy me on this head, I will heartily join with you in invectives against the increase of labour, and in the general sentiments of your essay on avarice and profusion.' Malthus did see some value in the notion of prudence, or moral restraint, both in itself, and as an argument which might be turned against Godwin.

> With the present acknowledged imperfections of human institutions, I by no means think that the greatest part of the distress felt in society arises from them. The very admission of the necessity of prudence to prevent the misery from an overcharged population, removes the blame from public institutions to the conduct of individuals. And certain it is, that almost under the worst form of government, where there was any tolerable freedom of competition, the race of labourers, by not marrying, and consequently decreasing their numbers, might immediately better their condition, and under the very best form of government, by marrying and greatly increasing their numbers, they would immediately make their condition worse. As all human institutions will probably be imperfect, and consequently always open to censure, it is not surely fair to charge them with evils of which, as far as I can judge, they are totally guiltless. And in all projected changes of human institutions, it appears to me of the highest importance previously to ascertain as nearly as possible how much evil is to be attributed to these institutions, and how much is absolutely independent of them.

The letter ends with an apology for its length and an expectation of future correspondence. Godwin's journal records no subsequent meeting until December 2, 1800 when he and Malthus were among the guests at a dinner at the publisher, Johnson's.[14] The next day, Godwin began to re-read the Essay on Population.

Between the time of Malthus's first publication of the Essay and Godwin's first reply in 1801, two of Godwin's former friends publicly denounced him. From January to June 1799, James Mackintosh delivered a series of lectures in Lincoln's Inn Hall entitled 'On the Law of Nature and Nations' in which he repudiated his original adherence to principles not unlike those of Godwin. Godwin was present at the lectures and rightly realised that some caustic remarks were being directed at him.[15] Dr Samuel Parr, a friend of both Mackintosh and Godwin, denounced Godwin's philosophy during the annual Spital Sermon preached on Easter Tuesday, April 15, 1801, before such notables as the Lord Mayor.[16] On May 18, Godwin began to write a reply to the mounting number of critics. It was directed mostly against Parr and Mackintosh who had not only criticised the philosophy, but also denounced the philosopher, a worse fault in Godwin's eyes. Thinkers might dispute the truth or falsity of respective doctrines, but there was no excuse to insult the author.[17] Furthermore, as the reaction to the French Revolution fully set in, a larger number of people saw Godwin as a symbol of the radical philosophy surrounding the French Revolution. He had remained silent for a number of years, but in 1801 he was forced to reply.

On June 18, he published Thoughts Occasioned by ... Dr Parr's Spital Sermon, etc., a pamphlet noted for its restrained and dignified tone. It prompted Coleridge to write in his copy:

> I remember few passages in ancient or modern authors
> that contain more just philosophy in appropriate, chaste,
> and beautiful diction than the five following pages.
> They reflect equal Honor on Godwin's Head and heart.
> Tho' I did it only in the Zenith of his reputation, yet
> I feel remorse ever to have spoken unkindly of such a man.[18]

Godwin treated Malthus with great deference. He said that originally he had not believed that the doctrines of Malthus seriously affected his own. However, he had been urged by his friends to reply:

> I approach, as I have already said, the author of the Essay on Population with a sentiment of unfeigned approbation and respect. The general strain of his argument does the highest honour to the liberality of his mind. He has neither laboured to excite hatred nor contempt against me or my tenets: he has argued the questions between us, just as if they had never been made a theme for political party and the intrigues of faction: he has argued, just as if he had no end in view, but the investigation of evidence, and the development of truth.[19]

For the sake of argument, Godwin assumed the ratios to be true. The issue was then whether the conclusions, that vice and misery were inevitable in every society, followed from these premises. Godwin argued that numerous practices existed which enabled men to regulate births. The ancients exposed babies or procured abortions. Another method was the extension of the legal age for marriage. In England, the poor treatment of children and the reluctance to marry at an early age acted as checks on the population. Furthermore, population was checked by the operation of virtue, prudence or pride.

If checks, based on prudence and moral restraint, could be found to operate in the present society, why could they not be expected to operate in a future society? As men progressed, they would become increasingly more prudent and thoughtful. Therefore, while Malthus's premises might be correct, his conclusions did not follow from these premises; a highly improved state of society thus remained possible.

If Godwin had realised the extent to which Malthus would be seriously received, he might have mounted more severe criticisms against him. It must be recalled that Godwin was replying to Malthus's first edition, which amounted to little more than a tract. However, presupposed in the ratios, and, at times, directly stated, was a conception of nature and nature's intentions which imposed on man, in whatever form of society, a scarcity of provisions for the satisfaction of his basic needs. This conception of nature set limits to human progress, and to much of an amelioration of the condition of the poor. That even moral restraint would not lead to unlimited progress, was not, perhaps, clear by this point, as Malthus had yet to use the concept, which appeared in the 1803 edition. This reply by Godwin, then, almost foreshadowed a second reply nearly twenty years later.

Godwin and Malthus remained on friendly terms at least until 1803. Godwin's journal records several meetings and on one occasion they were both guests for dinner at Johnson's.[20] In 1803, Malthus published the second edition of the <u>Essay on the Principle of Population</u>. In the preface he said that the first edition was written 'on the spur of the occasion,' while the present edition was a full discussion of the problem. Near the end of the preface, he drew attention to a basic change in the argument:

> Throughout the whole of the present work, I have so far differed in principle from the former, as to suppose another check to population possible, which does not come under the head either of vice or misery; and, in the latter part, I have endeavoured to soften some of the harshest conclusions of the first Essay. In doing this, I hope that I have not violated the principles of just reasoning; nor expressed any opinion respecting the probable improvement of society, in which I am not borne out by the experience of the past. To those who still think that any check to population whatever, would be worse than the evils which it would relieve, the conclusions of the former essay will remain in full force: and if we adopt this opinion we shall be compelled to acknowledge that the poverty and misery which prevail among the lower classes of society are absolutely irremediable.[21]

In this quarto edition, Malthus relegated criticism to the background and set his sights on establishing his own case.[22] However, he devoted a small chapter to Godwin's pamphlet of 1801.[23] He disagreed with Godwin's conception of the compatibility of their doctrines. 'But certainly,' he wrote, 'if the great principle of the essay be admitted, it affects his whole work, and essentially alters the foundations of political justice.'[24] Malthus argued that if Godwin's system were instituted, it would soon fall to pieces, because prudential restraint, in order for it to govern, must be based upon self-interest. Only then would it be sufficiently powerful to restrain men in general. Godwin replaced self-interest with a doctrine of benevolence, which, though necessary for the achievement of the new social order, might not be a sufficient motive to lead men to exercise moral restraint. To attempt to progress towards this new order would be, for Malthus, impossible, and the ratios would soon come into effect with the lapse of moral restraint. According to Malthus, then, progress and moral restraint could not proceed together; the doctrines of Malthus and Godwin thus remained incompatible.

Malthus published a fifth edition in June 1817, which probably led to Godwin's determination to write his second reply. In October, Godwin began to read Hazlitt's essay on Malthus, and he soon began reading Malthus's <u>Essay</u> and other works on the subject.[25]

On December 8, 1818 a small advertisement appeared in the <u>Morning Chronicle</u>:

> Speedily will be published
> An Answer to Mr Malthus's Essay
> in which the Question of Population as it
> Affects the Future Improvement of Society,
> **is fully considered**
> By William Godwin

<u>Of Population, An Enquiry concerning the Power of Increase in the Numbers of Mankind</u>, which did not appear until 1820, was a six hundred page attack on all aspects of Malthus's doctrine. At the outset, it criticized Malthus's scheme of ratios and checks on population which he had devised. Godwin worked hard to confute the evidence used by Malthus to support his points. Malthus's doctrines were based on flimsy statistical evidence, but so were Godwin's arguments in reply. Without the statistics for the United States, the geometrical ratio could not have been conceived. And there is no reason to believe that these statistics justify the 'law of nature' that population, when unchecked, increased in a geometrical progression. Furthermore, there is no convincing evidence that the means of subsistence increased at an arithmetical progression, or at any fixed rate. Indeed, the ratios, themselves, were merely imaginary constructions which happened to catch the public eye. For the geometrical progression to be valid, a constancy of sexual fecundity and desire must be assumed, which would be a highly speculative assumption. As Coleridge and many others had written, lust was not of the same class as hunger.[26]

Of interest is the manner in which the two combatants argued the relative merits of various regimes. Godwin considered ancient Sparta to be an example which refuted Malthus's principles. Here legislation encouraged the fastest possible increase in population, but the system of the great Lycurgus survived five hundred years.[27] Of Sparta, Malthus wrote:

> The preposterous system of Spartan discipline, and that unnatural absorption of every private feeling in concern for the public, which has sometimes been so absurdly admired, could never have existed but among a people exposed to perpetual hardships and privations from incessant war, and in a state under the constant fear of dreadful reverses of fortune. Instead of considering these phenomena as indicating any peculiar tendency to fortitude and patriotism in the disposition of the Spartans,

> I should merely consider them as a strong indication
> of the miserable and almost savage state of Sparta,
> and of Greece in general at that time.[28]

Godwin devoted a chapter to the Jesuit colony in Paraguay, showing that where favourable conditions existed, the size of the population did not increase in a geometrical progression.[29] Malthus wrote that 'even the missions of Paraguay, with all the care and foresight of the Jesuits, and notwithstanding that their population was kept down by frequent epidemics, were by no means totally exempt from the pressure of want'.[30] The actual facts in both cases may remain forever in dispute. What is important here is not the truth or the falsity of the basic data, but that both Godwin and Malthus drew their inferences from the same data. The old maxim that statistics may be used to prove anything might easily apply here. If Godwin discovered a society where the increase in population did not exceed the provision of food, Malthus would detect some form of vice and misery in that society which acted as a check on the rapid increase in population. Given these rules, one could not demonstrate the falsity of Malthus's ideas. Therefore, in this extensive reply to Malthus, Godwin was unable to refute him. What emerged, however, was not the soundness of Malthus's doctrine, but its absurdity in the manner he stated it. The Malthusian ratios were founded on fancy, and the arguments were circular.

Godwin wrote that the <u>Essay on Population</u> was unlike any published book in the history of political philosophy. Most philosophers discussed evils with the idea of proposing remedies for them, but, claimed Godwin, Malthus found that 'hunger and famine are the evils: vice and misery are the remedies'.[31] Malthus, he added, had attracted two types of converts: those who unwillingly were persuaded of the truth of his doctrines and those who found them useful. Of the latter, he wrote:

> They conceive it of the highest importance to put down once and for ever all impracticable speculations for the improvement of the political condition of man, and are anxious, not only that no overt attempts should be made towards such improvement, but that we should be deprived, if possible, of the dangerous indulgence of dreaming of it in the privacy of meditation and solitude. They regard the author as having performed an inestimable service by putting an end at once to all hopes of mankind ever bettering themselves. He has taught us an admirable lesson, by inducing us to rest satisfied as we are, and not to spend our strength in efforts, at once fruitless in the purposes at which they aim, and mischievous in the result. He has shown us the path of sobriety and reason.[32]

However, Malthus did propose to improve matters, and this led Godwin to consider Malthus's attitude towards the Poor Laws. Godwin charged that Malthus established two propositions: a) the poor had no right to support and b) the rich had a right to do what they pleased with their property. What Malthus intended as a way of improving society was in Godwin's view, the 'thinning of the ranks', and he proposed to achieve this by abolishing the Poor Laws.

Godwin wrote that Malthus should have enquired into the origin of the Poor Laws. These laws which began during the Reformation were substitutes for the older system of charity and benevolence practiced by the Church. The Poor Laws, said Godwin, 'were a penurious and scanty substitute for the vast sources of relief that were taken away, and they were absolutely required by the nature and state of society'.[33] On the Poor Laws, themsvelves, Godwin refrained from passing judgment:

> In England, those who are supposed unable to maintain
> themselves are aided from a general assessment; in
> France and some other countries, they are provided for in
> a different way. In both however they are under the
> protection of the law: I should prefer being the citizen
> of a country, where the deserted and the helpless should
> be <u>sufficiently taken care of</u> without the intervention of
> the state. But in England at least we are not yet ripe
> for this.[34]

The poor, Godwin believed, had a claim for support, one that was well-founded in Christian morality and practice. The rich had no right to do as they pleased, since no man had a right to do wrong, and the rich were merely stewards of the wealth they controlled. Godwin observed that 'the principle of population is no less pregnant with conclusions in favour of the riot and wastefulness of the rich, than for the oppression of the poor'.[35] Malthus may have justified luxury but he failed to stress duty.

Godwin's condemnation of Malthus reached a high point on the issue of wages. He charged that 'Mr Malthus is upon all occasions the advocate for low wages,' although Malthus, himself, 'ardently desired' to see an increase in the price of labour.[36]

> And so Swift in his own poignant style observes that,
> 'when the court of Lilliput had decreed any cruel
> execution, the emperor always made a speech to his whole
> council, expressing his great lenity and tenderness, as
> qualities known and confessed by all the world: nor did
> any thing terrify the people so much, as these encomiums
> on his majesty's mercy.'[37]

Malthus wrote that if the wages of the poor were sufficiently increased so that each worker could have a bit of meat for his table, the butcher's prices would rapidly increase with the increased demand. The increase in price would then make it difficult for the worker to buy the meat, and he would not be in an improved condition.

Godwin admitted that if every labourer in England were given twice as much money, prices would increase. However, the labourer going to market with his additional money would obtain more goods than he would if he were denied the increase, and he would stand in a better position against the rich. The rich would have to live with less luxuries. Furthermore, there was no reason to assume that the additional money would be spent on food. The labourer might consider clothing, comforts in the house, or an education for his children to be as important. Although the increase in money for the workers would not increase the commodities in the land, it would stimulate others to produce more goods. Progress in the improvement of men's conditions would soon be noted. 'Nothing could disturb this happy progress, but the geometrical ratio, an evil strong enough to disturb every thing, but which is nowhere to be found, and which exists only in the imagination of the libellers of the human species.'[38]

Malthus, concluded Godwin, presented a moral code consisting wholly of negatives:

> We must not preach up private charity. For charity, 'if exerted at all, will necessarily lead' to pernicious consequences.
> We must not preach up frugality. For the 'waste among the rich, and the horses kept by them merely for their pleasure, operate like granaries, and tend rather to benefit than to injure the lower classes of society.'
> We must deny that the poor, whatever may be the causes or degree of their distress, 'have a right to support.'...
> We must preach down marriage. ...
> What havoc do these few maxims make with the old received notions of morality![39]

Godwin accused Malthus of being revolutionary of human morality. Thus, Godwin concluded his book as the defender of the traditional

Christian teachings. 'If we embrace the creed of Mr Malthus,' he wrote, 'we must not only have a new religion, but a new God.'[40] Indeed, his most biting criticisms of Malthus were those based on common Christian maxims which Malthusian economists might prefer to ignore. His statistical attack on the ratios was less persuasive, because Malthus formulated his argument so as to preclude refutation by an appeal to facts.

Godwin did not argue his case from an idea of 'mind', with which he began his arguments in Political Justice. His science of politics seems less clearly a science of pleasure and pain, but more one of assessing the human situation in a practical manner and prescribing remedies. His superior position in the dispute arose from his use of common maxims to attack Malthus. However, these common maxims did not lead to the conclusion that man was 'perfectible' or necessarily capable of indefinite improvement, which was Godwin's original position. If he abandoned these arguments, he did not explicitly admit it. If he modified them to make them appear more acceptable, it must be doubted that his science of politics can be held in the same form as he originally intended. If he still held to his original conception, he is left with two systems of politics, which allege to explain all of the facts but are incompatible with each other.

Perhaps, the problem began with the Godwinian conception of a science of politics. Such a conception failed to appreciate the diversity of men and different societies. It might be suggested that the attempt in human affairs to seek realities which take a universal form and which are not immediately apparent to general observation may lead to the formation of unverifiable sciences.

The danger of this practice might not be so severe if the relationship between theory and practice is not as important as it is in human affairs. Godwin's science of politics was never intended to be 'other worldly'. The connection between theory and practice was as intimate as the relationship between science and technology in the non-human sciences.

Furthermore, the development of 'sciences' of politics eventually encourages both the revolutionary and the reactionary at the expense of the moderate. The moderate citizen or politician need only appeal to common sense on most issues. Utopian visions may guide him, but common sense is his tool in practical politics. The revolutionary or reactionary need to supersede common sense in a manner which ultimately replaces it with another view of politics. All evils in the world are said by some to be the result of the functions of certain institutions; all evils in the world are said by others to be necessary because of certain laws of nature. However, some men may be said to be evil, institutions notwithstanding, and men do change and some improve their lives. Common sense leads to a rejection of both Godwin and Malthus, as it was common sense which enabled Godwin to make his best criticisms of Malthus.

Godwin's reply to Malthus was treated in a small note at the end of the appendix to the 1825 edition of Malthus's work:

> Since the last edition of this Work was published, an answer from Mr Godwin has appeared; but the character of it, both as to matter and manner, is such, that I am quite sure every candid and competent inquirer after truth will agree with me in thinking that it does not require a reply. To return abusive declamation in kind would be as unedifying to the reader as it would be disagreeable to me; and to argue seriously

> with one who denies the most glaring and best attested facts respecting the progress of America, Ireland, England, and other States, and brings forward Sweden, one of the most barren and worst supplied countries of Europe, as a specimen of what would be natural increase of population under the greatest abundance of food, would evidently be quite vain with regard to the writer himself, and must be totally uncalled for by any of his readers whose authority could avail in the establishment of truth.[41]

In these few words, Malthus dismissed Godwin's entire argument. However, Godwin must also be blamed for this unfortunate circumstance, because of the weakness of his own case. Godwin's reply to Malthus was not a great success. What had taken him two years to write (he had planned to complete it in six months), fell, in many respects, 'dead-born from the press'. Nevertheless, Godwin was not one to sink quietly in defeat. In January 1821, he began to write a pamphlet in defence of his book. On January 22, 1821 this notice appeared in the Morning Chronicle:

> GODWIN ON POPULATION
> In a few days will be published, price 1s. A REPLY to the ECONOMISTS, in Defence of the Answer to Mr Malthus's Essay on Population.
>
> by William Godwin
>
> Printed for Longman, Hurst, Rees, Orme, and Brown, London. Of whom may be had, by the same Author, An Inquiry concerning the Power of Increase in the Numbers of Mankind, being an Answer to Mr Malthus's Essay, in One vol. 8vo. price 18s. boards.

No copies of what might be called Godwin's third reply to Malthus appear to have survived. However, the entire pamphlet is in manuscript form in Godwin's papers.[42] At the beginning he wrote:

> I have written a book in defence of human nature,
> and all that is dear to the human heart; Mr Malthus's
> Essay is the bitterest libel upon God and man that ever
> was penned. I have not entered the field of contention
> lightly; Mr Malthus was suffered to run his career
> almost unmolested for twenty years. I have not addressed
> myself to the passions and imagination of my fellow-beings;
> I have with much labour applied myself to collect a body
> of evidence which appeared to my mind irresistible.

Godwin declared in the 'Reply to the Economists' that after he had published his work on population, he realised that a party was being formed against it. 'This party was composed of a set of men, whom, to say the truth, I had nearly overlooked in the composition of my work, The Political Economists.'

> My Enquiry had been published but a very few weeks when
> I was informed that a leading man of this party had
> pronounced that he 'had read my volume and that it did
> nothing.' This was the first whisper of condemnation
> that reached me amidst the general congratulations that
> poured upon me from a variety of quarters. I was at the
> same time, I own, somewhat surprised at the obstinate
> silence of one or two old friends, adherents of that
> sect, to whom I had paid the compliment of sending a copy
> of my work, and requesting the favour in return of an
> early communication of their opinion founded on the perusal
> of it, whether favourable or otherwise.
>
> At length a somewhat clearer light broke in upon me;
> I received a letter from a heroic and generous friend at
> Edinburgh, who, having been upon his travels in England,
> had not examined my publication, but who thought it
> incumbent upon him to give me an estimation of how matters
> stood respecting it in the judgment of others. He had
> enquired of an acquaintance upon whose competence he could
> rely, what was the opinion entertained concerning
> Mr Godwin's answer to Malthus? The reply was 'I am sorry to
> say it is not approved of.' The next question was 'who is
> to review it in the Edinburgh Review?' The answer 'I rather
> think it will not be reviewed.'

Thus, the answer to Godwin was to be silence. This attitude was ostensibly adopted so as not to bring him more public disfavour. 'I disdain their **forbearance**,' Godwin declared. 'I disclaim their pity.' He suggested that their silence might be a consequence of their former acclamation of Malthus's doctrines; perhaps, they felt they could not retract, nor would they wish to do so as long as these ideas served a valuable social function. Godwin noted that the science of Political Economy was but a hundred years old, and that it was still in a highly undeveloped condition.

> But it happens to these gentlemen, in proportion to the infancy and unconcocted state of their study, to be insolent and overweaning. These men are drunk with their own petty speculations. I know some of them: with them, all that is interesting in the affairs of a community is debit and credit, and capital and stock: man and mind are but ciphers in their account, and go for nothing but as they happen to be placed in the great and all-embracing problem of the wealth of nations. They are described by Swift with surprising exactness: 'The universe in their estimation is nothing but a suit of clothes. [He should have added, an estate and implements withal]: in them we live, and move, and have our being: by all which it is manifest, that the outward circumstances must needs be the soul.'

In the pamphlet Godwin noted one critique of his book in a provincial newspaper, the Huntington Gazette (January 13, 1821). The critic had written that Godwin had failed to appreciate the role of capital in the determination of the population problem. Godwin replied that the argument of the political economists was that the operation of capital was the saving factor of mankind, because it did, in fact, keep births within the limits set by subsistence. Godwin questioned the origin and value of capitalism itself, and wrote:

Capital therefore has apparently no place in the original state of man. It has relation only to property and the unequal distribution of property. It has no existence among savages. It scarcely had any existence in Sparta; it was probably of small influence in Peru and Paraguay; and in that future state of man, that 'most beautiful form of society that imagination can conceive,' from which Mr Malthus set out in all his speculations, it would be neutralised, or rather annihilated. Capital has relation only to one accidental state of man: it has nothing to do with his beginning: and it must perish long before that consummation of all sublimary improvements, which may possibly arise, but which at any rate we are able to imagine.

In reality, the whole science of Political Economy has its origin in one of the vilest and most unnatural corruptions of human society. If there had never been such a thing as national debt, as money to be borrowed by one generation of men, to be squandered by them in wide-wasting war, and then to be restored over for payment, principal or interest, to their posterity, there never would have been such a science. With this it began: it has 'grown with its growth and strengthened with its strength.' And which will perish first, or first be thoroughly understood, is a problem that must be reserved for after-ages to solve.

The operation of capital, argued Godwin, is actually unconnected with Malthus's 'laws of nature'. Although in an economic system based on the accumulation of capital, population might not increase faster than subsistence, the same might be true where there was no operation of capital. Furthermore, since capitalism was a human institution, it could be changed, implying that the whole problem of population was more a problem of human governance than one of the operation of laws of human nature. Godwin concluded the 'Reply to Economists' by saying that even if the ideas of capital were true, Malthus's doctrines rested on the theory of ratios which Godwin believed he had refuted. Capital, therefore, was unrelated to the crucial problem at hand.

In February, the Monthly Review published a favourable review of Godwin's book, but the Edinburgh Review remained silent. Though he waited long, Godwin, however, was not to be neglected. The July issue of the Edinburgh Review attacked him with great asperity. The opening sets the tone for the rest of the review.

> We are surprised at this publication of Mr Godwin! Notwithstanding the prejudices which have prevailed against him on account of his moral and political theories, we have always felt a respect for his talents; and have thought that his reputation has been as much too low of late years, as it was too high soon after he wrote his Political Justice. The present work proves, either that we were wrong in the estimate of his powers, or that they are now greatly impaired by time. It appears to us, we confess, to be the poorest and most old-womanish performance that has fallen from the pen of any writer of name, since we first commenced our critical career.[43]

The remark about Godwin's powers being impaired cut deeply, as he had reached the age of sixty-five years. 'The Edinburgh Review, published a fortnight ago, contained a very scurilous and abusive account of my answer to Malthus,' he wrote bitterly to Mary Shelley. 'They began with saying, that I wisely held my tongue, and gave way to Malthus for twenty years, and that now I have fallen into my dotage, I have taken it into my head I can answer him.'[44] The Review admitted that at first it had intended to ignore his book:

> On first looking over Mr Godwin's work, we were certainly not disposed to pay such a compliment to his eloquence, aided even by the zest of abuse, as to think that it would make what was true appear to be false; and as the book was dear, and not likely to fall into the hands of the labouring classes, unless brought forward and quoted by others, which from the manner in which the subject is treated, could not have been expected, we had no thoughts

of noticing it. To our great surprise, however, we heard
that it had made some impression in London on a certain
class of readers; and, to our still greater surprise, we
learned from the papers, that upon occasion of a late
discussion of the Poor-Laws Amendment Bill, it had been
referred to by a member of the House of Commons as an elaborate
work, which, in the opinion of good judges, had shown that
Mr Malthus's statements respecting the rate of the increase
of population were quite unfounded.[45]

This state of affairs prompted the Edinburgh Review to publish a defence of Malthus. In strong language, it condemned Godwin's own use of strong language. Considerable space was also devoted to disputing the statistical arguments and methods. Then, Godwin was charged with two misrepresentations of Malthus's doctrines. The first was an insufficient attention to Malthus's use of the concept of moral restraint as a preventative check on population; the second, the assertion that Malthus believed in low wages. However, the Review did not attempt to answer the questions Godwin raised. For example, the reviewer pointed out that Malthus regarded misery and vice as consequences of excessive population, not the remedies for it.[46] But Godwin used the term 'remedies' to demonstrate his idea of the task of political science: to point out problems and suggest remedies. Malthus's remedy was 'moral restraint' which was reducible to vice and misery. If 'moral restraint', as used by Malthus, had any real meaning, the problem of population would not exist.[47]

'The Edinburgh Review lies,' wrote Shelley. 'Godwin's answer to Malthus is victorious and decisive; and that it should not be generally acknowledged as such, is full of evidence of the influence of successful evil and tyranny. What Godwin is, compared to Plato and Lord Bacon we well know; but compared with these miserable sciolists, he is a vulture to a worm.'[48] The debate continued, and in October 1821, Godwin received a pamphlet in his support which was written by a young friend, Henry B. Rosser.[49] Eventually, the Quarterly Review broke its silence and, in October, reviewed the book. 'He fared much better than in the Edinburgh, and was given part of the consideration due an intelligent writer, but the reviewer had no doubt that Malthus had spoken the last word on the subject.'[50]

As the debate continued, Godwin was not without a last word. In the Morning Chronicle of December 25, 1821, this passage appeared:-

> The increase [of the population of Ireland] since 1791, is therefore upwards of three millions. When we consider that Ireland has sent nearly as many emigrants to the United States as the rest of Europe taken together, and that the large stream of emigration is besides constantly flowing into both parts of this island from it, we need not go further for a proof of all that Mr Malthus has asserted with respect to the rate at which population may increase.

On January 11, 1822 there appeared in the Morning Chronicle a lengthy letter written by Godwin and signed L'AMI DES HOMMES.[51] Godwin's letter dealt with two problems. The first was the accuracy and the sources of the statistics used in the article, which, he argued, were highly deficient. Secondly, he questioned the application of Malthus's arguments to Ireland. In Ireland there was both a rapidly increasing population and a high incidence of vice and misery. This example, he thought, showed that the geometrical ratio worked in spite of vice and misery -- making the Malthusian system function too well.

> If Ireland, oppressed, rebellious, trampled upon, half-fed, half starved, multiplies as fast as America, I am afraid all schemes for keeping down population are gone forever. If Ireland thus multiplies, where shall we find a country in which population ought to be at a stand, or to decay?

Thus, with a question of statistics and a dispute over inferences, Godwin appears to have written his last piece on the problem of population. His concern with the subject spanned a period of nearly thirty years from his first reference in 1793 to his last in 1822. Population was a subject of great practical as well as theoretical importance, so it is perhaps understandable that the debate between Godwin and Malthus (and their respective followers) was more like a dispute between political factions than a dialogue between scholars seeking truth.

CHAPTER VIII

THE EARLY WRITINGS

In exploring the body of Godwin's writings on politics, a sharp distinction should be drawn between his practical and theoretical works, as Godwin himself intended. His practical writings reveal a man intensely concerned with the men, institutions, and events which constitute political activity. This concern stands in sharp contrast to the 'anti-political' character of his theoretical writings.

Godwin's early minor books and pamphlets are significant for several reasons: they demonstrate that many of Godwin's fundamental ideas had evolved before he wrote Political Justice; they also establish that by 1791, Godwin was already a writer of considerable merit. The History of the Life of William Pitt, Earl of Chatham (1783), Godwin's first publication, was a fair success and passed through two editions as well as being pirated in Ireland. The biography begins with an introduction dealing with the problem of impartiality in writing history. The term, 'impartiality', Godwin suggested, was an ambiguous one, and, perhaps, two kinds of impartiality existed:

> There is an impartiality, that embraces no party; that relates with the same spiritless and dispassionate tenour, the cruelties of a Nero, and the generous designs, and benevolent conduct of an Henri le grand. This is to be found, in the greatest perfection, in the

> dullest, and stupidest historians. Lover, as I am, of impartiality, I think it my duty, in this place, to advertise my reader that this kind of impartiality, I abjure, and I despise.[1]

Godwin favoured a different form of impartiality which he was able to explain only in rhetorical language:-

> But there is an impartiality; how shall I describe her? She is the native of no country; but a citizen of the world. She knows no personal regards; and she is superior to all party connections. She is deaf to the mandates of a court; and dead to the momentary gust of popular opinion. With a piercing eye, she looks through every disguise; and, with a discriminating spirit, she separates in the most dazzling and beautiful characters, the false brilliant, from the true. She seats herself in the chair of truth ... But then she is the farthest in the world from coolness and indifference. On the contrary, she treats every event, that comes before her, with deliberate, but energetic decision. Vice shudders, at her tribunal; and cruelty shrinks, into that abject, cowardly, trembling thing, that God and nature stamped her.[2]

In this first publication, Godwin was searching for a standard by which men were to be judged and history to be written, a standard both impartial and moral. He disdained the impartial writer who took no moral position and the writer of spirit who merely served party or faction. The man, soon to be characterised with an 'impartial benevolence' was the figure Godwin sought in this early work. The biography itself was not an inspiring one, and Godwin later referred to it as 'a very wretched attempt'.[3]

His next production was his first political pamphlet, A Defence of the Rockingham Party in their late Coalition with ... Lord North, which was published on May 5, 1783 and for which Stockdale, the publisher paid him five guineas.[4] There is, perhaps, some irony in the fact that this most 'political' of coalitions, what an historian recently labelled an 'uneasy alliance of discredited Whig and discredited Tory', should be supported by a writer, who, very early in his career, sought to place politics above faction.[5]

Godwin's argument in favour of the coalition was straight-forward and highly practical. His object was to establish the group led by Fox, the Rockingham party, as the best in Parliament, and then to show that only by the coalition with Lord North could it obtain power. He first argued that no alternatives existed for the Rockingham group besides the coalition with Lord North. The Bedford and Scottish parties were quickly dismissed as enemies to all reform. Lord Shelburne could not be dismissed so easily, because he had a certain reputation as an advocate of reform. Nonetheless, Godwin argued that Shelburne was very ambiguous, if not inconsistent, in his professions in favour of reform. He noted that Shelburne first raised suspicion among the reformers in 1778 when he opposed

American independence. Furthermore, when he controlled the government, he did not implement any of his proposals for parliamentary reform.

> In opposition, his declarations in favour
> of parliamentary reform seemed indeed very
> decisive. In administration, he was
> particularly careful to explain away these
> declarations, and to assure the people that
> he would never employ any influence in
> support of the measure, but would only
> countenance it so far as it appeared to be
> the sense of parliament. In other words,
> that he would remain neutral, or at most
> only honour the subject with a harangue,
> and interest himself no further respecting
> it.[6]

Godwin concluded that Lord Shelburne 'is a man, dark, insidious, and inexplicit in his designs; no decided friend of the privileges of the people; and in both respects a person very improper to conduct the affairs of this country'.[7] No effort was made to defend Lord North; but Godwin suggested that the dispute between Lord North and Fox had been somewhat moderated with the termination of the American war.

Next Godwin set out to praise the Rockingham faction, and he vigorously defended Fox against his critics.

> Men of formality and sanctity have complained
> of him as dissipated. They do not pretend
> however to aggravate their accusation, by
> laying to his charge any of the greater vices.

> His contempt of money, and his unbounded
> generosity, are universally confessed. Let
> such then know, that dissipation, so qualified,
> is a very slight accusation against a public
> man, if indeed it deserves a serious consideration.
> In all expansive minds, in minds formed for an
> extensive stage, to embrace the welfare and the
> interest of nations, there is a certain incessant
> activity, a principle that must be employed.
> Debar them from their proper field, and it will
> most inevitably run out into excesses, which
> perhaps had better have been avoided. But do
> these **excrescences**, which only proceed from the
> richness and fertility of the soil, disqualify
> a man for public business? Far, very far from
> it. Where ever was there a man, who pushed
> dissipation and debauchery to a greater length,
> than my Lord Bolingbroke? And yet it is perhaps
> difficult to say, whether there ever existed a
> more industrious, or an abler minister.... But
> Mr. Fox appears to me to possess all of the
> excellencies, without any of the defects of
> Lord Bolingbroke. His passions have, I believe
> never been suspected of having embroiled the
> affairs of his party, and he has uniformly
> retained the confidence of them all. His
> friendships have been solid and unshaken. His
> conduct cool and intrepid.[8]

Fox had also been accused of being too ambitious; but, for Godwin, ambition was something to be praised rather than condemned.

> He has been accused of ambition. Ambition is
> a very ambiguous term. In its lowest sense,
> it sinks the meanest, and degrades the dirtiest
> of our race. In its highest, I cannot agree
> with those who stile it the defect of noble minds.
> I esteem it worthy of the loudest commendation and
> the most assiduous cultivation.[9]

Godwin also praised Fox's supporters, including Burke. In Burke's case, however, he expressed certain reservations, as Burke was an advocate of 'aristocratical principles'.[10] The coalition itself was justified on the grounds of expediency. It was desirable that the Rockingham faction had power; the only workable alliance could be made between Lord North and Fox. Since the actual control of the government was to be in the hands of those of a liberal persuasion, the coalition was the best arrangement in light of the existing parties.

The degree to which Godwin himself was persuaded of the merits of the coalition remains unknown. Upon another occasion his tone might have been more subdued. However, when the coalition fell in 1784, Godwin wrote a second pamphlet entitled: <u>Instructions to a Statesman, humbly inscribed to the Right Honourable George Earl Temple.</u>[11] The East India Bills of Fox and Burke had passed the Commons, but the King, through Earl Temple, had influenced the Lords and the bills were defeated. The Fox - North coalition fell, and Pitt became Prime Minister. 'There can be no doubt', wrote Rose, the biographer of Pitt, 'that George III abused his power by seeking in an underhand way to influence the votes of the Peers'.[12] Godwin did not write to lament the passing of his favourites, but to direct a violent and sarcastic attack against the King's agent, Earl Temple. The pamphlet was constructed as a practical guide for the establishment of despotism, modelled on Machiavelli's _Prince_. Godwin suggested to Earl Temple certain techniques to be used to win over the King, the House of Commons and to guide his personal behaviour in order to bring chaos to the government. Such proposals included the use of invisible ink (milk) and having a key to the sovereign's bedchamber. Despite Godwin's doubtful advice, Pitt formed a government and Godwin's favourites were defeated in a general election.

Godwin had not at this time wholly devoted himself to a literary career. In 1783 he had returned for a spell to his original career in the ministry at Beaconsfield, but his attraction to 'the score of the infidel principles I had recently imbibed' from reading the French philosophers and a consideration of Priestley's Socinianism, led him to leave the ministry forever.[13] Next he decided to open a school, and on July 2 a curious pamphlet entitled _An Account of the Seminary that will be opened on Monday the Fourth Day of August at Epsom in Surrey_ was published.[14] The pamphlet was more an exposition of a philosophic point of view than a prospectus for a new school, and its contents were such that few English parents would consider sending their children to it.[15] Godwin was already using the language of Helvetius, d'Holbach, and Rousseau, and many of the theoretical ideas, later developed in _Political Justice_, first appeared in these pages.

By the summer of 1784, Godwin appears to have decided on a literary career. In several months he wrote three novels for which he was paid about thirty-five pounds.[16] The following year he became better established as a writer. Through the efforts of Dr. Andrew Kippis, whom he had known before he came to London, Godwin began to write the historical section of the New Annual Register, for which he was paid sixty guineas per year. At a meeting with Mr. Robertson and Dr. Kippis at the 'Crown and Anchor' in the Strand, the contract was sealed, and Godwin wrote the 'British and Foreign History' section from the 1784 edition until 1791 when he began to write Political Justice.[17] Godwin's yearly contribution to the New Annual Register amounted to approximately one hundred and fifty pages in small print and in double columns, summarising the world's events for the year.

At the same time he also began contributing articles to the English Review. As a result of these efforts, he was invited to contribute to the short-lived periodical The Political Herald and Review. This journal was established by Fox and Sheridan in 1785 to propagate their opinions, and Gilbert Stuart was appointed editor with Godwin and William Thomson as principal writers.[18] Stuart died the next year and Godwin became the editor. The journal failed at the end of 1786, and although Sheridan sought to revive it, Godwin relinquished the editorship. To survive, the journal would have had to be subsidised by the faction, and Godwin valued his independence more than the position.

Many of Godwin's contributions to the English Review and the Political Herald and Review were unsigned and cannot be identified. However, a series of letters in the Political Herald and Review, signed 'Mucius', have been found to have been written by Godwin.[19] His first letter was addressed to William Grenville, then Joint Paymaster of His Majesty's Forces, in which Godwin severely criticised Grenville and his faction for an attack they had made on Burke. The second letter was addressed to Burke, himself, urging him to reply to his critics. Burke, said Godwin, was, like Rousseau, too sensitive, and he disdained to attack his enemies who were beneath him in stature. Although Godwin had criticised Burke for giving too many speeches, he urged him now to exert himself in his own defence.

> A refined selfishness is in this case the noblest and most extensive benevolence. Talk, sir, of your services and your merits. Vindicate with energy and indignation your injured honour and eternal fame. ... Self-preservation is the first law of nature. Self-desertion is the disgrace and dishonour of the most consummate talents.[20]

In the other letters, Godwin frequently attacked Pitt. A typical remark: 'It has fallen to your lot, Sir, to new-model the constitution, to give to privilege and prerogative limits unknown before, and to open new channels for the exertions of aspiring ambition.'[21] His criticisms of Pitt were general ones against the administration. One issue, above all, held a prime position: the impeachment of Warren Hastings. Godwin accused Pitt of covering up evidence and of trying to prevent the impeachment. Godwin addressed one of his letters to Henry Dundas, Treasurer of the Navy, criticising him for speaking against Hastings in 1782 and then not voting against him in 1786.[22] He contrasted the actions of Pitt and Dundas in allegedly preventing the impeachment with the more virtuous Cicero who attempted to bring to justice wrongdoers in the provinces of the Roman Empire.

Godwin's writings for the <u>Political Herald and Review</u> were frankly partisan, though, as he would say, 'impartial' in the service of truth and justice. They were certainly polemical and, at times, violent. Although he could by no means be considered merely a spokesman for a faction, Godwin did take sides with Fox, Burke and Sheridan.

His contributions to the <u>New Annual Register</u> were more factual and less rhetorical. They were lengthy but well written accounts of events in Great Britain and abroad for each year. Until the events of the French Revolution took hold of the public, most affairs of interest revolved around either war, the impeachment of Warren Hastings, or reform. These annual essays stand in sharp contrast to Godwin's writings for the <u>Political Herald and Review</u>.

CHAPTER IX

THE FRENCH REVOLUTION

'This was the year of the French Revolution', wrote Godwin in 1789 in a note to his journal.

> My heart beat high with great swelling sentiments of Liberty. I had been for nine years in principles a republican. I had read with great satisfaction the writings of Rousseau, Helvetius, and others, the most popular authors of France. I observed in them a system more general and simply philosophical than in the majority of English writers on political subjects; and I could not refrain from conceiving sanguine hopes of a revolution of which such writings had been the precursors.[1]

The French revolution was indeed the major political event in Godwin's life. It prompted him to write <u>Political Justice</u>; it brought him great fame and notoriety; and it placed him on the stage of English public life. If these events stimulated Godwin, they also provided a testing ground for his doctrines and character. If consistency in a period such as this was a virtue, Godwin, perhaps more than most of his contemporaries, held to a consistent doctrine and course of action. Although in theory he opposed revolution, he supported the French in 1789. He also opposed any popular political action, especially that kind which distinguished the French Revolution from most revolutions in the past. At first sight, Godwin appears both to favour and to oppose the same principles. But one can see his position more truly if one recognises the distinction between his theoretical and practical writings. Although both dealt with the same subjects, Godwin's theoretical works were concerned with general themes, and his practical writings, specific issues and events. His practical works had the object of moving men to action as well as enlarging their knowledge.

Godwin recorded the events in France in yearly instalments for the <u>New Annual Register</u>. 'Whatever may be the ultimate consequences of the French Revolution', he wrote, 'its origin and progress constitute perhaps the most interesting subject of modern history.'[2] He regretted the excesses but realised that 'there is nothing so difficult to moderate and restrain as popular sentiment; and the vacillations of opinion are seldom regulated, but commonly vibrate from one extreme to another'.[3] Indeed, Godwin's closing lines on the events in France took the form of a warning that 'a free government may sometimes experience injury from too much confidence; but it is certain to be destroyed by a series of discord, disorder, and faction'.[4]

During 1789, Godwin attended a number of dinners which brought him into closer contact with leading Whigs and radical Dissenters. On November 4, he was present at the Old Jewry when Dr. Price gave his famous sermon 'On the Love of Our Country'.[5] While he followed the events in France, Godwin became increasingly concerned with the possibilities of reform of English political institutions. In this vein, on April 29, 1791, Godwin and Holcroft drafted letters to Sheridan and Fox on the Canadian constitution. Godwin wrote in his journal that the 'object of the ... letters was to excite these two illustrious men to persevere gravely and inflexibly in the career on which they had entered'.[6] Fox had said during the debate that he would not abolish a House of Lords in a country where it was established nor would he create one in a country where it did not already exist. 'This was by no means the only public indication he had shown how deeply he had drank of the spirit of the French Revolution.'[7] Godwin's letter was addressed to Sheridan but neither his nor Holcroft's letter to Fox appear to have been published.[8]

> Godwin's letter was as critical as it was encouraging.
>> Can you really think that the new constitution of France is the most glorious fabric ever raised by human integrity since the creation of man, and yet believe that what is good there would be bad here? Does truth alter its nature by crossing the Straits and become falsehood? Are men entitled to perfect equality in France, and is it just to deprive them of it in England? Did the French do well in extinguishing nobility, and is it right that we should preserve hereditary honours? Or are these questions so very trifling in their nature, so uninteresting to the general weal, that it is no matter which side of them we embrace?

The lengthy letter pressed Sheridan to be a firmer advocate of liberty. Godwin and Holcroft were pushing from one side; in a week, Burke attacked Fox from the other. The debate was over the

Quebec act, but the issue was the French Revolution. Burke and Fox split, and their friendship came to an end. Veitch says that the dispute led to the division of the opposition, and also to the beginning of a crystallisation of opinion in parliamentary ranks.[9]

At the same time that Godwin wrote the letter to Sheridan, he made his decision to write Political Justice. On March 19, he wrote to Robinson, the publisher of the New Annual Register and proposed this project for £1050.[10] At the end of June he dined with Robinson and the arrangements were soon made. His beginning Political Justice was an important personal step for Godwin. In his journal he wrote:

> This year was the main crisis of my life. In the summer of 1791 I gave up my concern in the New Annual Register, the historical part of which I had written for seven years, and abdicated, I hope for ever, the task of performing a literary labour, the nature of which should be dictated by anything but the promptings of my own mind. I suggested to Robinson the bookseller the idea of composing a treatise on Political Principles, and he agreed to aid me in executing it.[11]

Throughout 1792, Godwin worked on Political Justice. His journal recorded his daily reading spent primarily with such writers as Hume, Burke, Rousseau, Montesquieu, Helvetius, d'Holbach, Paine, bits of Bentham and Condorcet, and many others. He also read all Shakespeare's plays during the year. Although he remained politically active during this period, he devoted most of his time to his writing. Political Justice appeared early in 1793. During the week of May 25, the Privy Council debated the question of whether to prosecute the book, but it declined, primarily because the high price of the book (3 guineas) precluded much popular consumption. It was also a philosophic work both in intention and design.

The great popularity of the book has puzzled some critics. 'Political Justice was not published till 1793, and cannot be judged as an immediate reflection of the Revolution's influence', wrote Philip Anthony Brown. 'It is all the more remarkable because it appeared when optimism was ceasing to be popular.'[12] Indeed, the reaction was growing, but many minds were prepared for a serious study of first principles which Godwin supplied. Furthermore, he was seized upon by the young. 'He was the oracle of the young generation of many schools; and men as different as Wordsworth, Malthus, Shelley and Crabb Robinson, Chalmers the Scotch Theologian and Place the London Radical tailor, were altered for better or worse by reading William Godwin.'[13]

As a practical work, Political Justice was designed to act as a moderating force, combining a firm belief in libertarian ends, with a moderate conception of means. As Francis Place wrote, 'his book was laid before the public at a time of great excitement, and was intended to assist in allaying the excitement'.[14]

By early 1793, the political reaction in England had set in. Paine's Rights of Man had been successfully prosecuted for seditious libel the previous year; and the Birmingham riots of 1791 were signs that the populace could become violent when called to the defence of 'King and Country'. As individual liberties became more endangered, and liberty of speech, in particular, was threatened, Godwin took to the defence. In January 1793 he wrote four letters to the Morning Chronicle, signing them 'Mucius', the name he used to contribute to the Political Herald and Review. The newspapers were full of letters and news from France and England, and Godwin's letters did not appear until February and March.[15]

In the first letter Godwin began by recognising the great energy being expended to preserve the English constitution. He agreed that it was in grave danger, but questioned where the danger lay.

> What is the true meaning of this cry in favour of the Constitution? What part of the Constitution is it about which the attention of these new associators is engaged? It is the old boasted privilege of Englishmen; liberty of speech; but their attention is not engaged to confirm, but to destroy it. The Constitution is left at this moment almost without a defender; and those who sanctify their proceedings with its name, are taking the direct road to erect despotism upon its ruins.

Godwin's immediate motive for writing was the recent case of Daniel Crichton who, on January 8, had been sentenced to three months imprisonment and forced to give security of good behaviour amounting to several hundred pounds. Crichton, a tallow chandler, arrived in London from Scotland the evening before his arrest. The next day he became intoxicated, and in that condition he visited the Tower of London where he was heard to say: 'Damn the King. We have no King in Scotland, and we will soon have no King in England.' He was soon arrested and convicted of uttering treasonable and seditious words. 'Mr. Editor', wrote Godwin, 'the trial of Crichton must form an epoch in the history of our country.' What are the liberties of Englishmen? he asked. 'It is the liberty of a Portuguese, to be unmolested, as long as he attends solely to his private affairs, and refrains from thinking or speaking respecting the government of his country.' Godwin also attacked the use of spies and informers which had begun, he alleged, with a conspiratorial meeting at the Crown and **Anchor** on November 20, 1792.

> On that day, an Association at the Crown and Anchor Tavern, in the Strand, under the pretence of protecting liberty and property, formed a plan for overturning the Constitution. ... From that day we have been surrounded with spies; ... not merely the spies of Government, who might be marked, but every timid observer, and every rancorous disputant we may happen to encounter.

This association, the 'Society for Protecting Liberty and Property against Republicans and Levellers', was infiltrating all areas of English life, even the Attorney General's office, and its members were acting as spies and informers. They, Godwin claimed, were responsible for Crichton's arrest and conviction.

The second 'Mucius' letter was addressed to John Reeves, its chairman. He noted that Reeves and his association had almost silenced the reformers' popular propaganda activities. Godwin did not criticise him for this: 'You deprive the intemperate advocates of Reform of the instruments they were so forward to employ. You tell them, and you tell them true, that such instruments are disgraceful to a civilised community.' If his organisation had stopped by merely disarming its opponents, Godwin would have had no quarrel. 'I am no friend to force either on the part of the Populace or of Government.' But Reeves had gone too far and had distributed the most scurrilous and approbrious handbills against Paine and others, the tendency of which was to 'pull down the houses and destroy the property of Dissenters'. 'If it were possible that such machinations should be crowned with success, you should be inscribed, not perhaps on your tomb, but on the deathless page of history -- "Reeves, the assasin of the Liberties of Englishmen".' He also accused Reeves of destroying the English Constitution. 'You employ the vulgar artifice of raising a cry against Democrats and Levellers, and then hope, under favour of this cry, to strip us of every one of our privileges.'

Godwin's fourth letter was addressed 'To such persons as may be appointed to serve upon juries for the trial of seditious and treasonable words'. It was a plea to all prospective jurors to be honest in their deliberations and abjure favour. If the juror disagreed with the accused, he should remember that the other may be honest in his beliefs and not deserving punishment. He then called their attention to the fate of Daniel Crichton, the subject of the first letter.

> Countrymen and Britons, I ask not for the confidence of my readers, I desire to find you incredulous. The less easily you are satisfied and the more you enquire, the more will evidence accumulate upon you. Is the language I use the mere hackneyed language of declamation? Is the constitution in no danger from these trials ex officio? What constitution shall we have left, when the trial of Crichton has passed into precedent, and been confirmed by two hundred other verdicts obtained upon the same principle? Are you in love with the mere form of King, Lords and Commons, and careless about personal independence and security, for the sake of which only that form was cherished by your ancestors.

The English State Trials provided the crucial test of Godwin's abilities as a writer of political tracts. On May 5, 1794, Pitt, supported by Burke, and violently opposed by Fox, Sheridan, and Grey, demanded the suspension of Habeas Corpus, and it was granted. On May 12, Thomas Hardy, the founder and Secretary of the London Corresponding Society was arrested.

The previous day Godwin dined at Horne Tooke's with, among others, Thelwell and Richter, all three of whom were arrested during the next week. On May 15, Godwin called on Mrs. Thelwell and later met with Mackintosh. On the 18th, he and Holcroft, who had not yet been indicted, called on Horne Tooke in the Tower. During the spring and summer, Godwin frequently visited the prisoners, met with Holcroft, and called on such people as Joseph Gerrald, then at Newgate, and Mrs. Thelwell.

These were dangerous months, and Godwin acted with caution, always afraid of being the next to be arrested. On October 5, he dined with Holcroft, and the next day he went to Warwickshire to visit Dr. Parr 'who had earnestly sought the acquaintance and intimacy of the author of "Political Justice"'.[17] Meanwhile, the Lord Chief Justice Eyre had given a charge to the grand jury which returned indictments, on the day Godwin left London, against those already in custody and others who had not been confined. Among those named was Holcroft, who, upon learning of the indictment, dramatically surrendered himself in open court, 'a premeditated act of gallantry, which produced a great and salutary effect'.[18]

Godwin was sharply aware of the precariousness of his own position. Had Political Justice been of a more inflammatory tone, a bit cheaper, and had not Godwin consistently repudiated the activities of the reformers and advocated moderation, he might easily have been indicted. Furthermore, if the men on trial had been convicted, there is little doubt that Godwin would soon have been in the Tower or at Newgate. On October 13, he left Dr. Parr and hastened to London. The next day he called at Holcroft's house and after dining with Marshall, he went to Newgate to visit Holcroft himself. Two days later, October 16, he again visited Newgate. After a busy day on Friday, October 17, Godwin began to write Cursory Strictures on the Charge Delivered by Lord Chief Justice Eyre to the Grand Jury, October 2, 1794 which he hurriedly finished the next day. Cursory Strictures appeared in the Morning Chronicle on October 21 and was quickly reprinted in pamphlet form. If Holcroft's dramatic entrance had a salutary effect, Cursory Strictures helped to save the day. Godwin recorded the following note in his journal:

> To this pamphlet Mr. H[orne] T[ooke] frequently declared that he was indebted for his life. One day, in mixed company, having insisted that the author should tell him without circumlocution whether it were of his writing or no, and been answered in the affirmative, he called the author to him, and taking his hand, conveyed it suddenly to his lips, vowing that he could do no less by the hand which has given existence to that production. (May 21, 1795)[19]

Cursory Strictures was calm, dignified and directly to the point. It dealt strictly with the law of treason on which Eyre based his charge to the Grand Jury.[20] Godwin said that the English law of treason was embodied in the act 25 Edward III which confined treason to 'levying war against the King within the realm, and the compassing or imagining the death of the King'.[21]

He argued that the framers of the law wisely precluded arbitrary or constructive treason by providing the clause that 'if in any future time it might be necessary to declare any new treasons, that should only be done by a direct proceeding of parliament for that special purpose'.[22]

The Chief Justice had attempted to fit the current cases into the law, but Godwin questioned whether these cases could possibly fall under the law of treason. Even Eyre indicated that there was a difference.

> 'If a conspiracy to depose or imprison the King, to get his person into the power of the conspirators, or procure an invasion of the kingdom, involves in it the compassing and imagining his death, and if steps taken in prosecution of such a conspiracy, are rightly deemed overt acts of the treason of compassing the King's death', what ought to be our judgment, 'if it should appear that it had entered into the heart of any man, ... to design to overthrow the whole government of the country, to pull down and subvert from its very foundations the British Monarchy'....[23]

Thus, Eyre indicated that a distinction existed between the cases at hand and the traditional law of treason. He pointed to a clear difference in this second passage:

> 'That the crime of conspiring to overthrow the monarchy, is such an one, as <u>no lawgiver in this country has ever ventured to contemplate in its whole extent</u>. If any man of plain sense, but not

> conversant with subjects of this nature, should feel himself disposed to ask, whether a conspiracy of this extraordinary nature is to be reached by the statute of treasons? Whether it is a specific treason to compass and imagine the death of the King, and not a specific treason to conspire to subvert the Monarchy itself? I answer, that <u>the statute of Edward III, by which we are bound, has not declared this</u>, which undoubtedly in all just theory of treason is the greatest of all treasons, <u>to be a specific high treason</u>. I said <u>no lawgiver had ever ventured to contemplate it in its whole extent</u>'.[24]

The rhetoric and the argument of the Chief Justice in this instance was then used against him. Godwin argued that if, as Eyre said, there was a difference between the cases at bar and the law of treason, no matter what the exact nature of the difference might be, the cases did not fall under the law. If the court was bound by the law, it should not try the cases.

Eyre's entire argument was held together by the assertion that these cases fell under the law of treason because they involved what 'no lawgiver had ever ventured to contemplate', the total subversion of the government. Godwin argued that the purposes of associations for reform were not such that they led to a subversion of the monarchy. The Chief Justice had implied a concealed motive to the associations in so far as he admitted that the advocacy of parliamentary reform was neither treasonable nor unlawful. The Chief Justice had referred to the British Convention, saying that this meeting would not have been dangerous except for the example of a neighbouring country which was before the eyes of the nation. To this, Godwin retorted:

> This remark constitutes one of the most flagrant violations of the principles of executive justice, that was ever heard of or imagined. If the times require different measures of justice, we are already instructed by the act 25 Edward III, as to the proceeding fitting to be employed. 'The Judge', says the act, 'shall tarry, without going to judgment of the treason, till the cause be shown and declared before the King and his Parliament, whether it ought to be judged treason or other felony.' Parliament, the legislative authority of the realm, may make new provisions of law in accommodation to circumstances; but the Judges, the bare expounders of the law, are bound to maintain themselves in an atmosphere unaffected by the variations of popular clamour, ministerial vengeance, or the ever changing nature of circumstances.[25]

A reply was written to Godwin, supposedly by Judge Buller; the publication of the reply was indicative of the influence of *Cursory Strictures*. Godwin wrote an answer, but the *Morning Chronicle* declined to print it. It was published as a pamphlet and a few copies have survived.[26] The pamphlet against Godwin (who, of course, was not known to be the author) charged him with confusing the law and criticised him for attempting to influence the jurors. To the first criticism Godwin answered:

> I repeat, that every man condemned upon an adjudication of this sort, is condemned upon an *ex post facto* law; and that a more nefarious proceeding can scarcely be imagined, than that a man should be hanged upon an action which he did not know to be High Treason ... and which was not High Treason till it was made so by the adjudication under which he is executed.[27]

To the second criticism Godwin wrote that since the Chief Justice had published his charge to the jury, Godwin felt that it was an extra-judicial proceeding. Eyre thus assumed the status of an author and could be answered on that basis. Furthermore, 'it is impossible', he wrote, 'that this court, or you, Gentlemen of the Jury, should seriously imagine, that an investigation of truth in a most important crisis, can be mischievous.'[28] Finally, he said that numerous articles and pamphlets had been written against the prisoners, and he was merely redressing the balance.

Besides writing the pamphlets, Godwin visited Newgate nearly every day up to and during Hardy's trial. This, the first one, lasted eight days and the prisoner was acquitted. This result was a heavy blow to the government. In its second attempt, the trial of Horne Tooke, they also failed to obtain a conviction. Another attempt was made with Thelwall, with the same result. Godwin was present at the trials for a part of each day, and he spent the rest of the time calling on friends and relatives of the prisoners. He also continued to visit Gerrald who remained in Newgate awaiting transportation, and consulted with Gerrald's friends, Parr and Mackintosh.

The _Cursory Strictures_, together with the later 'Mucius' letters, conformed to a certain pattern which Godwin seemed to have followed in his practical political writings. All of his pamphlets dealt with particular issues, persons or laws, and general principles were woven into the fabric of the concrete discussions. Furthermore, Godwin wrote consistently in defence of English liberties which were endangered by the growing political reaction. He eloquently defended Muir and Palmer in the first Scottish trials, Gerrald in the trials after the British Convention, Daniel Crichton in the 'Mucius' letters, and the dozen defendants in the State Trials. He wrote, not of the 'rights of man', but of the rights of Englishmen; he preferred to preserve what was established than, at that time, attempt to introduce what might be more just. Godwin also repudiated all appeals to popular opinion, to the point of congratulating John Reeves for silencing the radical reformers. Thus, Godwin's position in his practical writings is a moderate one, inspired by a faith in human progress, but tempered by a prudential attitude towards the means of progress.

It is important that Godwin's position with regard to practical politics be understood, as his next pamphlet has been seriously misinterpreted. The occasion was the dispute with his friend John Thelwall which arose from Godwin's pamphlet, Considerations on Lord Grenville's and Mr. Pitt's Bills, opposing what became the Treason and Sedition Acts of 1795. Conditions in England were as desperate as in the previous year. The war with France was not succeeding, and the people were heard to shout, 'No Pitt', 'No War', 'Bread' as the King passed on his way to open Parliament.[29] Passions were high on both sides, though popular opinion strongly favoured the bills. The Morning Chronicle, however, published hundreds of petitions from the opposition. On November 20, overwhelmed by the events, the newspaper published this note.

> We trust to the indulgence of our many valuable
> Correspondents for the delay of their favours.
> They will see that it is obviously impossible to
> find room for papers of length, at a time when
> Ministers are hurrying through the stages of the
> two Bills, which give the death blow to the
> British Constitution, without allowing the respite
> of a single day. We hope they will accept of this
> excuse, without the necessity of individual reference.
> We have received from every part of the kingdom,
> matter to fill a volume on the subject of this
> daring attack on our liberties.

On the following day, the advertisement for Godwin's pamphlet appeared in the pages of the <u>Morning Chronicle</u>.[30]

> This day at noon will be published, price 2s 6d.
> Considerations on Lord Grenville's and Mr. Pitt's
> Bills concerning Treasonable and Seditious Practices
> and unlawful Assemblies
> **By a Lover of Order**
> Printed for J. Johnson, St. Paul's Church-yard.

That Godwin signed the pamphlet 'a Lover of Order' indicates his intentions. Striving for impartiality and rising above faction, he sought to establish a position which would enable both sides to avoid licence, on the one hand, and despotism on the other.

> In the present irritated and unnatural state of
> political affairs, while one party will not endure
> to hear of any cautionary restraints upon freedom,
> and another party, impressed with apprehensions of
> anarchy, conceives that scarcely any restraint can
> be too vigilant or severe; it is the object of the
> following examination of the bills lately introduced
> into Parliament by Lord Grenville and Mr. Pitt, to

> estimate their merits with the strictest
> impartiality. It is much to be desired,
> in moments pregnant with so important
> consequences, that an individual should
> be found, who could preserve his mind
> untainted with the headlong rage of faction,
> whether for men in power or against them;
> could judge, with the sobriety of distant
> posterity, and the sagacity of an enlightened
> historian; and could be happy enough to make
> his voice heard, by all those directly or
> remotely interested in the event.[31]

From this position, Godwin directed a strong attack against both the London Corresponding Society and the Treason and Sedition Bills of Lord Grenville and Mr. Pitt. He compared the Corresponding Society with the Jacobin Society in Paris and asserted that the former had copied the undesirable ways of the latter. After summarising the activities of the London Corresponding Society, he concluded that 'the government of this country would be unpardonable, if it did not yield a very careful and uninterrupted attention to their operations'.[32] He cautioned the reader to note that he did not question the purity of the intentions of the members of the London Corresponding Society, because 'to rail against men's intentions, is to take an undue advantage of popular prejudices.'[33] The task of the statesman was rather to be concerned with the welfare of the whole community, and to consider whether actions tend to produce the public good. Sending missionaries to propagandise among the people and holding huge rallies and meetings tended to create public disorder and tumult as well as creating a reaction against reform.

He then examined the series of lectures given by Thelwall (not mentioning Thelwall by name) during the previous two years in the Beaufort Building in the Strand. Godwin admitted that the object of the lectures was to promote reform.

> True, we must reform. There is scarcely a man in Great Britain so stupid, so bigoted, or so selfish, but that, if the question were brought fairly before him, he would give his suffrage to the system of reform. But reform is a delicate and an awful task. No sacrilegious hand must be put forth to this sacred work. It must be carried on by slow, almost insensible steps, and by just degrees.[34]

The public lectures did not in general, Godwin argued, further this kind of progress. Although the lecturer might begin with the best intentions, he soon was forced to abandon the quiet disquisitions and speculations which complemented gradual progress. This kind of lecture was not meaningful to an audience not accustomed to careful thinking. In the assembly hall, a different approach is necessary.

> Here men require a due mixture of spices and seasoning. All oratorial seasoning is an appeal to the passions. The most obvious seasoning of this sort is personality. The lecturer infallibly learns in a short time, to quit the thorny paths of science, and to inveigh against the individuals that exercise the functions of government. Their vices are painted in caricature; their actions are disfigured, and uniformly traced to the blackest motives; a horrible group is exhibited; all the indignant emotions of the human mind are excited. The audience do not hasten from the

> lecture-room, and hurry the minister to the lamp post; their passions are only in training for destruction. The cauldron of civil contention simmers, but is not yet worked up into the inquietude of a tempest.[35]

Godwin concluded:

> The London Corresponding Society is a formidable machine; the system of political lecturing is a hot-bed, perhaps too well adapted to ripen men for purposes, more or less similar to those of the Jacobin Society of Paris. Both branches of the situation are well deserving the attention of the members of the government of Great Britain.[36]

The question became just what sort of attention they ought to receive, and the Pitt and Grenville Bills received an eloquent condemnation. Grenville's Bill seriously affected the liberty of the press, and Pitt's, the right of assembly to demand redress of wrongs. The remedy, argued Godwin, was ten times worse than the disease and the words of the bills were such that art and science as well as pamphlets and agitation would become seditious. Godwin quoted passages from Hume and Rousseau which would be seditious under the bills, and noted that the destruction of the free expression of philosophical ideas would render progress impossible.

> A doctrine opposite to the maxims of the existing government may be dangerous in the hands of agitators, but it cannot produce very fatal consequences in the hands of philosophers. If it undermines the received system, it will undermine it gradually and insensibly; it will merely fall in with that gradual principle of decay and renovation, which is perpetually at work in every part of the universe.[37]

Godwin also criticised the bills on historical grounds, by arguing that they would destroy what public liberties had been established in recent centuries. However, what was of the greatest importance was his condemnation of the London Corresponding Society. It is, perhaps, an error to refer to this as merely a condemnation, as there is little reason to believe that Godwin intended his words to have solely a negative effect. The pamphlet was rather a defence of political theory, on the one hand, and gradual progress, on the other, both of which were threatened by the more radical reformers and the government. It was also a defence of the kind of practical political writing which Godwin had cultivated for the past twelve years, carefully written to produce results without stirring the passions or creating public turmoil. Although his words here were strong, the conditions in England at that time were precarious for a person of Godwin's convictions.

The critic of Godwin might point to these lines about the London Corresponding Society and wonder whether the defender of Muir and Palmer, the champion of Gerrald, the author of <u>Cursory Strictures</u> could have written them. The reply is that in the former instances Godwin was defending the very lives and personal liberties of men unjustly condemned. In this pamphlet, he was attempting to prevent laws from being passed. The difference in tone follows a difference in object. And a change in object requires a different approach. Thus, he cannot very well be charged with inconsistency on this point. Furthermore, Godwin had already opposed the Corresponding Society in his 'Mucius' letters in the <u>Morning Chronicle</u>, so that the attack on the reformers did not begin here.

Thelwall, of course, was most directly affected, and he immediately wrote to Godwin demanding to know whether he was the author of the pamphlet.

> ...[I]t is with difficulty that I can believe that William Godwin is the man who has taken the advantage of the alarm and fury of the moment to join the warhoops of slanderous misrepresentation against an individual whom every engine of Tyranny and Falsehood is at work to destroy -- that William Godwin is the man who has dared to accuse an individual, the purity of whose heart and the sincerity of whose benevolence he knows, of bringing the passions of men into training for lamp post massacres, and ripening them for purposes similar to those of the Jacobin Society of Paris -- that William Godwin is the man who has publicly [assassinated] the friend of whom he has so often, to his face at least been the private panegyrist, to a miserable enthusiast whose mind appears to have been a curious tissue of folly, madness, cowardice and hypocrisy.[38]

Godwin received the letter on November 28, a week after the pamphlet had been published, and he was asked to reply to the bearer of the letter.

> Your letter is much too extraordinary and much too angry for me to attempt to answer it properly by the bearer. Indeed, it would not be without great reluctance that I should engage in the tediousness of an epistolary correspondence on the subject, though I should most willingly engage in a personal explanation.

> I am most assuredly the author of the pamphlet you mention, and I am fully persuaded that it contains the sentiments of an honest man. There is not one word in it respecting you that I have not pressed upon your personal attention again and again with earnest anxiety. My favourite sentiments of you are not in the smallest degree altered, though I confess the undistinguishing fury of the letter before me is more than I can reconcile with these sentiments.
>
> I do not conceive that my frankness in acknowledging the pamphlet entitles you to the public use of my name. I would not advise anyone who has a respect for morality to enter upon a public discussion in the angry temper in which your letter is written. But you will, of course, do as you think fit, and contribute perhaps, as far as your powers may extend, to consign me also to the lamp-post.[39]

The next day, Thelwall having written again, Godwin wrote a terse reply.

> It is impossible for me to answer the farrago of abusive language you send me.
>
> If ever you should return to the esteem you once professed for me, you will be at all times welcome to my intercourse and explanation.
>
> There is not a word, in the pamphlet, reflecting upon your motives or your insincerity.
>
> There has been, and will be, before passing the Bills, time enough for you to answer my pamphlet, if you thought proper, three times over.
>
> There is but one part of your letter that I suspect of insincerity, where you affect seriously to charge me with timidity.[40]

Thelwall felt deeply insulted by what he conceived to be a personal attack on him and his activities. Godwin in turn became indignant with the abusive and threatening language of Thelwall's letters.

During this period, Godwin's life was particularly active and his journal records his preparation of a petition apparently in opposition to the Pitt and Grenville Bills as well as a visit to the House of Commons during one of the debates. He dined regularly at the home of Horne Tooke, besides visiting Mackintosh on frequent occasions. Early in 1796, Godwin dined with the Earl of Lauderdale, who had 'requested the favour' of his attendance, and soon regularly attended his parties in the company of Fox, Francis and other Whig members of Parliament. At this time he also became more intimate with Mary Wollstonecraft.

The dispute with Thelwall wore on. On December 22, 1795 the note 'Explanation with Thelwall' appears in Godwin's journal. Soon, a volume of Thelwall's periodical, the <u>Tribune</u>, in which he collected his lectures, was published, and the preface was devoted to a refutation of Godwin.[41] Although Thelwall did not say that Godwin was the author of the pamphlet, he said that it was written with the same 'daring excellencies' as <u>Political Justice</u> and he referred to 'Mr. Godwin' during the course of his essay.[42] He mentioned that the author and he had been friendly, but had disagreed over the merits of political lecturing. He objected to the severity of the attack upon himself, especially when he had lectured to small numbers of people and his series of lectures was nearly completed. If his lectures were truly seditious, the government might have closed his doors, but it chose not to regard them as lectures of this nature. He said that Godwin's arguments were absurd in excluding the lecture as a means of spreading knowledge, because it might occasion tumult and disorder. Although the lecture hall might not be the proper arena for the cultivation of truth, such a statement ignored the preparations made by the lecturer, and the information and stimulation he imparted to the student. Furthermore, there was, he argued, no reason to conclude that a lecture led, in any way, to the lamp-post.

Godwin decided to reply, and he wrote to Thelwall asking that his letter be inserted in the next number of the Tribune.[43] Godwin said that his remarks had two objects: to disavow any sinister intentions to the lecturer and to defend his own attack on political lectures. He added that the similes to which Thelwall objected might have been altered if he had been able to compose the pamphlet at leisure. Thelwall wrote a short preface and conclusion to the letter, accusing Godwin of some misrepresentations and, in addition, questioning his authority, as Godwin had attended only two of his lectures, and only one since the State Trials. However, the passion which initially accompanied the dispute appeared spent. In 1796, T. Amyot, a friend of Crabb Robinson, recorded this scene in Norwich.

> I had the supreme honour (and I am highly proud of it) to sit on the same bench with the arch-philosopher GODWIN at our assizes. I find myself about three inches taller and somewhat fatter from this Circumstance. Taylor, who sat between me and GODWIN, asked the latter if Ld. Chief Justice Eyre (two whom we sat opposite) knew his Person; he smiled and replied he believed he did. GODWIN while

at Norwich was reconciled to Thelwall at William Taylor's and I have since seen them walking together round our Castle Hill. Of course the former will no longer be accused of 'cherishing a feebleness of spirit,' nor will the latter be again compared to Iago. Like Gog and Magog or the two Kings of Brentford, they will now go hand in hand in their glorious schemes.[44]

Charles Cestre, biographer of Thelwall, is reponsible for the misrepresentation of Godwin's position.[45] Although he recognised the influence of Godwin on Thelwall, Cestre found 'an irreconcilable inner discrepancy of spirit between them. Godwin was essentially a thinker in abstracto.'[46] Cestre juxtaposed Thelwall and Godwin as the man of action and the closet philosopher respectively. This juxtaposition, I believe, is fundamentally misleading, because their dispute arose from the very practical question of political methods. Godwin had repudiated appeals to popular prejudice as a useful method of progress. This, in itself, would hardly classify him as a closet philosopher. It was for a similar reason that Francis Place resigned from the Corresponding Society in 1797, and he is not considered a thinker in abstracto.

Cestre bolstered his contrast of Thelwall and Godwin, by the use of a letter Godwin sent to Thelwall on September 18, 1794 while the latter was in the Tower.[47] Cestre wrote that 'when Thelwall was confined in the Tower, under threat of capital punishment, neither his sufferings nor his courage, nor the distress of his wife and child, caused Godwin to relent from the severity of his judgment'.[48] However, the letter was written the day after Godwin had met Mrs. Thelwall at the

Hazlitt's with whom he most certainly discussed the matter. It was sent to tell Thelwall that because of the political situation, he did not feel that a visit at that time would be wise. Godwin criticised Thelwall for using abusive language against his jailers, and urged him to be calm and benevolent. He also tried to persuade him to develop a simple, direct defence rather than one based upon citations of various philosophical authorities. Mrs. Thelwall printed the letter in her biography of her husband.[49] She used it to show the 'caution' and 'dismay' of the period, but never mentioned its importance in any dispute between Godwin and Thelwall. This is probably the correct view. Cestre called the letter 'one of the most striking examples of the influence of abstract thought on conduct', but it seems rather a highly prudential and practical assessment of political events.[50]

Cestre's misrepresentation of Godwin is significant not only because it has led a writer to assert that Godwin 'approved of the government's repressive measures and denounced the agitators and democrats, i.e. his own friends', but also because it confuses Godwin's intentions and ascribes to his practical writings characteristics which belong to the theoretical ones.[51] Godwin may have been an 'abstract' philosopher, but his practical writings, especially in this dispute with Thelwall, dealt in concrete terms with pressing political issues. Cestre's criticism has tended to confuse the distinction between the theoretical and the practical which enabled Godwin to be both a thinker <u>in abstracto</u> and an effective pamphleteer.

CHAPTER X

THE LATER WRITINGS

By 1796, Godwin's enthusiasm for the French Revolution had substantially cooled. He had already revealed this in the dispute with Thelwell, and in the Preface to the *Enquirer*, published in 1797, he clearly stated his position:-

> There is one thought more he is desirous to communicate; and it may not improperly find a place in this Preface. It relates to the French Revolution; that inexhaustible source of meditation to the reflecting and inquisitive. While the principles of Gallic republicanism were yet in their infancy, the friends of innovation were somewhat too imperious in their tone. Their minds were in a state of exaltation and ferment. They were too impatient and impetuous. There was something in their sternness that savoured of barbarism. The barbarism of our adversaries was no adequate excuse for this. The equable and independent mind should not be diverted from its bias by the errors of the enemy with whom it may have to contend.
>
> The author confesses that he did not escape the contagion. Those who ranged themselves on the same party, have now moderated their intemperance, and he has accompanied them also in their present stage. With as ardent a passion for innovation as ever, he feels himself more patient and tranquil.[1]

If Godwin's attitude had substantially moderated, little imagination is needed to conceive the state of English opinion generally towards France and the French Revolution. For the next years, Godwin and others who had supported the reformers were subjected to vicious abuse and calumny, especially in the highly effective <u>Anti-Jacobin Review</u>. In 1802, Thomas Robinson wrote to his brother Henry that 'the famous new philosophy of the French which seemed to promise a revolution in the world is I believe now almost without a disciple -- The Political Justice rests quite at ease upon the bookseller's shelf -- at Granham's auction, I think it sold for less than two shillings -- although there were booksellers present who came from Cambridge and Norwich'.[2] In these years, Godwin was to travel the road from public fame to notoriety without hardly moving a finger.

The general public attack on his character, though serious, seems not to have disturbed him as much as that initiated by some of his friends who had turned against him. In particular, he was injured by James Mackintosh and Dr. Samuel Parr with whom he had been very friendly during the events of 1794 and 1795. He had visited Dr. Parr at his home for a number of days as late as March 1796, and he continued to see Mackintosh regularly through 1798.

Mackintosh was the first to defect and then denounce Godwin in public which he did when he delivered his lectures 'On the Law of Nature and Nations' in Lincoln's Inn Hall from January to June

1799.³ Privately, however, Mackintosh had altered his position as early as December 1796 when he wrote dramatically to Burke:

> For a time indeed seduced by the love of what I thought liberty I ventured to oppose without ever ceasing to venerate that writer who had nourished my understanding with the most wholesome Principles of political wisdom. I speak to state facts -- not to flatter -- you are above flattery....
>
> Since that time a melancholy experience has undeceived me on many subjects in which I was then the dupe of my own enthusiasm. I cannot say ... that I can even now assent to all your opinions on the present politics of Europe. But I can with truth affirm that I subscribe to your general Principles and am prepared to shed my blood in defence of the Laws and Constitution of my Country. ...
>
> Whatever be the fate of this request /for visit with Burke/, I can only safely entrust the construction of so singular a step as that which I have now hazarded to such a mind as yourself. I am perfectly confident that you will not sofar punish my presumption as to expose me to the sneers of those who are less generous by disclosing any circumstance of this address.⁴

On January 19, 1797, Godwin called on Mackintosh, and the conversation was about Burke. That Mackintosh had told Godwin of his letter is highly unlikely, although he may have spoken of a change in his ideas. Whether Godwin attended the first lecture given by Mackintosh in January 1799 is not known.⁵ The lecture was published and upon reading it, Godwin immediately wrote to Mackintosh. The exchange of letters is of considerable importance for understanding Godwin's practical idea of the relationship which should exist between philosophers or men of letters in their various activities. Godwin conceived a class of cultivated gentlemen, differing, perhaps, in theoretical ideas, but agreeing to allow differences to exist and to debate these differences in a scholarly spirit. To this conception might be added the notion arising out of the dispute with Thelwall, that no gentleman ought to make popular appeals which might lead to tumult, and possibly, chaos and revolution. These principles were the practical guides which ensured intellectual progress, and possibly, moral progress without stimulating a reaction which threatened to destroy philosophy itself.

The first letter was written by Godwin on January 27, 1799.[6]

> I have just read with mingled emotions of pleasure and pain, your Discourse on the Study of the Law of Nature and Nations. My emotions of pleasure you will take, and you are well entitled to do so, as the just tribute of my admiration for the comprehensiveness of your talent and the profoundness of your discernment. An enquiry into the source of my emotions of pain will probably not be very interesting to you, and I therefore (except in one incidental particular) will pass it over in silence.

Will you give me leave to enquire (I hope you will not impute to an impertinence of disposition, a question I should scarcely have deigned to address to a less man than yourself) who are the speculators whom you designate with the following epithets — superficial and most mischievous sciolists — masters of fatal controversies — men who, in pursuit of a transient popularity, have exerted their art to disguise the most miserable commonplaces in the shape of paradox — promulgators of absurd and monstrous systems — of abominable and pestilential paradoxes — shallow metaphysicians — sophists swelled with insolent conceit — savage desolators?

If these epithets are meant to apply to Rousseau, Turgot and Condorcet, will you condescend to inform me how it is you have discovered that their motives were less pure and philanthropical, than those of Grotius, Puffendorf, Wolf, Burlamaqui, or Vattel? It would perhaps be presumptuous for me to suppose that any portion of this invective was designed to light upon myself, but, if it were, I must be permitted to answer that however weak my speculations may be, I am not conscious of their dishonesty.

Again, supposing the motives of the authors you seem disposed to treat as heterodox were less pure than those of the orthodox (and I hold no motives to be unmixed), is it the soundest and most manly way of refuting an author's paradoxes, to load his character with odium and his doctrine with a frightful catalogue of frightful consequences, pernicious and immoral? I am the more surprised at this in the discourse before me, as, in the personal intercourse which for years I have been so fortunate as to hold with you, I have always found you the closest, most dispassionate and candid disputant I ever encountered.

It seems that our personal intercourse is likely to be much diminished. I am sincerely and deeply grieved for the loss I am destined to sustain. You are not disposed to maintain the intercourse upon that footing of reciprocity, which is preserved by frequent, unequivocal demonstrations that it is mutually desired. But that is not to be wondered at; you probably did not find in it a reciprocity of advantage. I experienced essential benefits, which I might want the power, or be denied the good fortune, to be able to repay. I should really be happy to meet you as a literary antagonist; for I should rejoice to have the mistakes into which I have fallen corrected, and I know no man so competent to the task as yourself. But if you condescend to refute my errors, I should very earnestly wish that you would console me, by the liberality and generosity of your manner, for the philosophical patience which the task of seeing this system demolished would require in any human being. It would be a consolation, not to my personal feelings merely, but upon general principles. No man who, after having meditated upon philosophical subjects, gives the result of his reflections to the world, believes that, for having done so, he deserves to be treated like a highwayman or an assassin. And this sort of invective, I think upon further consideration you will not deny, contributes much more effectually to the spread of malignity and persecution, than of science and truth.

On the following day, Mackintosh wrote a conciliatory reply.[7]

... In all discussions of 'Speculative Principles' it is always a most unfair act of controversy to load the author whom we oppose with the 'immoral consequences' which we suppose likely to flow from his opinion, not to mention that it is a sorry and impertinent sophism to urge such consequences as an

argument against the truth of a speculative
proposition. But the case is very different
in moral and practical disputes. There the
consequences are everything and must be
constantly appealed to, especially by those
who, like you and myself, hold utility to be
the standard of morals. To apply this to the
present subject. With respect to you personally,
I could never mean to say anything unkind or
disrespectful. I had always esteemed both your
acuteness and benevolence. ... I, however, allow
that I should have confined these epithets, which
I apply to denote pernicious consequences, merely
to doctrines. Though these epithets, when they
are applied by men to men, are never intended to
convey any aspersion upon the moral or intellectual
character of individuals, but merely to describe
them as the promulgators of opinions which I think
false and pernicious, yet I admit that I should
not in any way have applied the epithets to men.

On February 3, Godwin replied to Mackintosh, the final letter in the exchange.[8]

... You certainly, as you say, have a right to state,
that certain opinions, on moral and political subjects,
if reduced, or attempted to be reduced to practice,
are of mischievous tendency. But I am not quite so
well satisfied that it is liberal, manly or tolerant,
to talk of the fatal consequences of broaching
certain opinions, or bringing them into the discussion.
... The friend of science will always be reluctant to
discourage men from the enunciation or support of
principles they apprehend to be true.

> ... I grant you have a right to impute bad consequences to my opinions or those of any other man on practical subjects. But I do not admit that you are to be commended or excused, when you style the authors you undertake to refute, sophists, shallow, superficial, conceited, and insolent. This is neither political with regard to yourself nor generous so far as they are concerned.
>
> You express a hope that we may exhibit the example, which is all too rare of men who are literary antagonists, but personal friends. I participate with you in this sentiment and the omission shall not rest with me, if it is not carried into action. But I conceive it to be still more worthy of our ambition, that we should afford the example of antagonists who, in the midst of their contention about principles and public good, know how to treat each other in their discourses and literary productions with a uniform liberality and respect. The reality of friendship cannot perhaps subsist without this. There is nothing that I have more constantly wished than a reform of the rancour of controversy; nor could I ever persuade myself to adopt the opinion of those, who say, that without this stimulant, our [?] would be unable either to excite the curiosity, or procure to themselves the suffrage of the public.

Mackintosh regretted his initial treatment of Godwin. In a letter written to a friend on December 9, 1804, he admitted his 'guilt' in the matter.

> If I committed any fault which approaches to immorality, I think it was towards Mr. Godwin. I condemn myself for contributing to any clamour against philosophical speculations; and I allow that, both from his talents and character, he was entitled to be treated with respect. Better men than I am, have still more wronged their antagonists

> in controversy, on subjects, and at times in which
> they might easily have been dispassionate, and
> without the temptation and excuse of popular
> harrangues. But I do not seek shelter from their
> example. I acknowledge my fault; and if I had
> not been withheld by blind usage, from listening
> to the voice of my own reason, I should long ago
> have made the acknowledgement to Mr. G., from
> whom I have no wish that it should now be concealed.[9]

In later years he was particularly solicitous about Godwin's welfare and helped to raise money for him when Godwin's business began to fail.

The key point at issue in this dispute was the manner of debating moral principles. Mackintosh urged that the practical consequences of a moral or political doctrine ought to be taken into account and the doctrine criticised if its consequences were injurious to the stability or perhaps the welfare of the society. Godwin argued that if the consequences of a moral doctrine became the decisive criteria of its value, no moral doctrine, critical of existing society and institutions, could become established. What was important was the truth or falsity of the doctrine, and only with the object of proving or disproving moral and political ideas could the science of politics progress. Although the consequences of a doctrine might be important, the injurious consequences of all moral and political ideas could be avoided by the presentation of these ideas in a calm, reasonable manner. In this way, the consequences of a theory need not become the deciding factor of its validity, because the consequences would only immediately affect the small number who took an interest in speculations of this kind. Thus, radical ideas might be talked about without threatening existing institutions.

If the dispute with Mackintosh ended with a satisfactory demonstration of his practical principles, Godwin's relationship with Parr only showed that his principles might not be universally applicable. It will be recalled that Godwin was visiting Parr when Holcroft was arrested for treason, and after the trials, Parr wrote to Godwin.[10]

> Your anxiety, dear Mr. Godwin, during Hardy's trial could not be more intense than mine, your joy at the close of it was not more rapturous, your approbation of the jury is not more warm, and your indignation against the judge seems to be less fierce.

Parr reminded Godwin that he did not support the British Convention but heaped lavish praise on the author of Cursory Strictures. Although Godwin and Parr might not have agreed on all issues, there was evidence of agreement on numerous points and particular evidence of Parr's admiration of Godwin. On January 3, 1800 in an effort to restore a declining relationship, Godwin sent Dr. Parr a copy of his new novel, St. Leon, asking him for his comments. He also criticised Mackintosh's lectures, and did it in a manner to draw out Parr's opinions of his friend's new enterprise. His letter was not answered, except in the form of Parr's Spital Sermon on April 15, Easter Tuesday at Christ Church before the Lord Mayor. The sermon was a direct attack on the philosophy of universal benevolence, and although Parr did not name Godwin in the text, the object of his criticisms was certainly clear. Godwin attempted to call on his old friend several times, but found him not at home. He finally wrote him a letter on April 24. He began by recalling his sending him St. Leon the previous January.

> This subject dismissed, I should then have mentioned your sermon of Easter Tuesday. I spoke in that letter of Mackintosh's [lectures], in which that gentleman, without the manliness of mentioning me, takes occasion three times a-week to represent me to an audience of a hundred persons, as a wretch unworthy to live. Your sermon, I learn from all hands, was on the same subject, handled, I take it for granted, from what I know of your character, in a very different spirit. I am sorry for this. Since Mackintosh's Lectures, it has become a sort of fashion with a large party to join in the cry against me. It is the part, I conceive, of original genius, to give the tone to others, rather than to join a pack, after it has already become loud and numerous.[11]

Several days later, Parr wrote a lengthy reply in which he expressed a desire not to see Godwin again. He accused him of misrepresenting Mackintosh, noting that Mackintosh, himself, had said that he did not personally attack Godwin. He also accused Godwin of making offensive remarks about his own character.

At the end of his letter, Godwin had asked Parr to list what made him think so unfavourably of him in 1800 after thinking so favourably of him in 1794. Parr said first that he had not sought Godwin's acquaintance with any zeal. He also objected to passages in Godwin's Enquirer which were hostile to religion. In addition, he said that he was shocked at the volume Godwin had written in memory of Mary Wollstonecraft. But a final remark was particularly strange: 'I had not then seen your eagerness and perseverance in employing every kind of vehicle to convey to every class of readers those principles which, so long as they appeared only in the form of a methaphysical treatise, might have done less extensive mischief.'[12] Godwin wrote some notes to Parr's letter objecting primarily to two points. First, he recalled Parr's zeal in desiring to know him, his insistence that Mackintosh bring Godwin to see him, and the numerous meetings which they enjoyed as late as 1798. He also pointed out that Parr knew his views on religion long before this dispute.

Godwin did not actually reply though he began a draft of a letter when his copy of St. Leon was returned.[13] His reply was reserved for his long pamphlet, Thoughts Occasioned by the Perusal of Dr. Parr's Spital Sermon, which was published on June 18, 1801. This publication has already been assessed in terms of the debate with Malthus. The first part, however, was devoted to an appraisal of the events of the French Revolution and criticism of Mackintosh and Parr.

In the pamphlet Godwin admitted that Political Justice was a child of the French Revolution. He also admitted that the revolution had proved a great disappointment. However, the many friends of the event had declared themselves so decisively that they held to their decision for a long time.

What was the consequence of this? Mr. Burke published his celebrated book against the French Revolution in 1790 they were unmoved. The powers of Europe began to concert hostile measures upon the subject in 1791: they were unmoved. Louis was deposed; monarchical government was prescribed in France: they were unmoved. In September 1792 scenes of execrable and unprecedented murder were perpetuated in the capital and many of the provinces: they scorned for the sake of a few private misdeeds to give up a great public principle. The head of Louis fell on the scaffold: still they were consistent. The atrocious and inhuman reign of Robespierre commenced; it continued from May 1793 to July 1794; almost every day was marked with blood; almost all that was greatest and most venerable in France was immolated at the monster's shrine; ... still these advocates ... were consistent. Down to the spring of 1797, when petitions were sent up from so many parts of England for the removal of the king's ministers, scarcely any of those persons who had declared themselves ardently and affectionately interested for the success of the French, deserted their cause.[14]

After these years, they now had turned to attack Godwin.

I am willing to yield to these men considerable praise for the constancy with which they persevered so long; as long perhaps as worldly prudence could in any degree countenance. But why, because I have not been so prudent as they, should I be made the object of their invective? I never went so far, in my partiality for the practical principles of the French revolution, as many of those with whom I was accustomed to converse. I uniformly declared myself an enemy to revolutions. Many persons censured me for this lukewarmness; I willingly endured the censure. Several of those persons are now gone into the opposite extreme. They must excuse me; they have wandered wide of me on the one side and on the other: I did not follow them before; I cannot follow them now.[15]

Godwin suggested that his former friends should have modestly admitted their mistakes rather than attack Godwin who would have accepted their change of opinion in silence. He criticised Mackintosh both for avoiding the use of Godwin's name, and thereby avoiding the necessity of refuting his arguments. With Parr he was more severe. He alleged that Parr, knowing full well that he, Godwin, had changed his views on the question of the importance of the domestic affections (in the preface to St. Leon), had nevertheless criticised Godwin's old view. He also pointed out that Parr had relied on Thomas Green's pamphlet against Godwin — but that pamphlet was critical of utilitarianism, a doctrine which Parr himself shared with Godwin. Next, Godwin carefully attempted to refute the philosophical issues raised by Parr, and in doing so he avoided any personal remarks against him. After the pamphlet had been published, there is no evidence that Godwin and Parr met again. In Parr's Memoirs, published in 1828, William Field assessed the Spital Sermon as follows:

> It is much to be regretted that, instead of a moral and religious disquisition, on the subject of which it professes to treat, the preacher should have allowed his discourse to assume the form of a personal attack, as already noticed, on a very distinguished writer and a friend; and still more to be regretted is the want of fairness and candour, so evident, in declaiming, vehemently and acrimoniously, against the errors of a system, even after those errors had been publicly acknowledged and abjured.[16]

If the controversy with Thelwall served to illustrate Godwin's ideas about practical politics, this dispute with Mackintosh and Parr illustrated his practical ideas about political philosophy. Where Godwin succeeded with Mackintosh, he failed with Parr. The cause of this failure could be attributed to Parr's personality, or it might be due to the difficulty, if not the impossibility, of ultimately developing a class of men of letters who agreed on the right to differ as long as differences were expressed in a reasonable manner. Parr apparently found this liberality incompatible with the establishment and maintenance of moral virtue.

After these incidents, Godwin devoted most of his attention to literary affairs, although he did not wholly neglect politics. In 1801, he married again and soon began a business selling and publishing books. This enterprise was a disastrous failure, and Godwin was soon so hoplessly in debt that he never recovered. He was bankrupt in 1825 and would have been so sooner but for the generosity of his friends. But this generosity was not unlimited, and Godwin's habits of borrowing money soon alienated many former admirers and supporters.

His financial position, more than any other factor, probably led to the diminution of his political activity. There was also the factor of his public reputation, the bitter fruit of the anti-Jacobin propaganda, but this should not have diminished his standing among the reformers. Financial distress led him to concentrate on literature and the numerous children's books that he wrote, leading him more into literary circles than political ones. He became the friend of Lamb, Hazlitt, Coleridge, Shelley and many others.

However, he did not entirely give up politics, and his journal records letters and visits exchanged with various luminaries of the day. In 1806, he published a lengthy letter on the occasion of the death of Fox. Godwin's admiration for Fox had been constant since 1784. Now, twenty-two years later, he wrote an essay on Fox's character. Kegan Paul referred to the letter as 'an excellent specimen of his style at this period of life, dignified and worthy of the great statesman'.[17] In it, Godwin wrote:

> For thirty-two years Fox hardly ever opened his mouth in Parliament but to assert, in some form or other, the cause of liberty and mankind, and to repel tyranny in its various shapes, and protest against the encroachments of power. In the American war, in the questions of reform at home, which grew out of the American war, and in the successive scenes which were produced by the French Revolution, Fox was still found the perpetual advocate of freedom. He endeavoured to secure the privileges and the happiness of the people of Asia and the people of Africa. In Church and State, his principles were equally favourable to the cause of liberty. Englishmen can nowhere find the sentiments of freedom unfolded and amplified in more animated language, or in a more consistent tenor, than in the recorded Parliamentary Debates of Fox. Many have called in question his prudence, and the practicability of his politics in some of their branches; none have succeeded in fixing a stain upon the truly English temper of his heart.[18]

In Godwin's papers is an essay written on the administration of 1806, when Fox briefly became Foreign Secretary, after the death of Pitt. There seems to have been some criticism of Fox's activities at that time, for Godwin concluded it with a defence of his policies and personality:

> These certainly are not the qualities of the man, of whom one should suspect that when in place he would forfeit all the well-earned praises that he had reaped while he was the organ of a senatorial minority. And accordingly, I affirm, that Mr. Fox was to an unprecendented degree the same man in office as out of office; and that while he breathed the air of a court, he imbibed neither the slavish and adulatory spirit, nor the crafty and insidious character, which are too often contracted in that atmosphere.[19]

In this essay, Godwin also reviewed his own principles of politics, carefully distinguishing between the speculative and the practical.

> 'In speculative politics, I indulge with great delight to my own mind (and I cannot easily persuade myself with injury to others) in meditating on what man can be, on all the good which our nature, taken in the most favourable point of view, seems to promise, and in endeavouring to trace in the wide and unexplored sea of future events, through what adventures and by what means that good (certainly in many of its branches exceedingly remote) may ultimately be brought home to us.'

On the other hand, practical political writing provided beacons to guide him in concrete issues and events. He stated that he was an enemy to revolution and 'practically' a friend of the English Constitution.

> I am therefore practically a friend to the English Constitution. Not that I regard it, as some men have done, as the model of all that is best in political government, and the consummation of human wisdom. But I find in it much that is good; and when I compare it with the governments of the countries that surround us, devoutly do I admire it. Were it much worse than it is, my principles would restrain me from assailing it with violence; but as it is, that patience and filial tenderness towards it which my principles enjoin, is made likewise agreeable to my inclinations. I would treat it as a robe bestowed on me for the most useful purposes; I would repair it where it became decayed; in those repairs I would change in some respects the fashion of it as my conveniency seemed to require; but the changes that took place (to however great a sum they might one day amount) should be, separately taken, gentle, temperate, almost insensible. From a pure system of feudal manners, which the English constitution at one time was, it has gradually adapted itself to a mercantile and considerably luxurious nation; and I neither expect nor desire that it should continue unchanged in times to come, any more than it has remained unchanged in ages past.

Godwin did not consider this avowal to be an abrogation of his earlier doctrines, and indeed his practical writings showed it to be a confirmation of what he had essentially believed for more than twenty years.

During this period, Godwin had not wholly turned his attention from French affairs. In 1801, he wrote optimistically of Napoleon. '... [W]e have seen an auspicious and beneficent genius arise, who without violence to the principles of the French revolution, has suspended their morbid activity, ... All the great points embraced by the revolution remain entire .... Every thing promises that the future government of France will be popular, and her people free.'[20] With such an opinion, his meeting Madame de Staël was bound to be memorable. He apparently became acquainted with her at Mackintosh's where he visited for tea on 17 September 1813. He called on her several times during the next month and was invited to dinner on October 18, with Lady Mackintosh, his friend John Curran, Crabb Robinson, and several others. Crabb Robinson summarised their conversation:-

> Godwin defended Milton with zeal, and when his submission to Cromwell was urged by Madam de Staël he even justified Cromwell too on some points. He admitted him to be a Usurper, but asserted him to be no Tyrant. This latter part of his conversation gave offense for as he soon after went away. Madam de Staël said to Lady Mackintosh, 'I am glad I have seen this man -- it is curious how the Jacobins ally themselves with tyrants -- and are their Apologists.' The others spoke favourably of Godwin and Lady Mackintosh said he had been harshly treated -- that he had since lived quite retired and had been ... excluded from Society.[21]

In 1815, Godwin argued that the French should not be coerced into choosing someone other than Napoleon. In a pamphlet entitled Letters of Verax, based on letters to the Morning Chronicle, he contended that the Allies had no right to violate that principle of non-intervention in the internal affairs of other nations. Of Napoleon, he now wrote:

> I was sufficiently disgusted with the character of Bonaparte as it had been displayed up to his exile to Elba; how far his character or his circumstances are altered now, I do not precisely know; but I could have been well satisfied that things had remained as they were settled in 1814.[22]

However, the actions of the Allies at this point, when the entire French nation appeared to favour Napoleon, was designed to destroy French liberty. Godwin called this a war unlike any other fought in history. 'It differs from all wars in the profligate principle which it takes for its basis, and which is unblushingly avowed -- that the sword shall never again be sheathed till the Government, now in full operation, and presiding over the enemy, shall cease to exist.'[23] This issue was the last in which Godwin revealed an active concern for French politics, though he continued to follow events there. He continued to show considerable sympathy for Napoleon although his expression of support was severely qualified.

During the twenty year period from 1800 to 1820, Godwin's actual political activity seems to have been slight, when compared with the preceding twenty years. However, it would be foolish to conclude that his influence had wholly waned. During this period, he came into contact with Shelley and Robert Owen. He also became friendly with Francis Place,[24] and although their relationship was a sorrowful story of Godwin borrowing money and being unable to repay, Place never denied the importance of Godwin or of his political writing. Godwin was also friendly with John Curran through whom he met William Cobbett.[25] His friendship with Coleridge grew much stronger during this period. With Hazlitt, Coleridge and Lamb, he frequently dined. Even his old friends, Horne Tooke and Thelwall, are still mentioned in his journal. His journal also notes numerous letters and visits with some of the Whig parliamentary leaders, but, unfortunately, examination of these exchanges reveals that they were mostly visits relating to Godwin's borrowing money or looking for a government position.

The one eminent English writer of his time with whom Godwin made little contact is Jeremy Bentham. In a letter to Francis Place he said that he envied him because of his acquaintance with Bentham which he, Godwin, had been trying to obtain for twenty years.[26] When Bentham died in 1832, Godwin wrote to Mrs. Gisborne (formerly Mrs. Reveley), an old friend, who had also known Bentham at one time, and she answered his request for an account of Bentham's life at the time she knew him.[27] Godwin may have met Bentham several times. Indeed, it seems impossible that with so many common friends that they could have avoided each other for such a long period. Godwin did send Bentham a copy of the book on population in 1820. However, Bentham, like Malthus, was one of the political economists, with whom Godwin was forced to contend. It is not surprising then that he did not become attached to Bentham, or, for that matter, James Mill. Although there were some who did not consider Godwin's doctrines incompatible with those of the political economists -- Mackintosh and Place are good examples -- both Godwin and the political economists seemed to have concluded that they were incompatible.

The relationship between Godwin and Shelley has been the subject of numerous books and essays, and it would be of little value to elaborate the facts of it here.[28] In one of his earlier letters, Shelley summarised the effect of Political Justice on him.

> It is now a period of more than two years since first I saw your inestimable book of Political Justice. It opened to my mind fresh and more extensive views; it materially influenced my character, and I rose from its perusal a wiser and better man. I was no longer the votary of romance; till then I had existed in an ideal world -- now I found that in this universe of ours was enough to excite the interest of the heart, enough to employ the discussions of reason; I beheld, in short, that I had duties to perform.[29]

Shelley may have been replying to this passage in a letter from Godwin written at approximately the same time in which the philosopher estimated the importance of his book.

> The Enquiry concerning Political Justice, may, unknown to me, be a mass of false principles, erroneous conclusions. To me, it appears otherwise. There is one principle that lies at the basis of that book: 'I am bound to employ my talents, my understanding, my strength, and my time, for the production of the greatest quantity of general good -- I have no right to dispose of a shilling of my property at the suggestion of my caprice.'[30]

Of greater interest perhaps in this chapter on Godwin's practical political ideas is his correspondence with Shelley during the latter's journey to Ireland to campaign for Catholic emancipation. He wrote at the time to Godwin describing his pamphlet, the <u>Address to the Irish People</u>:

> With these sentiments I have been preparing an Address to the Catholics of Ireland, which however deficient may be its execution, I can by no means admit that it contains one sentiment which <u>can</u> harm the cause of liberty and happiness. It consists of the benevolent and tolerant deductions of philosophy reduced into the simplest language, and such as those who by their uneducated poverty are most susceptible of evil impressions from Catholicism may clearly comprehend. I know it can do no harm; it cannot excite rebellion, as its main principle is to trust the success of a cause to the energy of its truth. It cannot 'widen the breach between kingdoms', as its attempts to convey to the vulgar mind sentiments of universal philanthropy; and, whatever impressions it may produce, they can be no others but those of peace and harmony.[31]

Godwin was unconvinced. After receiving Shelley's pamphlet, he replied in a long letter on March 4, 1812.

> In the pamphlet you have just sent me, your views and mine as to the improvement of mankind are decisively at issue. You profess the immediate objects of your efforts to be 'the organisation of a society whose institution shall serve as a bond to its members.' If I may be allowed to understand my book on Political Justice, it's pervading principle is, that association is a most ill-chosen and ill qualified mode of endeavouring to promote the political happiness of mankind. And I think of your pamphlet, however commendable and lovely are many of its sentiments, that it will either be ineffective to its immediate object, or that it has no very remote tendency to light against the flames of rebellion and war.[32]

Godwin added that only by 'discussion, reading, enquiry, perpetual communication', did man improve himself; it was not by organised societies or associations of any kind. However, Shelley was not convinced and sharply attacked Godwin in the next letter.

> I am not forgetful or unheeding of what you said of associations. But <u>Political Justice</u> was first published in 1793; nearly twenty years have passed since the general diffusion of its doctrines. What has followed? Have men ceased to fight? Have vice and misery vanished from the earth? Have the fireside communications which it recommends taken place? Out of the many who have read that inestimable book,

> how many have been blinded by prejudice!
> How many, in short, have taken it up to
> gratify an ephemeral vanity, and, when the
> hour of its novelty had passed, threw it
> aside, and yielded with fashion, to the
> arguments of Mr. Malthus![33]

Godwin hurriedly took up his pen to save Shelley 'from the calamities with which I see your mode of proceeding to be fraught.'[34] He also replied to Shelley's criticism.

> You say, 'what has been done within these
> last twenty years? Oh that I could place you
> upon the pinnacle of ages, from which these
> twenty years would vanish to an invisible
> point'. It is not after this fashion that
> moral causes work in the eye of him who looks
> profoundly through the vast and -- and allow
> me to add -- venerable machine of human society.
> But so reasoned the French Revolutionists.
> Auspicious and admirable materials were working
> in the general mind of France; but these men
> said, as you say, 'When we look on the last
> twenty years, we are seized with a sort of
> moral scepticism; we must own we are eager
> that something should be done'. And see what
> has been the result of their doings. He that
> would benefit mankind on a comprehensive scale,
> by changing the principles and elements of
> society, must learn the hard lesson, to put off
> self, and to contribute by a quiet but incessant
> activity, like a rill of water to irrigate and
> fertilise the intellectual evil. ...[35]

Shelley finally bowed to Godwin's wishes and the erring disciple returned to his best graces. He withdrew the pamphlets from circulation and prepared to leave Dublin. However, Shelley's acquiescence in Godwin's opinions did not mean that he agreed with his teacher. He believed that the associations that he recommended would enhance progress rather than retard it. 'My mind is by no means settled, on the subject of Associations', he wrote on March 18, 1812. 'They appear to me in one point of view useful, in another deleterious.'[36] And though his ideas for the organising of the illiterate may have been ill-timed, he thought that there was no reason to assume that they would lead to violence. On March 30, relieved at the turn in Shelley's actions, Godwin wrote that 'I can now look upon you as a friend. Before I knew not what might happen.'[37] Godwin continued to advise Shelley on this and numerous other topics, a correspondence, though marred by disputes about Godwin's many financial difficulties and Shelley's relationship with his daughter, which remained active and exciting to the end. This brief portion of the correspondence is the most instructive for understanding Godwin's practical ideas about politics. Again, he opposed the association, the faction, and all appeal to popular favour. The theme recalls the dispute with Thelwall or one of the later 'Mucius' letters.

Another important, though less known, relationship was established with Robert Owen. The friendship began on January 8, 1813, when the two men met at a dinner, which Coleridge also attended. On January 20,

Godwin's journal notes: 'Owen of Lanark calls', and he became a frequent visitor at Godwin's home. Unfortunately, little evidence of the substance of their conversations has been found, although they visited and corresponded regularly from 1813 to 1818 and occasionally afterwards.[38] It is possible that Godwin introduced Owen to Francis Place.[39] Owen listed Godwin among the 'literary men and women' who were friendly to his views, but did not single him out for special treatment.[40] Podmore, his biographer, has noted that 'those who are familiar with the Political Justice will recognise a striking similarity, extending in some cases to the actual phrases employed, between Godwin's philosophical conceptions and those expounded by Owen twenty years later'.[41] Indeed, when Owen was writing his New View of Society, he was a regular visitor at the Godwin household.

On the whole, Godwin had a considerable influence on many reformers. He attracted to himself the literary figures more than the political economists, although the latter were also to become the advocates of parliamentary and legal reform. Over the issue of population, these two groups locked horns, and the struggle was, as we have seen, a fierce one. That Bentham and Godwin did not have much contact, is also an indication of this conflict. They were both utilitarians, and, for this reason, people such as Mackintosh, Place, and Owen could actually have a position on both sides.

After the debate over population, Godwin's practical political activity nearly came to a halt once more. He was very poor after his bankruptcy and though his journal records meetings and correspondence with many eminent men of the period, his relationships were based either on sentiment for an old warrior or the circumstances that Godwin was seeking their assistance. One at a time, his old friends, Coleridge, Lamb, Mackintosh, Scott, and Hazlitt, and several others who were not his friends, Parr and Bentham, died. Finally, he was given the sinecure of Yeoman Usher of the Exchequer by Lord Grey in April 1833. At seventy-seven, he was enabled to pass his few remaining years at peace and in security. However, he had performed a final political act, either to gain his position, to demonstrate concern, or, perhaps, he was called upon to perform it. In his papers are fragments of a draft of a 'Representation to the King' expressing displeasure with the rejection of the Reform Bill by the House of Lords after the King had dissolved parliament and held a general election on the issue. Godwin saw the events as crucial to the future development of the English Constitution.[42]

CHAPTER XI

PROGRESS AND DEMOCRACY: THE MEANS

In these final chapters, the task is to gather the threads which together form the whole design of Godwin's political philosophy. Godwin was concerned with improvement or progress. He considered democracy to be the best form of government and one most likely to enable men to improve the moral and political conditions of their lives. There must clearly be a set of means to sustain this progress -- though Godwin may have thought of progress as an insensible process, he did not see it as an automatic one. Furthermore, progress means development towards an end or set of ends. Godwin frequently spoke of movement towards 'a state of civilisation'. This chapter will be concerned with the question of the means of progress, and the next with the end or ends.

In Godwin's last book of essays, published posthumously, there is a preliminary essay entitled 'On the Exoteric and Esoteric in Philosophy and Theology'.

> The Ancient Egyptians, the Pythagoreans, the leaders of the Hindoo religion in India, the Druids, and a number of speculative men in all ages, have been of opinion that there is one set of doctrines that it is convenient should be recommended to and imposed upon the vulgar, and another that should be communicated only to such as were found unquestionably worthy of that favour and distinction.

It has been supposed that a long train of previous initiation and trial should precede the communication of that system which is the ultimate result of the examination of the learned, and of those who were inclined and encouraged by means of elaborate research to enquire into the essence of things.

It was imagined that these men had purified themselves from the grosser elements of our kind, and might safely be trusted to look into the innermost sanctuary, and to see nature as it really is, stripped of those false colourings and that dazzling glare under which, for the most part, it appears to the ignorant.

A sort of strength of mind, which can only be the result of long discipline, has been supposed to be necessary to keep men in the path of right conduct by the force of the light of nature only, while the mass of mankind are conceived no otherwise to be held under sufficient restraint but by the terrors and bugbears which stand revealed to the eyes of the select few, but which are sufficient, when nothing else would suffice, to check the escapades and enormities of the ordinary race of men.[1]

Godwin could not agree that mankind was necessarily divided into two groups, the larger to be kept in ignorance by the smaller. There was no caste system natural to man:

All men are acknowledged to partake of a common nature, to have a right to deliberate respecting their system of action; and having deliberated, to conduct themselves accordingly. This is the most important revolution that has occurred in the history of the world. The equality of human beings as such, opens upon us the prospect of perpetual improvement. ... It opens to us the prospect of indefinite advancement in sound judgment, in real science, and the just conduct of our social institutions.[2]

The invention of printing insured that men would not regress, because the means of education were now in the hands of a larger part of the people. The attempt to erect a wall at this time between the wise and the unwise would be analogous to planting a hedge to confine birds.

The termination of the use of the exoteric and esoteric in philosophy and science had an analogy to changes in political organisation.

> The question is the same as that of political liberty and slavery. There was a time when it was held that it was only a privileged few that were to be the masters of their own actions, while the great majority was to be held in chains. ... This is, of all considerations, the most vital to the community of mankind. So long as we were divided into two classes, the master and the slave, both parties were corrupted -- the lower by the condition of their existence being precluded from the influence of almost every generous motive, every impulse of a loftier sort, and the higher impelled from the first hour of their moral existence to the practice of tyranny and despotism.[3]

Thus, the duality had evil effects in both philosophy and politics. Furthermore, it was wrong for religion, which was the great equaliser of mankind, to perpetuate these doctrines. In place of exoteric and esoteric doctrines, Godwin presented his arguments on a single level of discourse.[4] He attached a high value to the open pursuit of truth and the accumulation of knowledge; he disdained the salutary delusions advocated by Burke and the impostures approved by Rousseau.

> If there be any truth in the reasonings
> hitherto adduced, we are entitled to
> conclude that morality, the science of
> human happiness, the principle which
> binds the individual to the species, and
> the inducements which are calculated to
> persuade us to model our conduct, in the
> way most conducive to the advantage of
> all, does not rest upon imposture and
> delusion, but upon grounds, that discovery
> will never undermine, and wisdom never
> refute.[5]

Knowledge led to the increase of happiness; great pleasures were derived from the mere process of learning, besides the substance of various intellectual pursuits. 'Sublime and expansive ideas produce delicious emotions', he wrote. 'Knowledge contributes in two ways to our happiness: first by the new sources of enjoyment it opens upon us, and next by furnishing us with a clue in the selection of all other pleasures.'[6] Knowledge also led to the cultivation of virtue. The most virtuous man was he who chose the greatest amount of pleasures. In order to make these choices, knowledge was required.

For Godwin, the dissemination of knowledge was as important as its accumulation. The development of printing and the denunciation of two teachings in philosophy made the task easier than it was in the past. It was not by accident that Godwin considered sincerity to be the most important virtue in moral and political life.[7] He thought there was no need to dwell on the advantages of sincerity.

The innocence which its exercise produced, with the absence of caution and restraint, and the energy of disposition which resulted were manifestly evident. Besides, sincerity led to intellectual improvement. The hesitancy and fear connected with intellectual discourse were abandoned with the establishment of sincere intercourse between men, and an honest spirit of intellectual discovery and communication took its place. Furthermore, the practice of sincerity led to philanthropy.

Godwin distinguished several degrees of sincerity. The first was found in the person who considered it his duty to utter nothing which could not consistently be said to be true. The second was represented by the person who conceived his duty to utter nothing untrue <u>and</u> which might be **misconceived** by someone else. These were examples of 'negative' sincerity, compatible with systems of morality such as Rousseau's whose maxim, to do no injury to one's neighbour, combined with this active avoidance of deceit. However, there was a final degree of sincerity expressed in Cicero's maxim, 'utter nothing that is false and withhold nothing that is true'. This, urged Godwin, was the form which sincerity must take if it was to transform human society. Avoiding deception was not sufficient, and would contribute little to an honourable undertaking. 'If sincerity be, as we have endeavoured to demonstrate, the most powerful engine of human improvement, a scheme for restraining it within so narrow limits, cannot be entitled to considerable applause.'[8] In addition, to suppress information, an honourable practice within the maxim of doing no injury to others, produced evasiveness and ambiguity not suited to a virtuous disposition. 'Hence it appears, that the only species of sincerity which can in any degree prove satisfactory to the enlightened moralist and politician, is that where the frankness is perfect, and every degree of reserve is discarded.'[9] Godwin argued, in principle, for the unlimited exercise of sincerity. Yet, he put a limit to the doctrine with this maxim:-

> The rule respecting them must be, that, wherever a great and manifest evil arises from disclosing the truth, and that evil appears to be greater than the evil, to arise from violating, in this instance, the general barrier of human confidence and virtue, there the obligation of sincerity is suspended.[10]

This rule was applied by Godwin to instances when the utterance of a truth would result in one's immediate destruction. Nevertheless, the maxim expressed merely a limitation on the general rule and did not replace it.

Education, broadly speaking, was the method of disseminating knowledge, although sincerity opened the channels and established the proper dispositions for giving and receiving it. Godwin saw two aspects to a doctrine of education, the theoretical and the practical, as education, like politics, was an activity of man. He directed education more towards creating a particular kind of character and emphasised moral obligations more than the mastery of certain arts and sciences. The kind of character he sought to create was an enquiring and critical one. He believed that education should begin in the very early years of a child. 'Thus a diseased state of body, and still more an improper treatment, the rendering the child, in any considerable degree, either the tyrant or the slave of those around him, may in the first twelve months implant seeds of an ill temper, which in some instances may accompany him through life.'[11] During childhood, more important than actual happiness was an awakening of the mind which should take place during these years. Children need not acquire a particular kind of knowledge. Of greater value was the cultivation of an ability to think. The mind of a child should not be idle, as this created a laziness no subsequent education could mend. 'In a word, the first lesson of a judicious education is, Learn to think, to discriminate, to remember and to enquire.'[12]

It was also important to begin to cultivate certain talents. Godwin severely criticised the common opinion which discouraged the development of talents, usually expressed by saying that talents might be injurious to he who has them: good sense and a virtuous disposition were sufficient for happiness. Godwin replied:

> Talents are the instruments of usefulness. He that has them, is capable of producing uncommon benefit; he that has them not, is destitute even of the power. A tool with a fine edge may do mischief; but a tool that neither has an edge nor can receive it, is merely lumber.[13]

Genius, Godwin urged in the *Enquirer*, which enabled man to cultivate his talents was not born with the child, but was subsequently infused. The new-born child was very plastic and habits acquired before birth could be changed. That was another reason for careful attention to the early years of the child. 'There is perhaps nothing that has a greater tendency to decide favourably or unfavourably respecting a man's future intellect, than the question whether or not he be impressed with an early taste for reading.'[14] The pupil was thus a tabula rasa upon which impressions were made by the teacher. 'All education is despotism,' he wrote at one point.[15] 'The pupil is the clay in the hands of the artificer,' he wrote at another.[16] In *Thoughts on Man*, he modified this position somewhat. The child's mind was no longer a tabula rasa, the child no ball of clay. Although each child was born with a different disposition, Godwin retained most of his old view by arguing that all of them had talents.

> The result of these observations certainly strongly tends to support the proposition laid down early in the present Essay, that, putting idiots and extraordinary cases out of the question, every human creature is endowed with talents, which, if rightly directed, would shew him to be apt, adroit, intelligent, and acute, in the walk for which his organisation especially fitted him.[17]

Godwin did not repudiate the Helvetian view which he held at the time he wrote the Enquirer, twenty-five years before, that every person born into the world was capable of being made or becoming the equal of Homer or Newton. He objected to it now only because it was 'too vast and indefinite' a view, leaving neither the pupil nor the instructor with a compass to find the best road of learning.[18] Godwin's new principles required that each child be studied to determine what best suited his nature; each child might be suited to a different task, but all of them were capable of performing one task well, and all were 'endowed with faculties, apt, adroit, intelligent, and acute'.[19] This was a revision, but not wholly a rejection of Helvetian principles.

In teaching, Godwin said, what must be cultivated were the motives for learning. 'The best motive to learn, is a perception of the value of the thing learned.'[20] Godwin desired to break down the traditional barrier between teacher and pupil. 'This plan', he wrote, 'is calculated entirely to change the face of education.'[21]

> The whole formidable apparatus which has hitherto attended it, is swept away. Strictly speaking, no such characters are left upon the scene as either preceptor or pupil. The boy, like the man, studies, because he desires it. He proceeds upon a plan of his own invention, or which, by adopting, he has made his own. Every thing bespeaks independence and equality. The man, as well as the boy, would be glad in cases of difficulty to consult a person more informed than himself. That the boy is accustomed almost always to consult the man, and not the man the boy, is to be regarded rather as an accident, than any thing essential.[22]

Godwin claimed that his method would be very beneficial to the child. The child would have more independence; he would strengthen his sense of judgment by the frequent exercise of it; and he would develop a love of literature. Therefore, the substance of this basic relationship, whether between parent and child or teacher and pupil, was crucial to the development of the young. Godwin condemned the sort of deception which was very common in this relationship. 'Nothing tends effectually to poison morality in its source in the minds of youth, than the practice of holding one language and laying down one set of precepts for the observation of the young, and another of the adult.'[23] On these grounds, he criticised Rousseau whom he otherwise acknowledged as a great influence on his own ideas. 'His whole system of education is a series of tricks, a puppet-show exhibition, of which the master holds the wires, and the scholar is never to suspect in what manner they are moved.'[24] Godwin thus advocated sincerity in place of imposture in education as well as in politics and in day-to-day moral relationships.

Turning to a different level, he considered the study of the Classics to be an essential part of education. Modern writers learned how to think from the ancients, and although modern civilisation could exist without the study of the ancients, there were still good reasons for studying them. The Latin authors had great skill in the use of language and should be studied for that reason. The Latin historians, he argued, were among the best that ever lived. Furthermore, the best ages of Rome offered to the world the purest examples of virtue. 'Modern ages have formed to themselves a virtue, rather polished, than sublime, that consists in petty courtesies, rather than in the tranquil grandeur of an elevated mind.'[25]

Although Godwin opposed a national institution of education, he weighed the advantages and disadvantages of public and private systems. At home the child received sympathy, which was an important factor in encouraging study. At school he was alone in the midst of the crowd, and he might become selfish and sullen. Nevertheless, placing the child at school with his peers often stimulated him. Furthermore, the schools tended to stress fundamentals which were neglected or overlooked in private education.

Whether in his arguments about talents and genius, his discussion of classical education, or in his consideration of the merits of public or private education, Godwin continually stressed the development of virtuous character. This production of virtue was more important than the cultivation of the arts and sciences, themselves, for virtuous men were necessary for moral improvement. All men were capable of becoming virtuous; their institutions maintained prejudices which only education and reforms in relationships between men could eradicate. Godwin was not satisfied with the production of simple virtue. He desired the extensive cultivation of talents and development of men of genius.

> The affairs of man in society are not of so simple a texture, that they require only common talents to guide them. Tyranny grows up by a kind of necessity of nature; oppression discovers itself; poverty, fraud, violence, murder, and a thousand evils follow in the rear. These cannot be extirpated without great discernment and great energies. Men of genius must rise up, to show their brethren that these evils, though familiar, are not therefore the less dreadful, to analyse the machine of human society, to demonstrate how the parts are connected together, to explain the immense chain of events and consequences, to point out the defects and the remedy. It is only then that important reforms can be produced. Without talents, despotism would be endless, and public misery incessant.[26]

Godwin did not intend that men should drop their current affairs and apply themselves exclusively to the cultivation of talents and virtue. His theoretical teaching had a practical side to it which was more adapted to actual conditions. Yet, he did not consider his theoretical maxims wholly inapplicable to practice. Theory accounted for the general; practice dealt with the particular. Theory and practice, though different, were not antagonistic; they were complementary.

> Nothing can be more idle and shallow, than the competition which some men have set up, between theory and practice. It is true that we can never predict, from theory alone, the success of any given experiment. It is true that no theory,

> accurately speaking, can possibly be practical.
> It is the business of theory to collect the
> circumstances of a certain set of cases, and
> arrange them. It would cease to be theory if
> it did not leave out many circumstances; it
> collects such as are general, and leaves out
> such as are particular. In practice, however,
> those circumstances inevitably arise, which are
> necessarily omitted in the general process: they
> cause the phenomenon, in various ways, to include
> features which were not in the prediction, and to
> be diversified in those that were. Yet theory is
> of the highest use; and those who decry it, may
> even be proved not to understand themselves.[27]

Godwin would have men try to conform their actions to theoretical principles. However, they must also take into account practical consequences.

> General principles of morality are so far valuable,
> as they truly delineate the means of utility,
> pleasure, or happiness. But every action of any
> human being, has its appropriate result; and,
> the more closely it is examined, the more truly
> will that result appear. General rules and theories
> are not infallible. It would be preposterous to
> suppose that, in order to judge fairly, and conduct
> myself properly, I ought only to look at a thing
> from a certain distance, and not consider it
> minutely. On the contrary, I ought, as far as
> lies in my power, to examine every thing upon its
> own grounds, and decide concerning it upon its own
> merits. To rest in general rules, is sometimes a
> necessity which our imperfection imposes on us, and
> sometimes the refuge of our indolence; but the true
> dignity of human reason is, as much as we are able,
> to go beyond them, to have our faculties in act upon
> every occasion that occurs, and to conduct ourselves
> accordingly.[28]

Godwin, himself, did not fail to be prudential in his application of theory to practice. In this letter to Joseph Priestley, Godwin, then a Socinian, preferred not to announce his faith to the world.

> I am myself a Socinian. Convinced of the divine origin of Christianity, and yet, perfectly satisfied that it will not stand the test of philosophical examination, unless stripped of its doctrinal corruptions, I should be happy by every method which providence may seem to offer to be the humble instrument of dispelling them....
>
> I have only to add, that though I have been contented to appear openly to Dr. Priestley, it is my earnest desire to remain concealed from the rest of mankind. I have the honour, to be, Rev. Sir, your sincere admirer, and (as a Socinian) your obliged humble servant.[29]

Neither did Godwin believe that all incidents need be given publicity. When Fanny Godwin, Mary Wollstonecraft's illegitimate child, committed suicide, Godwin wrote this letter to Shelley:

> I did indeed expect it.
>
> I cannot but thank you for your strong expressions of sympathy. I do not see however that that sympathy can be of any service to me: but it is best.
>
> My advice and earnest prayer is, that you would avoid any thing that leads to publicity. Go not to Swansea. Disturb not the silent dead. Do nothing to destroy the obscurity she so much desired that now rests upon the event. It was, as I said, her last wish. It was the motive that led her from London to Bristol and from Bristol to Swansea.

> I said that your sympathy could be of no service to me. But I retract that assertion. By observing what I have just recommended to you, it may be of infinite service. Think what is the situation of my wife and myself, now deprived of all our children but the youngest; and do not expose us to those idle questions, which to a mind in anguish is one of the severest of all trials.
>
> We are at this moment in doubt whether during the first shock we shall not say that she is gone to Ireland to her aunts, a thing that had been in contemplation. Do not take from us the power to exercise our own discretion. You shall hear again tomorrow.
>
> What I have most of all in horror is the public papers; and I thank you for your caution as it might act on this.
>
> We have so conducted ourselves that not one person in our house has the smallest apprehension of the truth. Our feelings are less tumultuous than deep; God only knows what they may become.
>
> The following is one expression in her letter to us, written from Bristol on Tuesday. 'I depart immediately to the spot from which I hope never to be removed.'[30]

Godwin's disciples, especially in the 1790s were more literal in their conformity to the master's principles. The following letter from David Booth, who twenty years later assisted Godwin in the mathematical calculations to be used in the reply to Malthus and who wrote a reply of his own, demonstrated the problems associated with a more doctrinaire adherence to principle:

> For some time past, there has occasionally appeared in the Courier an address 'To The Friends of Liberty, Justice, and Humanity.' This address has attracted the attention of some in this neighbourhood, and as its object is to endeavour to procure pecuniary assistance for the families of the state prisoners, we suppose that a few pounds could be collected by us for that purpose. Meanwhile, it has been suggested that the names, to whom money is requested to be remitted, are not sufficiently known to us to ensure our confidence, and that a letter from <u>you</u>, stating your opinion of the <u>utility</u> of the subscription, would greatly influence its amount. -- Though ardent Friends to the extension of Human Happiness, and consequently anxious to assist in affording relief to the victims of Error, we wish not to promote the views of <u>Political Associations</u>. I write only in the name of a few, but that few are familiar with the principles of <u>Godwin</u> and <u>Holcroft</u>.[31]

These letters again emphasise the distinction between theory and practice.[32] Godwin believed that human behaviour ought to meet the standards he set. Nevertheless, he did realise that if all men met these standards there would have been a revolution in the organisation of society. Such a revolution would have been chaotic and tumultuous. To avoid chaos, change needed to be gradual. Godwin opposed, as we have seen, revolution and violence; he opposed factions and associations; only by the individual cultivation of knowledge and its dissemination, could mankind be improved.

Godwin did not oppose violence on principle. He seemed more concerned with the manner in which violence brought an end to progress. In his dispute with Thelwall, Godwin feared, not that the radical reformers were considered outside the law, but that discourses of philosophy, the writings of Rousseau and Hume, would also become illegal. The ban on philosophical writings would eventually bring an end to moral improvement. Hume wrote that the development of the arts and sciences, although initially requiring a free society, could be transplanted to societies which enjoyed no civil liberty.[33] Therefore, progress in the arts and sciences, once established, could flourish in soil not fertilised with freedom. Godwin implied that liberty, though, perhaps, unnecessary for the development of the arts and sciences, was necessary for the cultivation of virtue. However, a certain order must be established in society. Godwin preferred that it be order founded on democratic principles, although, in his theoretical, and, to a certain extent, his practical writings, he indicated that he would suffer the imposition of an Hobbesian sovereign to end a state of war which threatened the possibility of intellectual improvement. This sovereign might have to wield considerable power, because he would have to deal with a large portion of the society which Godwin intended should be liberated from prejudice. Godwin would, of course, be disappointed, if such sovereign power were to be instituted. He would say, as he did to Shelley, or earlier at the time of the terror in France, that men were not prepared for freedom. However, his only remedy was that which he abhorred.

There could be no progress without liberty; it also seemed that progress might not proceed without a measure of despotism. It remained for nineteenth-century theorists to argue that immediate tyranny was essential for ultimate liberty.

Another problem associated with the means of improvement concerned Godwin's treatment of the relationship between education and politics. We have seen that Godwin's attitude towards government did not lead to his devoting his life to education in a manner which excluded participation in politics. Indeed, in 1796, he even considered running for parliament, but eventually he dropped the idea.[34]

He also accepted a sinecure office with the government when it was offered in 1833. It is true that he refused to accept party or government money when it was offered to him in 1788, as he preferred to avoid a formal attachment to faction or government. However, he began to seek such a position, himself, as early as 1806, when he first began to be financially embarrassed. Other references in Godwin's writings of his attitude towards the English Constitution and certain political leaders suggest that he was not, in practical affairs, an enemy to government.

He conceived his position as one between the government and the people. His pamphlets were designed to reform the people or urge the people to reform the government; he never urged the government to reform the people.

Indeed, Godwin's only 'instructions to a statesman' were in the form of the sarcastic attack on Earl Temple's behaviour in bringing down the coalition of the Rockingham faction with Lord North. Thus, while Godwin was concerned with government, he did not wish to guide it, but rather to influence it through public media. His lines appeared in the *Morning Chronicle* rather than in the proceedings of Parliament. He hoped to break down the prejudices established by government by influencing and improving public opinion. This process of public education could only be carried on in a peaceful atmosphere; hence, Godwin's opposition to associations, factions, and any type of popular appeal to the illiterate which would only lead to violence.

In bringing together Godwin's idea of the means of progress and democracy, recalling an unfinished problem from earlier chapters is an excellent starting point. His initial argument, in *Political Justice*, for the perpetual improvement of man, rested on his conception of a science of politics. If men saw 'things as they are', they would be prompted to react in the proper manner, given an understanding of the utility of their actions. This ethical knowledge was open to all men, as little intellectual discipline was necessary. Progress became likely, if not inevitable, because of the intimate connection Godwin detected between seeing and knowing. The problem here was not that men with ethical knowledge frequently did not act in a virtuous manner. The problem lay more with the universality of the doctrine (which was a consequence of the close relationship between seeing and knowing).

That all men are capable of indefinite improvement, as a law of human nature, can be neither refuted nor proven. That some or even many men are capable of improving themselves and that institutions and practices of government are capable of being reformed is a more arguable position. That human nature is such that it does not preclude improvement is a proposition of even greater credibility. In *Political Justice* Godwin's idea of progress conformed to the first statement in terms of universality. In his reply to Malthus, his argument conformed more to the second and third. Malthus, however, conceived the ratios as based on universal laws of human nature (for example, the constancy of the sexual passions), and his argument was neither refutable nor provable. The ratios represented natural laws, and the activities of various societies were classified as 'checks' on the operation of these laws. Malthus could never conceive of the ratios as isolated exceptions to different and more variable relationships of population to subsistence, although this was as plausible as his 'scientific' laws.

Thus, both Malthus and Godwin initially conceived the science of man on grounds which were beyond reasonable refutation or proof. When Godwin afterwards used the argument that human nature was so constituted as not to preclude improvement, he could point to instances of improvement to make his point. Godwin thus abandoned his unprovable position. But did he abandon the science of politics? He would argue that he was consistent, that man was capable of unlimited improvement and, as a corallary, his nature did not preclude improvement. Yet, the different kinds of proof necessary for each rendered them different doctrines. The difference affected more than the rate of progress. It affected primarily the justification of the universality of progress. It also led to questions about the science of politics itself. If it was apparent that only some men in each generation sought to improve the standard of virtue in their lives, then questions must necessarily be raised as to whether 'seeing things as they are' plus an appropriate emotional response was itself the method of improvement and whether the process by which a man actually attempted to improve himself was within the grasp of all men, either because of circumstances or innate dispositions.

If these questions are decided against Godwin, he might still argue that there is nothing which precludes improvement in any given society. However, the process of that improvement might be different from that in which Godwin believed. He might be forced to include in his doctrine a concept of moral virtue based upon custom or habit, if the universality of the science of politics could not be established. If some men in a generation did not improve, it might be necessary that they were educated through habit to obey just laws and perform actions which contributed to the greatest happiness. Progress might not be possible without custom and habit, a position Godwin would loathe to accept, but one which the student of Godwin finds himself driven to recommend.

On a practical level, Godwin sought to influence statesmen through the public rather than influencing the public through statesmen. This was an inevitable conclusion from his conception of a science of politics and his attitude towards government. However, if the universality of the science of politics was questioned, this method of influencing the course of political affairs might also be questioned. There is no error or evil in influencing political affairs by educating the public. But this technique may not work, and it may even become dangerous. If there is no reason to assume that ethical knowledge will be absorbed and put to use by all members of a society, there must obviously be established some forms of moral authority to ensure that certain social divisions do not fester into serious open wounds. They may be connected with church, state, a variety of educational institutions, or they may merely be individuals who by their words and deeds influence a number of their fellows. In whatever manner this or these moral authorities function in society, they must be aware of the importance of government and the men who lead the government, and, hence play a very crucial role in the society, including the exercise of moral authority. Although government leaders may initially rise from the ranks of society and be educated as the rest of the public, wielding both sovereign power and moral authority, it would appear that they require additional knowledge of ethics and politics, of little importance to the average citizen. Thus, Godwin's system of education is not sufficient, because it does not account for the education of statesmen. But, if he developed a doctrine along these lines, he would be defeating his ultimate purpose of freeing man from the constraints of government. Godwin is left with a dilemma. He must risk giving sovereign power to men who may not be sufficiently trained to avoid abusing it, or postpone his goal of freeing man from the constraints of government. He appears to have chosen the former, and again this line of argument places Godwin in a difficult position of taking a narrow path between the best of regimes, a popular democracy, and the worst, a popular tyranny.

The danger of this practical argument is that it leads to two very imperfect groups in a society sharing both power and authority. A government of inadequately trained men holds sovereign power. A body of men of literary taste and ability controls the ear of the public, but disdains and discredits actual political power. In balance this arrangement may be productive of great civil liberty; the two groups would check each other's power. Governmental abuse would be brought before the public, the liberties of individuals, protected, and censorship, moderated. However, in a time of crisis, the **arrangement** might prove disastrous. A government afraid of revolution would strike first at the group which might have moderated this fear, for this group had the public ear. The literary men might extend their freedoms only to see them crushed during periods of crisis. Godwin was aware of this problem. His solution was the agreement of men of letters not to direct emotional appeals to the populace. Then, the government need not fear their power as it would never be used in a manner which would directly threaten the regime. Here is the reason for Godwin's attack on John Thelwall.

Godwin's solution is often criticised because he is interpreted to mean that by the **mere** appeal to reason, progress will take place. In fact, Godwin's doctrine was more pessimistic.

Government could not improve man's condition, and it brought with it evils of its own. The means of progress lay with this band of literary men, educated men of taste, who knew what contributed to the happiness of man and which were his greatest pleasures. However, if these men acted with precipitancy, or if they appealed to popular passions, they courted repression and the end of progress, or a revolution and civil war. Though the latter might change the regime, it was doubtful whether it would improve the moral standards of the people. Godwin advocated the use of rational arguments to persuade men to change their habits of life, not merely because he had great faith in the power of reason, but because he wisely realised that this was the only way to achieve a steady progress. He sailed between the Scylla of evil government influence and the Charybdis of radical reform by popular action. This is, perhaps, the liberal alternative to the philosopher-king, but it is not without serious problems of its own.

CHAPTER XII

PROGRESS AND DEMOCRACY: THE ENDS

Unlike such writers as Thomas More and William Morris, Godwin did not construct a utopia. He did not intend to sketch the end of progress, largely because he believed that there was no end to it, and by the time a truly advanced stage of life developed, his writings would be out of date. The science of politics would by then be far advanced, and his treatise would appear as some old books on medicine do to the modern eye.

However, one cannot write of progress without some conception of ends, however dim and distant. It is clear that he did not approve of the more primitive society based upon simple virtue. Nor did he approve of a wealthy commerical society based on an extensive division of labour. Godwin favoured a simple but cultivated life, the ingredients of which are summarised in these comments by Marguerite to Reginald in St. Leon.

> Let us at length dismiss artificial tastes, and idle and visionary pursuits, that do not flow in a direct line from any of the genuine principles of our nature! ... You, like me, are fond of luxuriant and romantic scenes of nature. Here we are placed in the midst of them. How idle it would be, to wish to change our arbours, our verdant lanes and thickets, for vaulted roofs, and gloomy halls, and massy plate? Alas, Reginald! it is I fear too true,

> that the splendour in which we lately lived
> has its basis in oppression; and that the
> superfluities of the rich, are a boon extorted
> from the hunger and misery of the poor! Here
> we see a peasantry more peaceful and less
> oppressed, than perhaps any other tract of the
> earth can exhibit. They are erect and independent, at once friendly and fearless.[1]

Here, Godwin seemed to echo the romantic voice of Rousseau. But, this picture of pastoral bliss was highly qualified by the sensitive but sensible Marguerite.

> Though I love the sight of the peasants, I
> would not be a peasant. I would have a
> larger stock of ideas, and a wider field of
> activity. I love the sight of peasants only
> for their accessories, or by comparison.
> They are comparatively more secure than any
> other large masses of men, and the scenes in
> the midst of which they are placed are
> delightful to sense. But I would not sacrifice
> in prone oblivion the best characteristics of
> my nature. I put in my claim for refinements
> and luxuries; but they are the refinements
> and purifying of intellect, and the luxuries
> of uncostly, simple taste.[2]

Disdaining luxury and attempting to eliminate the condition of poverty, Godwin sought a middle way, living a highly cultivated life according to simple tastes.

Godwin occasionally used the term 'civil' or 'civilisation' to explain the direction of progress. '"Civility", "civil" are...

terms which express a state of peaceable occupation, in opposition to what is military, and imply ... the absence of contention, uproar, and violence.'[3] Civility, then, implies a condition which Godwin also found in the necessary relations and activities of man in society.

> Society for the greater part carries on its own organisation. Each man pursues his proper occupation, and there are few individuals that feel the propensity to interrupt the pursuits of their neighbours by personal violence. When we observe the quiet manner in which the inhabitants of a great city, and in the country, the frequenters of the fields, the high roads, and the heaths, pass along, each engrossed by his private contemplations, feeling no disposition to molest the strangers he encounters, but on the contrary prepared to afford them every courteous assistance, we cannot in equity do less than admire the innocence of our species, and fancy that, like the patriarchs of old, we have fallen in with 'angels unaware' ....
> When we look at human society with kind and complacent survey, we are more than half tempted to imagine that men might subsist very well in clusters and congregated bodies without the coercion of law; and in truth criminal laws were only made to prevent the ill-disposed few from interrupting the regular and inoffensive proceedings of the vast majority.[4]

Society then had a natural quality of peace in most of its proceedings. Godwin, of course, admitted the need for criminal laws, but crime was regarded as an exception to the usual prevailing tranquility, and it involved a small number of persons.[5] The disposition which led to this condition of society was not love, as most men were strangers. Nor was it fear that governed. It was primarily 'forecast and prudence', a reluctance to risk security and respectability.

Godwin realised that there were many accounts of the evil character of man, and the histories of famous regimes exhibited them 'as if they were so many herds of ferocious animals, whose genuine occupation was to tear each other to pieces and to deform their mother-earth with mangled carcases and seas of blood'.[6] But, he insisted that these were only partial histories of human activity. The lives of most men were spent in peaceable labour. Agriculture was a symbol of peace and the most important activity in a civilised society. In addition, the skilled occupations -- the manufacturer, carpenter, mason, joiner, etc. -- were also peaceable, and so were the traders. Study, science and the production of literature were tranquil activities, as Godwin used the term. They were contrasted with the activities of soldiers and ministers of state, the histories of whom were replete with war and intrigue. These were not 'necessary' occupations, because society, formed by the need to provide subsistence for itself, did not require them.

> We all fall into our ranks. Each one is a
> member of a certain company or squadron. We
> know our respective places, and are marshaled
> and disciplined with an exactness scarcely less
> than that of the individuals of a mighty army....
> We are intent upon the peculiar employment to
> which we have become devoted. We 'rise up early,
> and lie down late', and have no leisure to
> trouble ourselves with the pursuits of others.
> Hence of necessity it happens in a civilised
> community, that a vast majority of the species
> are innocent, and have no inclination to molest
> or interrupt each other's avocations.[7]

Although society maintained men in a state of innocence, so to speak, Godwin did not consider civilisation to be wholly beneficial. '...[I]t is not less true that its immediate tendency is, to clip the wings of the thinking principle within us, and plunge the members of the community in which we live into a barren and ungratifying mediocrity.'[8] Only men of considerable talents and genius with a sincere dedication to high principle could transcend this condition. These men must lead their fellows to a transformation of this already 'civilised' society into one which secured happiness to the whole of its population. One of the first steps was the elimination of poverty.

> To the poor and the wretched the landscape of the
> earth will always be deprived of its more brilliant
> colours. They care no more for the scenes that
> would ravish with delight the eye of Rubens or a
> Claude, than the hawk does for the plumage of the
> bird that is his destined prey. And in like manner

> the faculties of the mind which are imparted
> indiscriminately to all classes, and in greater
> abundance than the supercilious and disdainful
> are willing to allow, are imparted in a great
> majority of instances in vain.... The life of
> the poor man is little else than one scene of
> dulness and ignorance, scarcely varied. ... [9]

The elimination of poverty, he argued, must be accomplished by teaching men that they did not own the property they controlled, but that they were merely stewards, enjoined to use this property in light of the general happiness.

Godwin defined 'civil' as a socially pacific quality in man, relating solely to that organisation of society which was necessary for subsistence and the cultivation of the arts and sciences. He divorced it from the more 'political' meaning associated with its Latin root. The citizen, as Godwin saw him, was pacific, not because of the character of his political institutions, but in spite of them. His civility was wholly unrelated to the laws he lived under, or the customs and habits generated by these laws. However, civilisation was not sufficient, as it developed by that kind of labour which also produced mediocrity.

Godwin was an ardent advocate of equality. This served to break down the distinctions between the classes of people which had been considered by some to exist by the dictates of nature. However, he also favoured an aristocracy of talents and virtue which was the product of the cultivation of talents and genius. Godwin saw no incompatibility between the doctrines, the latter being possible as the result of the former and bound together with an idea of equity in the treatment and development of all men.[10] This aristocracy was partially the product of civilisation and wholly its guide. Although it consisted of the most virtuous and refined persons, these persons were also limited by the imperfections of civilisation itself.

The most significant virtue for guiding conduct in this aristocracy was sincerity, even more so here than in relations between the refined and the vulgar where some more prudential considerations might have to be introduced. The aristocracy should carry on its affairs in a reasonable manner, deciding problems by discussions and persuasion rather than by force and violence or even violent language. Here, Godwin's term 'common deliberation' comes into effect. However, the imperfections of civilisation, if not man, were, as we have seen, keenly felt in Godwin's own practice of sustaining an aristocracy of talent and virtue. If Mackintosh and Southey ill-treated Godwin, so did Parr. If he quarrelled with Thelwall, so did he quarrel with Holcroft, Shelley and Place. It would perhaps be in error to conclude with Rousseau that vanity, false pride and other passions of a similar nature were responsible for the development of the arts and sciences, and, hence, the aristocracy of talents might exist, at the least, in a state of war or, at best, in a state of peace based on a balance of interests. Yet, it is difficult to find in Godwin's case much stability in agreeing to disagree reasonably merely on that principle alone. Granted that men acted sincerely and openly in all their dealings, there still seems to be something missing in the aristocracy of talents which would seem to ensure only a brief period on the stage of life.

At the root of the matter was Godwin's conception of virtue, more suitable for the poet and the philosopher than for society as a whole. Here was a virtue which could not guide a Brutus who, though loving Caesar, loved Rome even more. Godwin frequently admired the virtue of the ancients and contrasted it to the petty courtesies of modern virtue. But he did not copy ancient virtue, or, at least, he omitted the element of patriotism. Rousseau said that we should be taught by Socrates and led by Cato, preferring the latter to the former.[11] A society of patriots might sustain itself, but a society of philosophers perhaps could not. Neither could a society of poets and philosophers to whom Godwin gave inspiration. It is no accident that around Godwin gathered the great poets and literary men of his period. Although many turned against him, they drank enough to be intoxicated with the spirit of poetic virtue. It is also no accident that Godwin's theoretical writings gave little inspiration to statesmen, as their intentions were to make the tasks of the statesmen superfluous. He inspired the reformer, the critic, the poet, the man who stood beyond the pale of the establishments of church and state and school and the traditions they engendered. The advantages and disadvantages of his doctrine of virtue have been amply discussed in many places throughout the thesis. A second idea of virtue may be required, one that not only inspires genius but also serves to hold communities together and allows simple ideas of justice and morality to take their place among common men, who by disposition or circumstance, failed to cultivate their artistic talents. Godwin was aware of this need in his practical writings, and indeed, it is this awareness which probably led him to distinguish carefully between his theoretical and practical writings. However, he failed to make this element a part of his theoretical writings, as it would be fatal to his science of politics which would liberate all men from such prejudice, custom, and habit. Both progress and democracy depended on men 'seeing things as they are'; yet seeing things as they are may, as I have argued, not lead to progress and democracy. If the means are problematical, so must be the ends. Godwin might have given greater attention to that state of man and society which would enable us, in retrospect, to admire human progress.

In summary, Godwin never designed a utopia, although he suggested the outline of the ends of progress. He rejected the simple virtue of primitive society, the ostentatious luxury of modern societies, and aimed at a society which combined simple tastes with an extensive intellectual cultivation. He elevated 'civilisation', ridding the term of its political meaning, and argued that civilisation was the basis of peaceful society. However, civilisation also spawned mediocrity, and Godwin argued that progress rested primarily with the aristocracy of talents and genius which must be developed within the society. It is doubtful, however, that this aristocracy can hold together and, in addition, guide the rest of society. Although Godwin admired ancient virtue, he stripped it of its political meaning, substituting a poetic virtue in its place. It is doubtful whether such virtue can sustain human progress, and the question of the <u>ends</u> of progress still remain an open one.

CHAPTER XIII

GODWIN'S CONTRIBUTION TO POLITICAL PHILOSOPHY

All writing about politics is not philosophic. The articles written by the journalist in the daily newspapers are clearly less philosophic than Godwin's Political Justice. Yet, it is only with difficulty that Godwin's writings can be called contributions to political philosophy. Although Godwin might be considered a philosopher in the sense of a man who seeks wisdom, his political writings cannot be placed in context with more philosophic writings. His most theoretical work, Political Justice, is more a study of politics than a study of philosophic problems in general. We might recall that Godwin's moral philosophy and psychology were set forth only to provide a foundation for his political theory, and Godwin never published a work which examined these principles in themselves.

This omission, so to speak, cannot properly be considered a failing. Did not Rousseau omit a treatise on basic philosophic principles from his writings? Did not Burke argue the absolute incompatibility of metaphysical speculation and political discussion? Although Burke and Rousseau may have been at odds in conceiving the proper level for writing about politics, they agreed on the problematic relationship of political theory to the whole of philosophy. Godwin seems closer to Rousseau and Burke than to the correspondent in the daily newspaper. His separation of political writing from the whole of philosophy does not follow from disinterest or ignorance of philosophy. It proceeds rather from the intention to establish a 'political science' which meets different criteria than philosophic writings about politics. Godwin's treatment of problems of psychology and moral philosophy indicate a concern with these subjects insofar as they assist him in establishing his political principles with greater certainty.

Godwin's political science, as evidenced in Political Justice, is by his own admission rigidly deductive. Beginning with 'first principles' of psychology (which seemed to him self-evident), he deduces his doctrines of justice, duty, property, revolution, etc. His method differs, for example, from Aristotle's whose Politics is written to reflect his conception of the hybrid character of the study of politics (as science, art, and action).[1] In addition, Aristotle's political teaching is intimately connected to a consideration of numerous actual regimes, and his arguments seldom supersede the frame of reference provided by his examination of these regimes. Godwin, on the other hand, refers to actual regimes in a metaphorical sense. His method is analogous to mathematics in its attention to rigorous deduction, and it certainly has little in common with Aristotle. Godwin's method is closer to Hobbes's both in attention to rigorous deduction and in conceiving political philosophy as a science.[2] Although Godwin admitted that he had not completed this science, he had little doubt of the desirability of a high degree of exactness and completeness. However, the exactness

in Political Justice does not seem to apply to the doctrines
themselves. For example, Aristotle's analysis of justice in
the Nicomachean Ethics, though perhaps ambiguous, would seem
to explain and account for more situations when questions of
justice are raised. We find an exactness in the refinement
of Aristotle's doctrine of justice which is missing in Godwin.
For Godwin, the meaning of justice consists in a simple definition:
'that impartial treatment of every man in matters that relate to
his happiness, which is measured solely by a consideration of the
properties of the receiver, and the capacity of him that bestows'.[3]
The virtue of this definition is not in its explanation of the
meaning of justice (for which we might better turn to Aristotle or
Plato) but in its provision of a standard which might in theory be
applied to all persons and in all regimes. Although Godwin realised
that his theory could not itself solve actual problems, as specific
instances must take into account more than the general rule, he
still argued that in theory the standard was applicable to all
instances where a question of justice was raised. That is, no
question of human relations could be raised which would exclude
Godwin's standard, although an actual decision could not be worked
out with reference only to that standard. In this light we may see
why Godwin did not discuss in Political Justice the actual constitutions
of different regimes. Actual regimes differ in their commonly held
opinions of justice and the best organisation of society. These
opinions constitute the prejudices or customs which guide the
behaviour of men in different societies, and they differ as societies

differ. Godwin sought to replace these opinions with a clear standard which could be universally applied. His science of politics is designed to replace opinion, to supersede prejudice and imposture, and its scientific character lies with its universal application. Hence, Godwin's science of politics is closely related to a universal 'social engineering' or 'social technology'.

This view of Godwin's political science is confirmed when we recall that while Godwin sought to develop a rational science, he insisted that reason be in accord with feeling or passion. A rational science which must also be in accord with passion is somewhat paradoxical; a rational science would seem to be complete when it is purely rational. However, if the science of politics was intended to be scientific in the sense that it set standards applicable without alteration to all men and at all times, the need to appeal to feeling becomes evident. Unless this standard is acceptable to all men, including the great many whose morals are based on feeling, Godwin's doctrine would not be 'scientific' in the manner he conceived it.

Although Godwin has been labelled a 'closet-philosopher' and, indeed, he preferred the peace of private life to the storms of the public stage, his philosophy is not one which we might preface: 'My kingdom is not of this world', as Godwin proclaimed the world as his kingdom. 'Political passions rendered universal, coherent, homogenous, permanent, preponderant', as Julien Benda put it, have an important place in Political Justice.[4] However, we must recall that Godwin conceived a portion of his writing, including <u>Political Justice</u>, to be 'speculation' as opposed to his practical writing in the pamphlets and newspaper articles; and I have argued that the distinction between the theoretical and the practical is necessary to render intelligible the whole of Godwin's doctrine. But I have not yet fully explained the relationship between the two levels. We have seen that Godwin intended his political theory to have an application, and, thus, both the theoretical and the practical writings share this feature of applicability. They differ, it seems, in this respect: the practical writings contain arguments intended for <u>immediate</u> application on a <u>limited</u> scale; the doctrines in his theoretical writings have <u>potential</u> application on a <u>universal</u> scale. Godwin's theoretical writings, while they contain the foundations of an ideal society, are thus not utopian in the strict meaning of the term -- 'nowhere' -- for Godwin intended the ultimate realisation of his speculations.

We should recognise that Godwin's distinction between the theoretical and the practical is not philosophic but tactical. Godwin's classification differs from Aristotle's distinction between science and art or Kant's distinction between the 'pure' and the 'practical'. This should be obvious as both the theoretical and the practical writings deal with similar problems, but only in a different manner. This 'strategy' so to speak has the merit of moderating the impact of a revolutionary doctrine. As we have seen, it was sufficiently successful to enable Godwin to avoid imprisonment at the time of the State Trials in 1794. However, the distinction between the two levels does not lead to a formal classification of two kinds of discourse.

Godwin was well aware that his theoretical writings were designed to create a revolution in society. However, we recall that he listed study and science among the peaceful pursuits of man, as one of man's 'civilising' activities. We are then faced with a doctrine which intends to be revolutionary and which at the same time pretends to be pacific. The idea of a peaceful revolution, though now a commonplace notion, is paradoxical, for revolution contains the element of struggle which is clearly opposed to pacificity. Godwin, I believe, failed to take fully into account the potential conflict implicit not only in his own doctrine but also in all political philosophy.[5] Although the philosopher may prefer to live in peace and though he may contribute to the civilisation of his society, doubtless a latent antagonism presents itself as the demands of the search for truth are not always compatible with the demands of society. We must acknowledge a certain potential conflict which accompanies the philosopher to the market place. We should certainly acknowledge the potential conflict if he is accompanied by a revolutionary doctrine. Even Godwin's separation of his writings into the theoretical and the practical fails to appreciate fully the latent hostility between the demands of society and the demands of philosophy. His failure stems from the fact that Godwin is more an 'intellectual' or a 'man of letters' than a philosopher in the full meaning of the term. The intellectual in Godwin's theory occupies the highest rank in the 'scale of pleasures'. It is significant that benevolence is the main characteristic of the highest rank of pleasure, for Godwin might have put contemplation in its place. But the life of the intellectual is one of action as well as contemplation; and action eventually supersedes contemplation or study. The most pleasurable actions are those performed with benevolent intentions, that is, those performed to serve the common good of man. The specific task of the intellectual is to educate people to 'see things as they are'. Thus, the interests of the intellectual who acts from benevolent motives are identical with the interests of society. The conflict which the philosopher might find in serving both the interests of man and the interests of truth does not seem to pose a problem for the intellectual and it did not pose one for Godwin. Intellectual activity, even political science, is for Godwin a peaceful activity as it harmonises with the needs of society.

Godwin's political science may thus be seen as a way of superseding political philosophy. Its value lies in its utility and the political scientist is the man of benevolence whose writings will contribute most to the improvement of society. However, the supersession of political philosophy by political science makes it difficult to evaluate the latter in terms of the former. How can Godwin's simple idea of justice be compared to the whole analysis of justice in Plato's Republic? Without attempting this kind of comparison, we might instead examine political science in terms of its own standards. The political science can claim validity as long as it 'explains' certain 'facts' of society and government. That is, so long as the doctrine provides a theoretical solution to the problems of increasing population, by answering any question we might raise, it can claim to be valid. However, as we discovered in the population dispute, it is possible for two opposing doctrines to explain the facts, for we are never certain which, of opposing theories, explains more facts (as new facts are always being turned up to be explained). One way of avoiding the problem is to stress the tentativeness and limited value of any theory which attempts to explain the facts of social life.[6] However, this solution seems only to avoid the problem rather than solve it; the problem is the explanatory power of a science of politics itself i.e., whether a computation of social principles which satisfies the student as to its accountability and logical rigour is a method adequate to deal with social and political problems. Godwin himself was satisfied that this method of proceeding was the most fruitful until it became clear that several 'sciences' might be devised to explain the same facts, such as economists today devise different mathematical models to explain the facts of modern economies. This seemingly academic difficulty soon became a political one (as the sciences were intended to be applied) and the 'sciences' of population represented two rival political opinions. One way of mitigating the effects of this condition is, as I have already noted, to stress tentativeness and a critical approach to the problem. However, political groups would never have seized upon the doctrines in the first place, if it were in their interest to be critical. Thus, theories, whose merit lies in their application, always run the risk of being transformed into party creeds.

Godwin's theory has been aptly called 'utilitarian', but his utilitarianism is different from other similar theories, particularly 'Benthamite' utilitarianism. Unfortunately Godwin's doctrine is sketched only in outline, and this prevents a full analysis of his ideas. Most students of Godwin have emphasised his arguments against the doctrine of self-love, which though affording some contrast to 'Benthamite' utilitarianism, do not distinguish the whole of Godwin's doctrine. Although he is concerned with a science of pleasure, Godwin does not conceive this science in <u>quantitative</u> terms, but rather in terms of a hierarchy of <u>qualities</u> of pleasure. This conception, in effect, leads Godwin to set limits or compute certain dimensions of pleasure.[7] He makes no effort in treating the 'science of pleasure' to break down 'pleasure' into basic constituent elements in the manner of Bentham.[8] His scale of pleasure has within it a certain unity which is missing not only in Bentham's theory but also in John Stuart Mill's. While Mill would prefer to be Socrates dissatisfied than a pig satisfied, he did not go far as to say what might satisfy Socrates. Mill makes the qualitative distinction between the pleasures appropriate to a pig and those appropriate to a philosopher, but the pleasures appropriate to each category remain unlimited.[9] Godwin is not altogether clear on this point. On the one hand, he states that the greater pleasure is always to be preferred to the lesser one. 'It must be admitted in every system of morality, not tainted with monastic prejudices, but adapted to the nature of intelligent beings, that, so far as relates to ourselves, and leaving our connection with the species out of the consideration, we ought not to refuse any pleasure, except as it tends to the exclusion of some greater pleasure.'[10] On the other hand, though Godwin does not depart from hedonism, he qualifies himself, if only because men live not alone but in communities. However, he in fact limits the quantity of pleasures which can be enjoyed.

> But it has already been shown, that the difference in the pleasures of the palate, between a simple and wholesome diet on the one hand, and all the complexities of the most splendid table on the other, is so small, that few men would even think it worth the tedium that attends upon a change of services, if the pleasure of the palate were the only thing in question, and they had no spectator to admire their magnificence. 'He who should form himself, with the greatest care, upon a system of solitary sensualism, would probably come at last to a decision, not very different from that Epicurus is said to have adopted, in favour of fresh herbs, and water from a spring.[11]

The impetus for prescribing the extent of pleasure arises initially from Godwin's dissatisfaction with the doctrine of self-love. The 'science of pleasure', like the idea of benevolence, is designed to transcend the narrowness of the doctrine of self-love and establish what Godwin calls that 'one thing, or series of things, that constitutes the true perfection of man'.[12] The 'science of pleasure', like the science of politics, enables man to perfect himself by pointing out the best combinations of pleasure and pains, and does not leave 'every man to pursue his own particular taste, which is nothing more than the result of his education, and of the circumstances in which he happens to have been placed, and which by other lessons and circumstances may be corrected.'[13]

> No man is entitled to complain of my sober and dispassionate expostulations respecting the species of pleasure he thinks proper to pursue, because no man stands alone, and can pursue his private conceptions of pleasure, without affecting, beneficially or injuriously, the persons immediately connected with him, and, through him, the rest of the world. Even if he had persuaded himself that it is his business to pursue his own pleasure and that he is not bound to attend ultimately to the pleasure of others, yet it may easily be shown that it is, generally speaking, the interest of each individual, that all should form their plan of personal pleasure with a spirit of difference and accommodation to the pleasure of each other.[14]

Godwin does not proceed to elaborate the dimensions of the proper pursuit of pleasure which the science of pleasure prescribes. But one point is clear: he conceives the pursuit of pleasure to be limited by both the demands of other men and by an idea of the best arrangement of all pleasures. This limitation is the basis of his conflict with the political economists. By limiting man's claim to property in the first instance to basic subsistence, he sets limits to the enjoyment of certain pleasures. This limitation eventually leads to the distinction between necessities and luxuries. The recognition among the people of this limitation on the pursuit of pleasures associated with the enjoyment of luxury is the product of the dissemination of knowledge and the cultivation of virtue. Virtue, in its appreciation of the greatest happiness of man, consists of a mode of conduct which acknowledges this limitation on pleasure. We might similarly conceive of Godwin's idea of justice. The practice by just and virtuous men of this ethical restraint renders superfluous the coercive institutions of government which might be more necessary to a society which did not recognise such a limit on the enjoyment of physical pleasures. Thus, Godwin's liberalism stems more from a conception of the restraint of certain passions than from a conception of the free satisfaction of various desires. Government, for Godwin, may be restricted, as restraint becomes more extensive in the community. This view of the relationship of government to society is different from that usually found in English liberal thought. For example, the Lockean argument for limited government is concerned more with restrictions on government to facilitate the free satisfaction of certain desires than with restrictions of human pleasures in order to limit the necessity for government.

Godwin's hedonism thus gives coherence to his social and economic theory. However, his understanding of the best political regime does not proceed solely from his conception of the unity of pleasure. Although Godwin's distinction between necessities and luxuries leads to a conception of society where the extremes of poverty and opulence disappear, Godwin's preference for democracy may be ill-founded. Nature may not have provided enough to relieve all men of the necessity for hard labour so that they might participate in public affairs. The natural provision for man determines the limits and extent of progress. It also determines the degree of popular participation in a regime. I have suggested that Godwin's understanding of nature's provision for man leads him to conceive of progress as an activity more natural than it might actually be. Not only does this render progress somewhat more problematic than Godwin believed, but it also leads us to question the value of his idea of democracy. Godwin did not realise that the amount of human artifice necessary to free men from the need to labour might itself create conditions inimical to democracy.

Godwin's utilitarianism, in conjunction with his idea of nature, thus provides the framework for his political science. Neither here nor in his arguments more specifically about politics do we discover original ideas which have never been previously encountered. Godwin's contribution to political science lay less with the discovery of new principles than with the new arrangement of principles already discovered. This arrangement is productive of not only a novel doctrine but also a revolutionary one. It is revolutionary, not because it countenances revolution, but because it combines conventional ideas in a manner to transform them into revolutionary ideas. Consider, for example, Godwin's understanding of the relationship between law and justice. Godwin, as we know, is concerned with justice; hence the title of his best known work. In light of Godwin's intention to re-establish the link between ethics and politics, we might expect Godwin's justice to be something which estimates the just qualities of positive law. Justice might stand above law as something to which men might appeal when positive law does not seem to meet equitable standards. But Godwin has justice do more; he sees a conflict between law and justice; and he believes that an understanding of justice will ultimately supplant the need for law itself. The replacement of law by a standard of justice is indeed a radical doctrine. Yet, it is the foundation of Godwin's liberalism insofar as a just society may be free from law and government.

A second example is the relationship between liberty and virtue. Godwin would have all men act virtuously; and to be virtuous is to act according to rules which consider the greatest happiness of the greatest number. Godwin would also have men question all authority so that they are free from prejudice and habit. However, the rule of virtue has an authority of its own. Godwin combines the doctrines by arguing that men must be free from prejudice in order to understand what is truly virtuous. Hence, virtue is less a set of rules for right conduct than, when combined with liberty, a set of rules for the transformation of conduct. Furthermore, Godwin does not emphasise 'political' virtue which would necessarily contain the element of patriotism. His idea of virtue ignores the 'political' and stresses poetic virtue. The poet envisages the 'golden age' and the kind of virtue appropriate to that age. Liberty is necessary for the realisation of this virtue much as the poet cannot be productive when he is constrained. Thus liberty makes the virtuous life possible, because it enables men to discard habits and customs not conducive to virtuous conduct. Applied to all men, the combination of liberty and virtue leads to the achievement of the 'golden age', or the full transformation of society.

Another example is Godwin's idea of democracy. We have seen that he does not intend democracy to mean a form of government in which the people exercise sovereign power, for there is no sovereign. Nor is it intended to be the government which best represents the interests of the greatest number of people.

Democracy, for Godwin, represents the regime which has extended a full measure of liberty to all of its citizens; it is the last regime before all politics and government disappear. The fully democratic society is thus fully libertarian. It is not an alternative and workable regime to monarchy or aristocracy, as its very existence presupposes a transformation of human nature.

After he wrote Political Justice, Godwin did not directly return to these themes in a manner which would emphasise their revolutionary nature. Perhaps, he began to see political science in a more moderate light. Godwin lived in a world which was basically pre-revolutionary in terms of the numerous political movements of the nineteenth and twentieth centuries. He was stimulated, however, by the first of the European revolutions, and though his heart beat high with the swelling sentiment of liberty in 1789, he prudently realised that his heart was not beating in time with the vast majority of his countrymen. Godwin's moderate attitude towards the French Revolution, and towards innovation in general, besides the cautious tenor of his practical writings, gives an air of moderation, even conservatism, to his ideas. As we look back upon Godwin, he seems even complacent, although we realise the revolutionary implications of his theory.

CHAPTER I

1. Letter from Godwin to Lady Caroline Lamb, February 25, 1819, published in C. Kegan Paul, William Godwin: His Friends and Contemporaries, 2 Vols., London, 1876, II. p.266.

2. Abinger Mss. Bodleian Library, Dep. b. 226/12. Essay written in 1806.

3. British Library Additional Manuscripts 35, 145, f.109 Place to J. Hume (1829).

4. Abinger Mss. Dep. b. 227/4. October 24, 1824.

5. Enquiry concerning Political Justice, 3rd ed., 1798, Preface to First Edition, p. v. All quotations are from the photographic facsimile, ed. F.E.L. Priestley (Toronto 1946). Political Justice will hereafter be cited as P.J., and Professor Priestley's commentary will be cited as Priestley, P.J., III.

6. P.J. Preface to First Edition, p.xi.

7. See, for example, Elie Halévy, The Growth of Philosophical Radicalism, trans. by Mary Morris, London, 1928, pp.199-200.

8.   Abinger Mss. Dep.c.537. Note: October 10, 1824.

9.   'From what has been said the humble pretensions of the contents of the present volume are sufficiently obvious. They are presented to the contemplative reader, not as dicta, but as the materials of thinking. They are committed to his mercy. In themselves they are trivial; the hints of enquiry rather than actual enquiries: but hereafter they may be taken under other men's protection, and cherished to maturity'. *The Enquirer, Reflections on Education, Manners, and Literature. In a Series of Essays*, London, 1797, p.viii.

10. Abinger Mss. Dep.b.227/2. June 8, 1801.

11. Abinger Mss. Dep.b.227/4. June 1, 1830.

12. Quoted in the editor's preface to *Essays, Never Before Published*, London, 1873, p.v. (afterwards *Essays*).

13. For this publication, most references to the microfilm have been checked against the original manuscripts and references to the originals have been made in the notes. On occasion, it has not been possible to locate the original, and the microfilm reference is retained.

CHAPTER II

1. <u>P.J.</u> I.I.v. pp.83-5.

2. <u>Essays</u>, p.259. **Cf.** John Stuart Mill: 'The words ⟦Nature, natural, etc.⟧ have thus become entangled in so many foreign associations, mostly of a very powerful and tenacious character, that they have come to excite, and to be the symbols of, feelings which their original meaning will by no means justify; and which have made them one of the most copious sources of false taste, false philosophy, false morality, and even bad law'. 'Nature' in the <u>Essential Works of John Stuart Mill</u>, **ed.** Max Lerner, New York, 1961, p.367.

3. <u>Essays</u>, p.268.

4. <u>Ibid</u>., p.266.

5. <u>Ibid</u>., pp.264-5.

6. Godwin's formulation of the dependence of society and civilisation on the faculty of reasoned speech was closer to Plato and Aristotle than to his contemporaries. In the <u>Politics</u> 1253a, Aristotle wrote: 'The mere making of sounds serves to indicate pleasure and pain, and is thus a faculty that belongs to animals in general: their nature enables them to attain the point at which they have perceptions of pleasure and pain, and can signify those

perceptions to one another. But language serves to declare what is advantageous and what is the reverse, and it therefore serves to declare what is just and what is unjust. It is the peculiarity of man, in comparison with the **rest** of the animal world, that he alone possesses a perception of good and evil, of the just and the unjust, and of other similar qualities; and it is association in these things which makes a family and a polis' (Barker trans.). However, Godwin regarded only society and not the entire polity to be natural. The separation of the two is a more recent idea. With the classical view, contrast Hume who found language established by convention and must presuppose the existence of society which in itself is an artificial arrangement. A Treatise of Human Nature, Bk.III, Pt.II, §II. Rousseau, however, never made a final decision on the question. 'Quant à moi, effrayé des difficultés qui se multiplient, et convaincu de l'impossibilité presque démontrée que les langues aient pu naitre et s'établir par des moyens purement humains, je laisse à qui voudra l'entreprendre la discussion de ce difficile problème, lequel a été le plus nécessaire de la société déjà liée à l'institution des langues, ou des langues déjà inventées a l'établissement de la société'. 'Discours sur l'origine de l'inégalité parmi les hommes' in Du Contrat Social, Paris, 1962, (Editions Garnier Frères), pp.55-6. However, he does lean towards the position that society precedes the full development of language. 'Quoi qu'il en soit de ces origines, on voit du moins, au peu de soin qu'a pris la nature de rapprocher les hommes par des besoins mutuels et de leur faciliter l'usage de la parole, combien elle a peu préparé leur sociabilité. ...' p.56. That is, nature did not provide a sufficient usage of speech to enable it to be the foundation of society.

7. Among the many topics of conversation with his friends, Godwin noted 'the intention of nature'. See Abinger Mss. Journal, entry for November 6, 1795, Dep.e.202.

8. Mandeville, Fable of the Bees, ed. Kaye, 2 vols., Oxford, 1924, I, p.345.

9. Bk.I, Ch.2 in Godwin, Of Population, p.9.

10. See: Aristotle, Politics 1256b: 'Property of this order is evidently given by nature to all living beings from the instant of their first birth to the days when their growth is finished. ... Accordingly, as nature makes nothing purposeless or in vain, all animals must have been made by nature for the sake of man'. And Aristotle argued that these were sufficient to provide subsistence and the good life. However, he was not extravagant in his claims for natural abundance. He rejected a description of nature by Solon, that 'there is no bound to wealth stands fixed for men' (Barker Trans.).

11. Cf. Aristotle, <u>Politics</u> 1256b.

12. Godwin did not conclude that because nature was generally beneficent, there was no evil in natural things. He certainly acknowledged the evil of hunger, famine and disease which sprang from natural conditions. See <u>P.J.</u> I.I.ii.p.7. However, these conditions were considered minimal as opposed to those created by human institutions, and, especially, war.

13. J.B. Bury has explained this blending by saying that Godwin 'entertained the same pessimistic view of some important sides of civilisation as Rousseau, and at the same time adopted the theories of Rousseau's opponents, especially Helvetius. His survey of human conditions seems to lead inevitably to pessimism; then he turns round to proclaim the doctrine of perfectibility'. <u>The Idea of Progress</u>, London, 1920, p.226.

14. <u>P.J.</u> I.I. ii-iii. pp.6ff.

15. <u>P.J.</u> I.I.iv. p.26.

16. See: <u>P.J.</u> I.I.iv. pp.26ff.

17. <u>P.J.</u> I.I.v. p.55.

18. *Ibid.*, p.56.

19. *Ibid.*

20. *P.J.* I.IV.x. p.431.

21. *P.J.* I.I.v. p.58.

22. *P.J.* I.I.v. p.70.

23. Hume, *Enquiry concerning Human Understanding*, Sect.II, Selby-Bigge edition, p.17.

24. *P.J.* I.I.v. pp.71-2.

25. Morris Ginsberg, *Essays in Sociology and Social Philosophy*, 3 vols., III, 'Evolution and Progress', London, 1961, pp.2-3.

26. *Ibid.*, p.53.

27. For an opposite view which holds that the rationalist fails to take into account experiential knowledge, cf. Michael Oakeshott, *Rationalism in Politics*, London, 1962.

28. David Hume, <u>A Treatise of Human Nature</u>, III, Pt.III, §II, quoted in D.H. Monro, <u>Godwin's Moral Philosophy</u>, London, 1953, p.49.

29. Dated May 12, 1794 and not published until the second edition, London, 1796.

30. Monro, p.36.

31. <u>P.J.</u> Summary of Principles, I. p.xxvi.

32. <u>Thoughts occasioned by the Perusal of Dr. Parr's Spital Sermon, etc.</u>, London, 1801, p.31.

33. Aristotle, <u>Nicomachean Ethics</u>, II, 1103a 14ff.

34. <u>Life of Geoffrey Chaucer</u>, London, 1803, I. p.17.

35. <u>Essay on Sepulchres</u>, London, 1809, p.82.

36. B.L. Add. Mss. 35,145 f.109.

37. Thomas Green, <u>An Examination of the Leading Principle of the New System of Morals</u>, London, 1799, Preface to 2nd Edition, pp.ii-iii.

38. <u>Ibid.</u>, p.16.

39. P.J. I.IV.xi. p.440.

40. Abinger Mss. Dep.b.228/9: 'The Enquiry concerning Political Justice I apprehend to be blemished principally by three errors. 1. Stoicism, or an inattention to the principle, that pleasure and pain are the only bases upon which morality can rest. 2. **Sandemanianism,** or an inattention to the principle, that feeling, and not judgment is the source of human actions. 3. The unqualified condemnation of the private affections'. Pollin states that this was probably written around 1799-1800, Education and Enlightenment in the Works of William Godwin, New York, 1962, p.41.

41. Enquirer, p.104.

42. 'Utilitarianism', in Essential Works, p.197.

43. P.J. I.IV.xi. pp.444ff.

44. Ibid., p.445.

45. Ibid., pp.445-6.

46. Ibid., pp.446-7.

47. Ibid., pp.447-8.

48. <u>Ibid</u>., Summary of Principles, p.xxvi.

49. See note 40.

50. <u>P.J.</u> Summary of Principles, p.xxvi.

51. Helvetius, <u>De L'Esprit</u>, Essay I, Ch.I.

52. Monro, p.36.

53. <u>P.J.</u> I.IV.x. p.424.

54. <u>Ibid</u>., p.425.

55. <u>Ibid</u>., p.427.

56. <u>Ibid</u>., p.429.

57. Quoted from the <u>Essay on Human Understanding</u>, in <u>Thoughts on Man</u>, pp.210-11.

58. <u>P.J.</u> I.IV.x. p.429.

59. <u>Ibid</u>., p.431.

60. <u>Ibid</u>., p.432.

61. *Thoughts on Man*, p.219.

62. *Ibid*., p.220.

63. *Ibid*., pp.220-1.

64. Monro, p.14.

65. *P.J.* I.IV.x. p.422n. In his *Account of the Seminary that will be opened on Monday, the Fourth Day of August at Epsom in Surrey*, written in 1783, Godwin writes: 'It has, I think, been fully demonstrated by that very elegant philosopher, Mr. Hutcheson, that self-love is not the source of all our passions, but that disinterested benevolence has its seat in the human heart' (pp.48-9). A contemporary of Godwin records this account of a lecture given by the famous political economist, Dugald Stewart: 'We had an admirable lecture on Godwin's system; in the discussion of which Stewart displayed, with his usual eloquence, more than usual acuteness; at least it was quite a new view of that system to me, to consider it a *reductio ad absurdum* of Hutcheson's principle of universal benevolence'. *Memoirs and Correspondence of Francis Horner M.P.*, ed. by Leonard Horner, 2 Vols. London, 1843, I. p.101. Godwin's doctrine might also be found in Joseph Priestley's essays on *Hartley's Theory of the Human Mind* (2nd Edition 1790) p.xxxii: 'According to this hypothesis all our passions are first *interested*, respecting our own pleasures or pains; and this sufficiently agrees with our observation: and

they become <u>disinterested</u> when these complex emotions are transferred by association to other persons or things. Thus the child loves his nurse or parent by connecting with the idea of them the various pleasures which he has received from them, or in their company; but having received the most happiness from them, or with them, when they themselves were cheerful and happy, he begins to desire their happiness and in time it becomes as much an object with him as his own proper happiness'. Among the French, said Godwin, all the philosophers declared with more or less explicitness for the doctrine of self-love. 'It is no wonder that Rousseau, the most benevolent of them, and who most escaped the general contagion, has been driven to place the perfection of virtue in doing no injury'. <u>P.J.</u> I.IV.x. p.436.

66. Monro, p.21.

67. Hume, <u>Treatise of Human Nature</u> (ed. Selby-Bigge), Bk.III. Pt.II. §I., p.479.

68. 'Some readers of my graver productions will perhaps, in perusing these little volumes, accuse me of inconsistency; the affections and charities of private life being every where in this publication a topic of warmest eulogism, while

in the Enquiry concerning Political Justice, they seemed to be treated with no indulgence and favour. In answer to this objection all I think it necessary to say on the present occasion, is that, for more than four years, I have been anxious for opportunity and leisure to modify some of the earlier chapters of that work in conformity to the sentiments inculcated in this. Not that I see cause to make any change respecting the principle of justice, or any thing else fundamental to the system there delivered; but that I apprehend domestic and private affections inseparable from the nature of man, and from what may be styled the culture of the heart, and am fully persuaded that they are not incompatible with a profound and active sense of justice in the mind of him that cherishes them'. St. Leon, 4 vols., London, 1800, I, pp.ix-x.

CHAPTER III

1. <u>P.J.</u> I. II. i. p.124.

2. 'Tous coururent au-devant de leurs fers, croyant assurer leur liberté; car, avec assez de raison pour sentir les avantages d'un établissement politique, ils n'avoient pas assez d'expérience pour en prévoir les dangers: ...
Telle fut or dut être l'origine de la société et des lois, qui donnèrent de nouvelles entraves au foible et de nouvelles forces au riche, détruisirent sans retour la liberté naturelle, fixèrent pur jamais la loi de la propriété et de l'inégalité, d'une adroite usurpation firent un droit irrévocable, et, pour le profit de quelques ambitieux, assujettirent désormais tout le genre humain au travail, à la servitude et à la misère'. pp. 78-9.

3. <u>P.J.</u> I. I. i. pp. 4-5.

4. Maurice Cranston, <u>Freedom, A New Analysis</u>, London, 2nd Edition, 1954, p.79.

5. <u>P.J.</u> I. II. ii. p.126.

6. <u>P.J.</u> Summary of Principles, p.xxv.

7. <u>P.J.</u> I. II. ii. pp.126-7. Originally, Godwin posed the question in terms of the archbishop and one's own father or brother, and he attempted to show the greater importance of universal benevolence.

8. <u>P.J.</u> I. II. ii. pp.130-1.

9. See Hobbes, <u>Leviathan</u>, Ch. XV; Hume, <u>A Treatise of Human Nature</u>, Bk.III, Pt.II, §2.

10. <u>P.J.</u> I. II. iii. p.143.

11. <u>Ibid.</u>, p.146.

12. <u>Ibid.</u>, p.145.

13. <u>Ibid.</u>, p.147.

14. <u>Ibid.</u>

15. <u>P.J.</u> Summary of Principles, p.xxv.

16. Thomas Paine, <u>The Rights of Man</u>, Pt.1, in <u>The Life and Major Writings of Thomas Paine</u>, ed. P.S. Foner, New York, 1961, p.316.

17. P.J. I. II. v. pp.158-9.

18. P.J. I. II. iv. p.149.

19. P.J. I. II. v. p.161.

20. Ibid., p.162.

21. Ibid., p.165.

22. Ibid., p.167.

23. Ibid., p.168.

24. Ibid., p.169.

25. P.J. I. II. vi. p.175.

26. P.J. I. III. ii. p.190 and n.

27. David Hume, Essays, Pt.II, Essay 12 (Green and Grose edition).

28. Ibid.

29. P.J. I. III. ii. p.190.

30. Ibid., p.192. See also Rousseau, *Du Contrat Social*, Bk. III, Ch.XV.

31. *P.J.* I. III. ii. p.193.

32. *P.J.* I. III. iii. p.195.

33. Ibid., pp.195-6.

34. Ibid., p.210.

35. *P.J.* I. III. iv. pp.214-5.

36. Ibid., pp.215-6.

37. Ibid., p.217. Godwin excluded legislation from the functions of government. He wrote: 'Legislation, as it has been usually understood, is not an affair of human competence. Immutable reason is the true legislator, and her decrees it behoves us to investigate. The functions of society extend, not to the making, but the interpreting of law; it cannot decree, it can only declare that, which the nature of things has already decreed, and the propriety of which irresistibly flows from the circumstances of the case'. *P.J.* I. III. v. p.221.

38. *P.J.* I. III. vi. pp.227-8.

39. Ibid., p.228.

40. Ibid., p.230.

CHAPTER IV

1. *P.J.* II. V. i. pp.6-7.

2. *P.J.* II. V. iv. p.32.

3. *Ibid.*, p.33.

4. *P.J.* II. V. viii. p.69.

5. *P.J.* II. V. x. p.87.

6. *Ibid.*, p.90.

7. *Ibid.*, p.91.

8. *P.J.* II. V. xiii. p.104.

9. See Burke's remarks generally in *Reflections on the Revolution in France*.

10. *P.J.* II. V. xiv. p.114.

11. *Ibid.*, p.116.

12. *Ibid.*, p.119.

13. <u>Ibid.</u>, pp.118-19.

14. <u>Ibid.</u>, p.121.

15. <u>Ibid.</u>, p.122.

16. <u>Ibid.</u>, p.123. See Harvey C. Mansfield Jr., 'Rationality and Representation in Burke's Bristol Speech', <u>Rational Decision Nomos VII</u>. ed. Carl Friedrich, N.Y., 1964. pp.197-216.

17. <u>P.J.</u> II. V. xxiv. p.209. The second approach was suggested to Godwin by Swift's <u>Gulliver's Travels</u>.

18. <u>P.J.</u> II. V. xv. p.124.

19. <u>Ibid.</u>, p.125.

20. <u>Ibid.</u>, p.128.

21. Rousseau, <u>Du Contrat Social</u> Bk.II. Ch.VII (translation mine).

22. In the account of the life of Numa, Plutarch stated that Lycurgus, Numa and others might or might not have had advice from the gods. That is, they might have deliberately used prejudice to gain favour with the people. Plutarch thus did not give a definite answer. Rousseau did (citing Machiavelli, not Plutarch), and, in this sense, he was in error. Furthermore, Lycurgus did use exhortation and persuasion, even though he might also have used divine sanctions. See: <u>Plutarch's Lives</u>,

23. <u>P.J.</u> II. V. xv. p.131.

24. <u>Ibid</u>., p.133.

25. <u>Ibid</u>., p.135.

26. Rousseau, <u>Du Contrat Social</u>, Bk.III, Ch.IV.

27. <u>P.J.</u> II. V. xvi. p.152.

28. <u>P.J.</u> II. V. xvii. p.154.

29. Paine, <u>Rights of Man</u>, Pt.II. (Foner edition), p.400.

30. Montesquieu, <u>Esprit des lois</u>, Bk. XX. Ch.2.

31. Immanuel Kant, <u>Perpetual Peace</u>, trans. Helen O'Brien, Grotius Society, London, 1927, p.41.

32. <u>Ibid</u>.

33. Montesquieu, Bk.IX. Ch.2.

34. <u>Ibid</u>., Bk.IX. Ch.1.

35. Paine, <u>Rights of Man</u>, Pt.I. p.285.

36.   *P.J.* II. VIII. vi. pp.481-2.

37.   Godwin's solution is similar to Rousseau's which is usually contrasted with Kant's. 'So whereas Rousseau's solution to the problem of war was in the establishment of the good society, Kant, who found the root of war in man's nature, not in society's 'denaturation' of man, could not halt, so to speak, the imperative of peace with setting up of ideal states. Hence the league for eternal peace, which Kant's philosophy required'. Stanley Hoffman, 'Rousseau on War and Peace', *American Political Science Review*, Vol.57, (1963) p.332.

CHAPTER V

1. See: Isaiah Berlin, *Two Concepts of Liberty*, Oxford, 1958.

2. *P.J.* I. IV. i. pp.258-9.

3. See: David Fleisher, *William Godwin, A Study in Liberalism*, London, 1951; George Woodcock, *Anarchism*, New York, 1962, pp.60-94; also Woodcock, *William Godwin, A Biographical Study*, London, 1946.

4. *Enquirer*, p.86.

5. See: Maurice Cranston, *Freedom, A New Analysis*, Pt. III.

6. *P.J.* I. IV. viii. p.385.

7. Abinger Mss. Dep.b.229/9. Note dated February 1800.

8. *Thoughts on Man*, p.226.

9. *Ibid.*, p.231. Godwin notes that Lord Kaimes in his *Essays on the Principles of Morality and Natural Religion* (1751) first used the phrase.

10. *Ibid.*

11. *Ibid.*, p.234.

12. *Ibid.*, pp.237-8.

13. *Ibid.*, p.240.

14. **P.J**. II. VI. i. p.215.

15. Godwin's doctrine of liberty has been compared with John Stuart Mill's essay on the same subject. See: F.E.L. Priestley, III. p.43 and n, referring to Godwin's idea of individuality and Mill's concept in Chapter III of On Liberty. See also: Plamenatz, The English Utilitarians, Oxford, 2nd Edition, 1958, p.129: 'It is in this second chapter, full of the most excellent liberal arguments, that Mill comes closest to the position taken up by Godwin in Political Justice'.

16. See Chapter III.

17. **P.J**. I. IV. i. p.251.

18. *Ibid.*, p.253.

19. *Ibid.*, pp.262-3.

20. *Ibid.*, p.260.

21. *P.J.* I. IV. ii. p.268.

22. *Ibid.*, pp.269-270.

23. *Ibid.*, p.272.

24. *Ibid.*, pp.273-4.

25. *Ibid.*, p.278.

26. *Ibid.*, p.284.

27. See: *P.J.* I. IV. iv.

28. Hume, *Essays*, Pt.II, Essay 13.

29. *P.J.* I. IV. iii. p.287.

30. *P.J.* II. VII. i. p.324.

31. *P.J.* II. VII. iii. pp.340-1.

32. *P.J.* II. VII. iv. p.348.

33. *Ibid.*, p.351.

34. P.J. II. VII. v. p.360.

35. Ibid., p.366.

36. P.J. II. VII. vi. p.385.

37. Ibid., pp.390-1.

38. P.J. II. VI. i. p.216.

39. Paine, Rights of Man, Pt.II. Ch.IV, p.375.

40. Paine, Rights of Man, Pt.I, p.279.

41. P.J. II. VI. vii. pp.286-7.

42. Ibid., p.286.

43. Ibid., p.289.

44. Ibid., p.291.

45. Ibid., p.294.

46. P.J. II. VI. viii. pp.296ff.

47. Ibid., p.298.

48. *Ibid*., p.302.

49. *On Liberty*, Ch.V. See: E.G. West, 'Liberty and Education: John Stuart Mill's Dilemma', *Philosophy*, XL (1965), 129-42.

50. *Caleb Williams* (1838 edition), p.143. However, Godwin regarded liberty to be more important than riches; it is better to be free and poor than rich and a slave to one's wealth. (p.209).

51. *Essays*, p.219.

52. *Ibid*., pp.219-20.

53. Berlin, p.13.

54. See: *Life of Geoffrey Chaucer* (1803), I. pp.13ff.

55. Hume's argument is that the initial development of the arts and sciences can take place only in a free society, though they can be transplanted to a society without civil liberty. *Essays*, Pt.I. Essay 14.

56. *P.J.* II. VII. iii. p.340.

57. See: J.L. Talmon, *The Origins of Totalitarian Democracy*, London, 1952.

CHAPTER VI

1. Jeremy Bentham, *A Fragment on Government and Introduction to the Principles of Morals and Legislation*, ed. Wilfred Harrison, Oxford, 1948, pp.74-5.

2. See: William C. Proby, *Modern Philosophy and Barbarism: Or a Comparison Between the Theory of Godwin and the Practice of Lycurgus*, London, 1798, pp.43f.

3. See: *P.J.* II. VIII. viii (Appendix), pp.503-4. 'The conclusion of the progress which has here been sketched, is something like a final close to the necessity of manual labour.... It was one of the laws of Lycurgus, that no Spartan should be employed in manual labour. For this purpose, under his system, it was necessary, that they should be plentifully supplied with slaves devoted to drudgery.... We shall end in this respect, oh immortal legislator! at the point from which you began'.

4. An emphasis on the production of wealth and contrast between the civilised society and the primitive one is found in Locke: 'There cannot be a clearer demonstration of any thing, than several Nations of *Americans* are of this, who are rich in Land, and poor in all the Comforts of Life; whom Nature having furnished as liberally as any other people, with the materials

of Plenty i.e. a fruitful soil, apt to produce in abundance, what might serve for food, rayment, and delight; yet for want of improving it by labour, have not one hundreth part of the Conveniencies we enjoy: And a King of a large and fruitful territory there feeds, lodges, and is clad worse than a day labourer in England'. <u>Two Treatises of Government</u>, II. §41. Summarising the condition of the hive in which the bees lived in luxury and idleness, motivated only by vices such as avarice, vanity, and fickleness, which created a powerful and cultivated society, Mandeville wrote:

> 'Thus Vice nurs'd Ingenuity
> Which join'd with Time and Industry,
> Had carry'd Life's Conveniencies,
> Its real Pleasures, Comforts, Ease,
> To such a Height, the very Poor
> Liv'd better than the Rich before,
> And nothing could be added more'.

<u>The Fable of the Bees</u>, I, p.26. Adam Smith developed the same thought when writing of the consequences of the division of labour. '...[A]nd yet it may be true, perhaps, that the accommodation of an European Prince does not always so much exceed that of an industrious and frugal peasant, as the accommodation of the latter exceeds that of many an African king, the absolute master of the lives and liberties of ten thousand naked savages'. <u>An Inquiry into the Nature and Causes of the Wealth of Nations</u>, ed. Cannan, 2 vols. London, 1904, I, p.14.

5. Mandeville is credited with placing great emphasis on the utility of luxury, arguing that it produced riches, provided employment and that no nation without necessity, followed a policy of national frugality. See: Mandeville, I, pp.107ff. Godwin regarded Hume as a follower of Mandeville on this issue: 'Hume (__Essays__; Part II, Essay II.) has endeavoured to communicate to the Mandevilian system his own lustre and brilliancy of colouring. But it has unfortunately happened, that what he adds in beauty he has subtracted from profoundness'. __P.J.__ II. VIII. vii. pp.490n-491n. His doctrine might be considered a refinement of Mandeville's. 'Luxury, when excessive, is the source of many ills; but is in general preferable to sloth and idleness, which would commonly succeed in its place, and are more hurtful both to private persons and to the public. When sloth reigns, a mean uncultivated way of life prevails amongst individuals, without society, without enjoyment. And if the sovereign, in such a situation, demands the service of his subjects, the labour of the state suffices only to furnish the necessaries of life to the labourers, and can afford nothing to those who are employed in the public service'. __Essays__, Pt.II. Essay 2.

6. Kingsley Martin, __French Liberal Thought in the Eighteenth Century__, London 1929, p.238.

7. 'Morelly and Mably completely rejected the current individualism and declared that happiness is to be found only in an organized society where individual satisfaction is deliberately subordinated to the public good'. Martin, p.242.

8. Robert Wallace, <u>Various Prospects of Mankind, Nature and Providence</u>, London, 1761. William Ogilvie, <u>An Essay on the Right of Property in Land</u>, London, 1781. Wallace, was referred to by Godwin as 'an antagonist of Hume' in their dispute over the question of population (<u>P.J.</u> II. VIII. iii. p.459n). Wallace wrote: 'The establishment of property in lands, has been attended with many disadvantages; it seems indeed to have been one great source, not only of those calamities, but of those vices, which have been so sensibly felt and so loudly complained of in every age. ... Being ignorant and destitute of experience in what is called the state of nature, feeling the evils of their defenceless and indigent condition; having abundance of room in these early days, and not foreseeing the evils to which the establishment of property would give occasion, they unfortunately had their first recourse to this expedient, instead of agreeing to an equitable distribution of labour, and to a community of goods. ... Instead of dividing the lands among particular persons, might they not have consented to labour them in common and share equally of the fruits' (pp.109-10).

Wallace went on to construct a utopian society, but at the end he abandoned it because the perfect system would stimulate an increase of population which would flood the earth. While his utopia was unachievable, it could nevertheless serve as a model for statesmen. Ogilvie presented a striking attack on the idea of unlimited rights to property in land. There were two foundations to the right of property: the right to occupy a piece of land as a man's equal share of the soil, and the right to appropriate the fruits of labour on the land. He said that in rude societies, the second right was neglected, while in more advanced societies, the first right was neglected to the disadvantage of the lower classes. He relied on state action to maintain a system of equality.

9. Joseph Priestley, <u>An Essay on the First Principles of Government</u>, London, 2nd edition, 1771. Thomas Paine, <u>Agrarian Justice</u>, London, 1817 edition. Priestley wrote: 'The very idea of property, or right of any kind, is founded upon a regard to the general good of the society, under whose protection it is enjoyed; and nothing is properly <u>a man's own</u>, but what general rules which have for their object the good of the whole, give to him' (p.41). Paine wrote: 'The life of an Indian is a continual holiday, compared with the poor of Europe; and on the other hand it appears abject when compared to the rich. Civilisation, therefore, or that which is so called, has operated two ways, to make one part

of society more affluent, and the other part more wretched than would have been the lot of either in a natural state' (p.5). The commercial society was a mixed blessing for mankind. While it benefited a certain portion of the society, it also caused a larger portion to live in a condition of poverty. 'Poverty, therefore, is a thing created by that which is called civilised life. It exists not in the natural state. On the other hand, the natural state is without the advantages which flow from Agriculture, Arts, Sciences, and Manufactures' (p.5). Paine's solution, like Ogilvie's, was a practical one. The state ought to give each man a sum of money when he comes of age to compensate him for his loss of an equal share of the land. The compensation would be paid for out of a special fund administered by the state.

10. *P.J.* II. VIII. i. p.422.

11. *P.J.* II. VIII. iii. pp.453ff.

12. Ibid., p.457.

13. Ibid., p.460.

14. Ibid., p.466.

15. Enquirer, p.162.

16. *Ibid.*, p.214.

17. *Ibid.*, pp.215-216.

18. *Ibid.*, p.217.

19. *Ibid.*, p.219.

20. See: Thomas R. Malthus, *First Essay on Population 1798*, London, 1926 (Royal Economic Society Reprint), p.174; Proby, p.17.

21. See discussion of rights and duties in Chapter III above.

22. *P.J.* II. VIII. ii. p.449.

23. *Ibid.*, p.433.

24. *Ibid.*, p.434.

25. *Ibid.*, p.435.

26. *Ibid.*, p.436.

27. *Ibid.*, pp.436-7.

28. *Ibid.*, p.438.

29. *P.J.* II. VIII. iv. pp.469ff.

30. *P.J.* II. VIII. v. p.475.

31. For similar ideas see Wallace, p.52.

32. *P.J.* II. VIII. vi. p.485.

33. See: Mandeville, I, p.25. Kingsley Martin wrote: 'Avarice, for centuries repudiated by the Catholic Church as a sin, became in the new philosophy a virtue whereby the indulgence of each man's desire to do the best for himself proved also to be best for the public welfare'. (p.221).

34. See note 5.

35. *P.J.* II. VIII. vii. p.491.

36. *Ibid.*, pp.492-3.

37. *Enquirer*, Pt.II. Essay II.

38. *Ibid.*, pp.177-8.

39. Max Beer, *A History of British Socialism*, 2 vols., London, 1919, I, p.119.

40. In this sense, Godwin's economic doctrine was close to Aristotle's.

41. *Enquirer*, p.171.

42. *Ibid.*, p.173.

43. *P.J.* II. VIII. viii. Appendix, pp.499-500.

44. *Ibid.*, p.501.

45. *P.J.* II. VIII. viii. Appendix pp.513-4.

46. Karl Marx, *Economic and Philosophical Manuscripts*, in Erich Fromm, *Marx's Concept of Man*, New York, 1961, p.95.

47. *Enquirer*, p.167.

48. 'It is generally agreed that leisure, or in other words freedom from the necessity of labour, should be present in any well-ordered state'. Aristotle, *Politics*, 1269a (Barker translation).

49. *Ibid.*, p.64n.

50. G.D.H. Cole, <u>A History of Socialist Thought</u>, I. London, 1953: 'Godwin wanted, not so much to make property collective, as to do away with the very conception of it'. (pp.27-8).

CHAPTER VII

1. See: Wallace, pp.114ff.

2. Thomas Paine used the population argument to say that man cannot return to the savage state. The development of the arts and sciences have enabled more people to live on the earth. It would be impossible to feed this additional population in the savage state. See: *Agrarian Justice*.

3. *P.J.* II. VII. ix. p.516.

4. *Ibid.*, p.518.

5. Malthus, *First Essay on Population 1798*: 'The most important argument that I shall adduce is certainly not new. The principles on which it depends have been explained in part by Hume, and more at large by Dr. Adam Smith. It has been advanced and applied to the present subject, though not with its proper weight... by Mr Wallace: and it may probably have been stated by many writers that I have never met with' (p.8).

6. *Ibid.* See Ch. XVIII.

7. *Ibid.*, p.11. Of interest is the manner in which he conceived a law of nature: 'These two laws ever since we have had knowledge of mankind, appear to have been fixed laws of our nature; and, as we have not hitherto seen any alteration in them, we have no right to conclude that they will ever cease to be what they now are, without an immediate act of power in that Being who first arranged the system of the universe; and for the advantage of his creatures, still executes, according to fixed laws, all its various operations' (pp.11-12).

8. *Ibid.*, pp.13-14.

9. *Ibid.*, pp.2-3.

10. *Ibid.*, p.177.

11. *Ibid.*, p.254.

12. *Ibid.*, p.261.

13. Letter is printed in Kegan Paul I. pp.321-5.

14. Godwin's journal records subsequent meetings, December 7, 1800, January 3, 1801, April 14, 1801. Abinger Mss. Journal, Dep. e. 205.

15. The dispute with Mackintosh is fully discussed in Chapter X.

16. The dispute with Parr is fully discussed in Chapter X.

17. *Cf.* Plato, *Charmides*, 161c.

18. Copy in the British Library, also quoted in Ford K. Brown, p.172.

19. **Thoughts occasioned by ... Dr. Parr's Spital Sermon, etc. p.55.**

20. March 17, 1802 -- Smith and Malthus call
    October 20, 1802 -- Dine at Johnson's [Godwin and Malthus among those listed as guests]
    January 19, 1803 -- Meet Malthus
    February 17, 1803 -- Meet Malthus
    Abinger Mss. Journal, Dep. e.206.

21. **Preface** to second edition, pp iii, **vii**.   See: K.Smith, *The Malthusian Controversy*, London, 1951, pp.37ff.

22. Coleridge, writing in the margin of his copy of the Quarto edition (second): 'And of course you wholly confute your former pamphlet, and might have saved yourself the trouble of making up the present quarto. Merciful God, are we now to have a Quarto to teach us, that great misery and great vice arise from Poverty and that there must be Poverty in its

worst shapes wherever there are more mouths than loaves and more heads than grains! -- The whole question is this: Are Lust and Hunger both alike passions of physical Necessity, and the one equally with the other and independent of the Reason and the Will? Shame upon our Race, that there lives the individual who dares even ask the Question? S.T.C.' Copy in the British Library, p.vii.

23. Malthus (second edition), Bk III. Ch III.

24. Ibid., p.380.

25. Abinger Mss. Journal, Dep. e. 215-16. There has been some discussion of the originality of Godwin's arguments, especially by Hazlitt who wrote: 'I wrote a book in defence of Godwin some years ago, one-half of which he has since stolen without acknowledgement, without even mentioning my name....' (Hazlitt to Leigh Hunt, April 21, 1821) in Ford K. Brown, The Life of William Godwin, London 1926 p.334n. Godwin has been defended most recently by W. P. Albrecht, 'Godwin and Malthus,' Publication of the Modern Language Association, LXX (1955) 552-6 where he points out that the two were aiming at different ends, Godwin's being to refute the ratios. Albrecht also points out that the ideas they shared were not original with either Godwin or Hazlitt.

26. For a full discussion of the ratios, see: K. Smith, pp.209ff. See also note 22 above.

27. Of Population, pp. 76-84.

28. Malthus (Sixth Edition, Reprinted 1890), p.51.

29. Of Population, pp. 71-5.

30. Malthus (Sixth Edition), p.34.

31. Of Population, p.518.

32. Ibid., p.517.

33. Ibid., p.559.

34. Ibid., p.560.

35. Ibid., p.561.

36. Ibid., p.598.

37. Ibid.

38. Ibid., p.603.

39. Ibid., p.622.

40. Ibid., p.623.

41. Malthus (Sixth Edition), p.586.

42. **Microfilm Reel 76, Abinger Mss.**

43. 'An Inquiry concerning the Power of Increase in the Numbers of Mankind, Being an Answer to Mr Malthus's Essay on that Subject,' Edinburgh Review, Vol.XXXV (1821), p.362.

44. Abinger Mss.Dep.c. 524, Letter to Mary Shelley, October 10, 1821.

45. Edinburgh Review, pp.363-4.

46. Ibid., pp.374-5.

47. See: Francis Place, Illustrations and Proofs of the Principle of Population, London, 1822. Place concluded that moral restraint would lead to a compatibility between the doctrines, and he said that Godwin's reply in 1801 was the proper one. Though he criticised Malthus for some of his extreme statements, Place pointed out numerous passages in both writers and argued that they were in basic agreement. However, the student of the problem is bound to wonder why Malthus rejected Godwin's first reply. It may be recalled that the issue turned not merely on moral restraint, but on the motives for moral restraint. These

motives, according to Malthus, had to be founded on self-interest to be effective. If founded on benevolence, they became too weak and the system fell prey to other checks. Place ignored this argument and failed to see that Malthus did not regard his own doctrine as compatible with Godwin's.

48. Quoted in F.K. Brown, pp.334-5.

49. Henry Blanche Rosser, <u>Pamphlet in Support of William Godwin Against Malthus</u> London 1821.

50. Brown, p.336.

51. Godwin's Journal records his beginning to write the piece on December 30. Abinger Mss. Dep.e. 218-19.

CHAPTER VIII

1. *Life of William Pitt, Earl of Chatham*, pp.ix-x.

2. *Ibid.*, pp.x-xii.

3. F.K. Brown, p.16.

4. Kegan Paul, I. p.20. See: Jack Marken, 'The Canon and Chronology of William Godwin's Early Works', *Modern Language Notes*, LXIX (1954), pp.176-180.

5. J.H. Plumb, *England in the Eighteenth Century (1714-1815)*, (Penguin Books), 1950, p.189.

6. *Rockingham Party*, pp.13-14.

7. *Ibid.*, p.16.

8. *Ibid.*, pp.24-6.

9. *Ibid.*, p.26.

10. *Ibid.*, p.30.

11. The pamphlet published January 5 is very rare and the only known copy of it is in the Yale University Library. This summary of it is taken from Jack Marken, 'William Godwin's Instructions to a Statesman', <u>The Yale University Library Gazette</u>, Vol. 34 (1959) 73-81.

12. J. Holland Rose, <u>William Pitt and the National Revival</u>, London, 1912, p.148.

13. See: Kegan Paul, I. p.19.

14. 'On quitting Beaconsfield in August, I formed the plan of a school, for which I was offered some pecuniary assistance, and I actually hired a furnished house for the purpose at Epsom in Surrey, and published a pamphlet in recommendation of my plan: but I never secured a sufficient number of pupils at one time to induce me to enter upon actual business'. Quoted in Kegan Paul, I. p.20.

15. See: George Woodcock, <u>William Godwin</u>, for a good summary of the pamphlet. p.21f.

16. See: Kegan Paul, I. pp.20-21. The titles are <u>Damon and Delia</u>, <u>Italian Letters</u>, and <u>Imogen, A Pastoral Romance</u>.

17. See: Kegan Paul, I. p.21. Jack W. Marken, 'William Godwin's Writing for the New Annual Register', Modern Language Notes, Vol.68 (1953), pp.477-9. The position was a good one, and when Godwin abandoned the job, Dr. Kippis, himself, took it. The New Annual Register was a rival to the more conservative Annual Register and during some of the time Godwin wrote for it, his rival was Edmund Burke. See F.K. Brown, pp.28-9.

18. Jack W. Marken, 'William Godwin and the Political Herald and Review'. New York Public Library Bulletin, Vol.65, (1961) 517-533.

19. Ibid., pp.523-4 for letter Godwin wrote identifying himself as Mucius. F.K. Brown incorrectly identifies him as Ignotus whom Marken has identified as Thomson. See: F.K. Brown, p.28. Marken has positively identified the following contributions: Vol.I. pp.175-182, 321-329; II. 175-183, 241-49; III. 19-24, 81-98, 268-275, 330-346, 401-416.

20. Political Herald and Review, I. pp.328-9.

21. Ibid., II. p.175.

22. Ibid., II. pp.402-411.

CHAPTER IX

1. Kegan Paul, I. p.61.

2. New Annual Register (1791), p.3.

3. Ibid.

4. Ibid., p.118.

5. F.K. Brown, p.35.

6. Kegan Paul, I. p.67.

7. Ibid.

8. Ibid., p.75; see Pollin, p.281.

9. G.S. Veitch, The Genesis of Parliamentary Reform, London, 1913, pp.179-80.

10. See Kegan Paul, I. pp.68, 81. Abinger Mss. Journal, Dep.e.198.

11. Kegan Paul, I. p.67.

12. Philip Anthony Brown, The French Revolution in English History, London, 1918, p.43.

13. *Ibid.*, p.44.

14. British Library, Add. Mss. 35,145, f. 109 to J. Hume, 1829. See also '... for there are passages in Godwin against rash rebellion and the anarchy of revolution more impressive, if less emotional, than anything in Burke'. H.N. Brailsford, *Shelley, Godwin and their Circle*, London, 1913, pp.21-2.

15. Letter I, February 1, 1793 signed Mercius (probably a mistake). Letter II, February 8. Letter III, March 26. Letter IV, March 30. His journal indicates that they were written on January 16-18 (Abinger Mss. Journal, Dep.e.200).

16. At this time, *Caleb Williams*, Godwin's most famous novel, was published. The publishers, afraid of possible government action, omitted Godwin's preface which noted the despotisms of his society. The preface was printed in the 2nd edition.

17. Kegan Paul, I, p.118.

18. Alexander Stephens, *Memoirs of John Horne Tooke*, II, p.140.

19. Abinger Mss. Journal, Dep.e.201, f.41, dated January 29, 1809. See: Stephens, II, p.140.

20. Brailsford wrote: 'The letter shows none of Godwin's speculative daring, and his gift of cold and dignified eloquence is severely repressed. He wrote to attain his immediate end, and from that standpoint his pleading was a master-piece. A certain deadly courtesy, a tone of quiet reasonableness made it possible for the most prejudiced reader to follow it with assent'. (pp.46-7).

21. *Cursory Strictures*, p.4.

22. *Ibid*., pp.4-5.

23. *Ibid*., p.7, quoting p.6 of C.J. Eyre's charge to the Grand Jury.

24. *Ibid*., p.8, quoting p.6 of C.J. Eyre's charge to the Grand Jury.

25. *Ibid*., p.15.

26. *A Reply to An Answer to Cursory Strictures, supposed to be wrote by Judge Buller*, London, 1794.

27. *Ibid*., pp.4-5.

28. *Ibid*., p.5.

29. Veitch, p.325.

30. On December 11, another edition was published at 1s 6d., this one advertised as written by a 'Lover of Order, Author of Cursory Strictures on the Charge Delivered by Lord Chief Justice Eyre, October, 2, 1794'.

31. <u>Considerations on Lord Grenville's and Mr. Pitt's Bills Concerning Treasonable and Seditious Practices and Unlawful Assemblies, By a Lover of Order</u>, London, 1795, pp.1-2.

32. <u>Ibid</u>., pp.14-5.

33. <u>Ibid</u>., p.15.

34. <u>Ibid</u>., p.17.

35. <u>Ibid</u>., pp.20-21.

36. <u>Ibid</u>., p.22.

37. <u>Ibid</u>., p.38.

38. Quoted in Charles Cestre, <u>John Thelwall</u>, London, 1906, pp.137-8.

39. <u>Ibid</u>., Appendix, p.203.

40. <u>Ibid</u>., p.204.

41. John Thelwall, The Tribune, London, 1796, Vol.II.

42. Ibid., pp.vii, x.

43. Tribune, III, p.101.

44. Letter from T. Amyot to Henry Crabb Robinson, Letters (1725-1799), 16 August 1796, Dr. Williams Library, f.78.

45. The misrepresentation of Godwin began with Charles Cestre's biography of Thelwall, published in 1906. Cestre had in his possession some unpublished correspondence between Godwin and Thelwall and he used it to criticise Godwin severely (pp.131ff). From here it passed to Ford K. Brown's biography of Godwin and from there into all the studies of him and the period. See: Brown, pp.97-103. Kegan Paul never mentioned the dispute because most of the material was in the Thelwall papers to which he did not refer.

Cestre also wrote that 'Godwin, and Thelwall had common friends and had met several times' (p.131). They were more intimate than is here implied. Between the end of the State Trials and the dispute over Thelwall's speech, Godwin recorded the following meetings: December 5, 7, 10, 12, 15, 18, 20, 1794; January 2, 15, 17, 26, 31, 1795; February 2; March 5, 31; May 7; June 11, 12, 18; September 6; October 8, 15. Prior to the State Trials they visited as frequently. Abinger Mss. Journal, Dep.e.201-2.

46. Cestre, p.132. Contrast: 'For Thelwall as for Godwin, the supreme possession that dignifies man, is his reason'. B.S. Allen, 'Godwin's Influence upon John Thelwall', Publication of the Modern Language Association, XXXVII (1922) p.667.

47. Cestre reprints letter in full in Appendix I, pp.201-3.

48. Cestre, pp.134-5.

49. Mrs. Thelwall, The Life of John Thelwall, London, 1837, pp.204ff.

50. Cestre, p.135.

51. Max Beer, History of British Socialism, I, p.115.

CHAPTER X

1. <u>Enquirer</u>, pp.ix-x.

2. <u>Letters</u>, August 16, 1802 in Dr. William's Library.

3. 'His reputation for radicalism was still such that the Benchers of the Inn refused his permission to speak there; the intervention of Pitt, himself a Bencher, was ineffectual; and only the efforts of Loughborough, then Lord Chancellor, were influential enough to get him the use of the hall of his own society'. F.K. Brown, p.166.

4. Both this draft of the letter and Burke's actual reply are in the British Library. <u>Add. Mss</u>. 52,451B f.28, Letter to Burke, December 10, 1796.

5. F.K. Brown, pp.166-7, quoting Hazlitt, states that he attended. Godwin's journal indicates that he attended the meetings on February 20, and 23, or possibly read the lectures on these days, but he has left no record of attending the lectures in January. His letter is written upon having <u>read</u> the lectures. Abinger Mss. Journal, Dep.e.203-4.

6. Kegan Paul, I. p.328, erroneously wrote that this letter was not preserved. (Woodcock, also made the same mistake, p.163). Not only was it preserved, but it was also in large part published by Godwin himself in his Thoughts occasioned by ... Dr. Parr's Spital Sermon, p.13. The original letter is in the British Library, Add. Mss. 52,451B, f.32.

7. Kegan Paul, I. pp.328-30.

8. Abinger Mss. (Microfilm) Reel 75.

9. Robert James Mackintosh, Memoirs of the Life of Sir James Mackintosh, 2 vols., London, 1835, I. pp.134-5. Godwin kept a copy of this letter in his papers. Coleridge disliked Mackintosh because he had apostatised and referred to him as the 'great Dung-fly Mackintosh.' Letter to Godwin May 21, 1800. Abinger Mss. (Microfilm) Reel 74. Kegan Paul reprints the whole letter except for this reference to Mackintosh which he discreetly omits (II. pp.2-4).

10. Parr to Godwin, November 10, 1794. Kegan Paul, I, p.136.

11. Ibid., p.378.

12. Ibid., p.383.

13. *Ibid.*, pp.386-7.

14. *Thoughts Occasioned by a Perusal of Dr. Parr's Spital Sermon*, pp.4-5.

15. *Ibid.*, p.5.

16. William Field, *Memoirs of the Life, Writings, and Opinions of the Rev. Samuel Parr, LL.D.*, 2 vols. London, 1828, I. pp.401-2.

17. Kegan Paul, II. p.152.

18. *Ibid.*, pp.153-4.

19. Abinger Mss. Dep.226/12.

20. *Thoughts Occasioned by a Perusal of Dr. Parr's Spital Sermon*, p.6.

21. Henry Crabb Robinson, *Diary*, Dr. Williams Library, October 18, 1813, f.89-90. Godwin and Madame de Staël met again twice: at Mackintosh's for tea on November 28, and Godwin called on her on December 6. See Abinger Mss. Journal, Dep.e.213.

22. *Letters of Verax to the Editor of the Morning Chronicle on the Question of a War to be Commenced for the Purpose of Putting an End to the Possession of the Supreme Power in France by Napoleon Bonaparte*, London, 1815, p.12, See: Burton R. Pollin, 'Godwin's Letters of Verax,' *Journal of the History of Ideas*, XXV (July 1964) pp.353-73.

23. *Letters of Verax*, p.16.

24. For an account of their relationship, see: F.K. Brown, pp.249-6.

25. At Curran's death, Godwin wrote a 'Memoir of John Philpott Curran,' published in the *Morning Chronicle* on October 16, 1817. Godwin met Cobbett with Curran on October 24 and 29, 1811. Abinger Mss. Journal, Dep.e.211.

26. F.K. Brown, p.322.

27. Kegan Paul, II, pp.314-20.

28. For a brief summary, see: H.N. Brailsford's chapter on Shelley and Godwin, pp.168-85.

29. Percy Bysshe Shelley, *Letters from Percy Bysshe Shelley to William Godwin*, London, Privately Printed, 1891, Vol.I, p.11. January 10, 1812. Most of these letters also appear in Ingpen's more popular edition of Shelley's letters.

30. M.S. 75. Godwin to Shelley, n.d. Written between January and March 1812.

31. Shelley, pp.27-8 January 28, 1812.

32. Kegan Paul, II, p.204. March 4, 1812.

33. Shelley, pp.41-2, March 8, 1812.

34. Kegan Paul, II. p.207, March 14, 1812.

35. Ibid.

36. Shelley, p.53, March 18, 1812.

37. Kegan Paul, II. p.207. March 30, 1812.

38. Abinger Mss. Journal, Dep.e.212.

39. Ibid. See entry February 7, 1813. 'Call on Place with Owen.'

40. Robert Owen, The Life of Robert Owen, Written by Himself, London, 1857, I. p.212.

41. Frank Podmore, Robert Owen, A Biography, 2 vols., London, 1906, I. p.119.

42. Abinger Mss. Dep.b.227/1.

CHAPTER XI

1. <u>Essays</u>, pp.3-4.

2. <u>Ibid</u>., p.6.

3. <u>Ibid</u>., pp.5-6.

4. Cf. Jeremy Bentham: 'He may therefore in this respect find himself in the condition of those philosophers of antiquity, who are represented as having held two bodies of doctrine, a popular and an occult one: but, with this difference, that in his instance the occult and the popular will, he hopes, be found as consistent as in those they were contradictory; and that in his production whatever there is of occultness has been the pure result of sad necessity, and in no respect of choice.' <u>Introduction to the Principles of Morals and Legislation</u>, Preface.

5. <u>P.J.</u> I. IV. v. p.306.

6. <u>Ibid</u>., p.308.

7. 'Burke made the first of the virtues prudence. Godwin would have given sincerity that place.' Brailsford, p.106.

8. _P.J._ I. IV. vi. p.340.

9. _Ibid._

10. _Ibid._, Appendix I. p.355.

11. _Enquirer_, p.4.

12. _Ibid._, p.6.

13. _Ibid._, pp.8-9.

14. _Ibid._, p.31.

15. _Ibid._, p.60.

16. _Ibid._, p.74.

17. _Thoughts on Man_, p.36.

18. _Ibid._, p.42.

19. _Ibid._, pp.43-4.

20. _Enquirer_, p.78.

21. *Ibid.*, p.80.

22. *Ibid.*

23. *Ibid.*, p.105.

24. *Ibid.*, p.106.

25. *Ibid.*, p.41.

26. *Ibid.*, p.10-11.

27. *P.J.* I. IV. vi. Appendix I. p.344.

28. *Ibid.*, p.345.

29. Abinger Mss. Dep.b.227/2. Written between 1785-7.

30. Abinger Mss. Dep.c.524. Letter to Shelley, October 13, 1816.

31. Abinger Mss. Dep.b.228/5, Booth to Godwin, May 25, 1799.

32. W.C. Proby's pamphlet against Godwin is entitled *Modern Philosophy and Barbarism: or a Comparison Between the Theory of Godwin and the Practice of Lycurgus*, London, 1798. This comparison is possible only if the distinction between theory and practice is deliberately ignored.

33.   Hume, Essays, Pt.I, Essay 14.

34.   Abinger Mss. Dep.b.229/8.

CHAPTER XII

1. *St. Leon*, Vol.1, pp.226-7.

2. *Ibid.*, pp.228-9.

3. *Essays*, pp.42-3.

4. *Thoughts on Man*, pp.112-13.

5. *Ibid.*, p.112.

6. *Ibid.*, p.118.

7. *Ibid.*, pp.122-3.

8. *Ibid.*, p.123.

9. *Essays*, pp.35-6.

10. A contemporary, (Rev) Charles Findlater, argued the opposite, believing Godwin himself to be a refutation of the doctrine of equality. See: *Liberty and Equality: A Sermon or Essay ... to which is subjoined an Appendix Containing an Analysis of, and some Observations on, Godwin's System of Society in his Political Justice*, London, 1800, p.42.

11. See: Rousseau, 'A Discourse on Political Economy' (Everyman Edition), pp.246-7.

CHAPTER XIII

1. See: Aristotle, <u>Nicomachean Ethics</u>, VI.

2. 'According to Hobbes's own view, the application of mathematical method to political philosophy means that politics is now for the first time raised to the rank of a science, a branch of rational knowledge'. Leo Strauss, <u>The Political Philosophy of Hobbes</u>, Chicago, 1952, pp.136-7.

3. <u>P.J.</u> I. II. ii. p.126.

4. Julien Benda, <u>La Trahison des Clercs</u>, trans. <u>The Betrayal of the Intellectuals</u>, Boston, 1959, p.7. Cf. 'Originally, philosophy had been the humanizing quest for the eternal order, and hence it had been a pure source of humane inspiration and aspiration. Since the seventeenth century, philosophy has become a weapon, and hence an instrument. It was this politicization of philosophy that was discerned as the root of our troubles by an intellectual who denounced the treason of intellectuals. He committed the fatal mistake, however, of ignoring the essential difference between intellectuals and philosophers. In this he remained the dupe of the delusion which he denounced. For the politicization of philosophy consists precisely in this, that the difference between intellectuals and philosophers -- a difference formerly known as the difference between gentlemen and philosophers on the one hand, and the difference between sophists or rhetoricians and philosophers, on the other -- becomes blurred and finally disappears.' Leo Strauss, <u>Natural Right and History</u>, Chicago, 1953, p.34.

5. 'The reason Plato wanted the philosophers to become the rulers of the city lay in the conflict between the philosopher and the polis, or in the hostility of the polis toward philosophy.... Politically, Plato's philosophy shows the rebellion of the philosopher against the polis. The philosopher announces his claim to rule, but not so much for the sake of the polis and politics ... as for the sake of philosophy and the safety of the philosopher.' Hannah Arendt, 'What is Authority', <u>Between Past and Future</u>, London, 1961, p.107.

6. See: W.G. Runciman, <u>Social Science and Political Theory</u>, Cambridge, 1963, p.175. Sir Karl Popper, <u>The Open Society and its Enemies</u>, Princeton, 1950, <u>passim</u>; <u>The Logic of Scientific Discovery</u>, London, 1959, <u>passim</u>; <u>The Poverty of Historicism</u>, London, 1957, <u>passim</u>.

7. 'La doctrine d'Épicure sur le plaisir est donc parfaitement cohérente et conséquente avec elle-même. Il faut seulement, pour bien l'entendre, se rappeler que le plaisir n'est pas, comme on l'a dit si souvent, un simple état négatif. Il faut aussi avoir presente à l'esprit cette conception de toute la philosophie grecque anterieure, d'après laquelle le plaisir n'est pas une <u>quantité</u>, capable de croître indéfiniment, mais une <u>qualite</u>, parfaitment determinée,

definie ou, comme dit Épicure lui-même, une limite, <u>peras</u>. On a commis une, grave erreur lorsqu'on a approché la doctrine d'Épicure de l'utilitarisme anglais, qui assigne pour but suprême à l'activité humaine la plus grande somme de plaisirs. Sur quelques points de details il peut y avoir des coincidences entre l'Épicurisme et le Benthamisme; sur la question essentialle, la défenition du plaisir, il y a une opposition radicale.' Brochard, 'La theorie du plaisir d'apres Épicure,' <u>Études de philosophie ancienne et de philosophie moderne</u>, Paris, 1926, pp.273-4. 'The application of a real inductive philosophy to the problems of ethics, is as unknown to the Epicurean moralists as to any of the other schools; they never take a question to pieces, and join issue on a definite point. Bentham certainly did not learn his sifting and anatomising method from them'. John Stuart Mill, <u>Mill on Bentham and Coleridge</u>, ed. Leavis, London, 1950. pp.54-5.

8. John Stuart Mill (ed. Leavis), p.48: 'Bentham's method may be shortly described as the method of detail; of treating wholes by separating them into their parts, abstractions by resolving them into Things, -- classes and generalities by distinguishing them into the individuals of which they are made up; and breaking every question into pieces before attempting to solve it.'

9. See: John Stuart Mill, 'Utilitarianism', in the <u>Essential Works of John Stuart Mill</u>, p.197. 'Bien moins encore les Utilitaires consentiraient-ils à suivre Épicure dans ses théories sur le bonheur du sage et la direction des pensées. Ce n'est pas par un effort du vouloir, par un sorte d'auto suggestion, finalment par un jeu de l'imagination qu'ils veulent atteindre félicité. Il leur faut des joies plus solides et en quelque sorte plus palpables. Stuart Mill a pu dire qu'il 'vaut mieux être un Socrate mécontent qu'un pourceau satisfait'; il n'a pas dit que le sage peut être heureux dans la taureau de Phalaris'. Brochard, p.288. Cf. A.J. Ayer, <u>Philosophical Essays</u>, London, 1954, pp.252-3.

10. <u>P.J.</u> II. VIII. i. p.425.

11. <u>Ibid</u>.

12. <u>P.J.</u> I. IV. xi. p.443.

13. <u>Ibid</u>., p.442.

14. <u>Ibid</u>., pp.442-3.